The Abduction of Dinah

The Abduction of Dinah
Genesis 28:10—35:15 as a Votive Narrative

DANIEL HANKORE

☙PICKWICK *Publications* • Eugene, Oregon

THE ABDUCTION OF DINAH
Genesis 28:10—35:15 as a Votive Narrative

Copyright © 2013 Daniel Hankore. All rights reserved. Except for brief quotations in critical publications or reviews, no part of this book may be reproduced in any manner without prior written permission from the publisher. Write: Permissions. Wipf and Stock Publishers, 199 W. 8th Ave., Suite 3, Eugene, OR 97401.

Pickwick Publications
An Imprint of Wipf and Stock Publishers
199 W. 8th Ave., Suite 3
Eugene, OR 97401

www.wipfandstock.com

ISBN 13: 978–1–61097–991–7

Cataloguing-in-Publication Data

Hankore, Daniel;

    The abduction of Dinah : Genesis 28:10—35:15 as a votive narrative / Daniel Hankore

    x + 262 p. ; 23 cm. Includes bibliographical references and index

    ISBN: 978-1-61097-991-7

    1. Bible. O.T. Genesis—Criticism, interpretation, etc. 2. Vows in the Bible. 3. Dinah (Biblical figure). 4. Jacob (Biblical patriarch). I. Title.

BS1199.R27 H29 2013

Manufactured in the USA

I wish to dedicate this work to my beloved wife Dero Dutamo, to my beloved children, and to all Bible translators with full appreciation.

Contents

Acknowledgments | ix

1 Introduction | 1
2 Boundaries of the Jacob Story and Its Literary Structure | 18
3 The Concept of נדר "Vow" in the Hebrew Scriptures | 43
4 Vow-Making of Jacob as a Metarepresentation | 88
5 Vow Granting and Vow Fulfilling | 126
6 Dinah Story as an Adverse Consequence of the Unfulfilled Vow | 163
7 Conclusion with Remarks on Implications for Translation | 202

APPENDIX 1: Hebrew, Israel, and Jew | 213
APPENDIX 2: Translation of Genesis 28:10–22 | 220
APPENDIX 3: Institution of Tithing | 222
APPENDIX 4: Interviews about the Vow and "Rape" of Dinah | 225
APPENDIX 5: Conditionals and Metarepresentation | 229
APPENDIX 6: Some Real-Life Stories of Abductive Marriage among the Hadiyya People | 232
APPENDIX 7: Excursus on Translating Gen 28:10—35:15 | 236

Bibliography | 247
Scripture Index | 255
Author Index | 259
Subject Index | 261

Acknowledgments

FIRST OF ALL, I give all the glory and honor to God for all the inexpressible kindness, mercy, and inspiration he gave me in this research. I sincerely acknowledge that it is God's goodness which helped me finish this dissertation.

I also want to express my deep appreciation and thanks to all who contributed to the success of this dissertation in one way or another. However, I would like to thank the following in a special way. My deepest appreciation and thanks go to my supervisor Professor Ronald J. Sim for the wonderful guidance he gave me so that I finish this dissertation successfully. I acknowledge that it is a privilege to work under his supervision. My heartfelt thanks and appreciation also goes to Professor Gordon Wenham for encouraging me and guiding me throughout this dissertation with great interest. Sincerely it is a privilege to have him as my external supervisor. I desire to emulate his good Christian scholarship. My warmest thanks also go to Dr. Mike Gibson for helping me in doing the same. His sincere advice and guidance in this research significantly contributed to the success of this dissertation.

I also would like to thank the Ph.D. committee at AIU, Translation department of AIU, and Tyndale House staff in Cambrdge for all their helpful assistances in relation to this research. I would also like to extend my sincere thanks to Doctor George Huttar for taking time to read some of the chapters of this dissertation and for giving me very helpful comments.

I would like to express my sincere thanks, appreciation, and gratitude to SIL Africa Area, Wycliffe Africa Area, and SIL Ethiopia Branch for all their assistance in many ways in relation to this research. Without their support I wouldn't be able to do this research.

I would also like to express my special thanks and gratitude to my beloved wife and supporter Dero Dutamo and my beloved children for their patience and for all their kind assistance throughout this research.

Acknowledgments

Particularly I feel I am in heavy debt to my wife in this regard. I would also like to express my sincere thanks to those who kindly cooperated for my interviews.

Finally, as a non-mother-tongue speaker of English Language I would like to express my sincere appreciation to Alizon Cleal and other various individuals who have given me editorial assistance and I take full responsibility for all the remaining matters of style in this work.

1

Introduction

Introduction

THE PROCESS OF UNDERSTANDING a text from the narrator's point of view is crucial for the tasks of interpretating and translating the Bible. If the translator's understanding of a narrative from the narrator's point of view is erroneous, then the whole process of translating the message into another language may also fall into error. This poses Bible translators a difficult challenge: "How can we understand the narrator's point of view of the biblical stories which are culturally, geographically, and historically remote from our own?" There is no easy answer to this question. However, from the outset, I presuppose that an African perspective when reading the Scripture complemented by relevance-theoretic parameters may contribute to answering it. Reading Genesis 28:10—35:15 in the light of Hadiyya culture and relevance theory will help in its interpretation and translation.

Understanding the utterance of a discourse must precede the translation process, so I will attempt to explain the intended utterance of Genesis 28:10—35:15 in depth first, before proposing in brief how to translate it. Thus, I wish to show that a correct understanding of the concept of the ancient Israelite vow in the framework of a social institution is fundamental to reading and translating Genesis 28:10—35:15 and this same votive framework will assist us to explain the relevance of Genesis 34 to the Jacob story.

A comparison of different translations of the Jacob narrative unit of 28:10—35:15 in general and the Dinah story in particular show that the story has often been mistranslated because the episodes are treated as if they were isolated episodes. One may wonder what is the cause for the mistranslation. The obvious answer is that this narrative unit and its component episodes were misread because of assumptions the readers brought to the text when trying to respond to it. I wish to show that the whole story is a coherent narrative unit and to demonstrate how the coherence of the narrative is developed. Each episode of the story, including the Dinah story, is a componential part or a building block of Jacob's votive narrative. Chapters 3 and 6 will show that an understanding of the institutions of vow and marriage is vital for explaining this coherence.

Many critical readers of the story wonder: "What is the relevance of the Dinah story to the narrative of Jacob?" Different biblical scholars propose different answers to this question as the following examples show: the Dinah story does not have any significant relationship to the Jacob story;[1] it was intended to be an example of banning exogamous marriage;[2] it was intended to challenge the militant attitude to outsiders;[3] etc. However, the question to be asked regarding these answers is, what are the textual evidences provided by the narrator/communicator in this particular narrative discourse?

I argue that Genesis 34 was not thrown into the Jacob narrative accidentally; rather there must be a communicative intention which the narrator wished to achieve by including the Dinah story at this particular location in the Jacob narrative. This presumptive communicative intention must have been manifested through the *ostensive signals of the communicative intention* for including it. This is the question to be addressed.

Hence, since the main reason for the mistranslation and misinterpretation of the story was misreading of the same, most of my discussion is spent explaining that Genesis 28:10—35:15 is a coherent narrative unit of which the Dinah story is an integral part. I believe my explanation will help the translators in a significant way.

It will be shown that the Dinah story is an intentionally included congruent part of the votive narrative of Jacob which comprises Genesis 28:10—35:15. This hypothesis will be substantiated by the close reading of the whole narrative unit from the narrator's point of view as it is manifested by his linguistic/public representation. His mental representation of the story, manifestly represented in his linguistic organization of the

---

1. Brueggemann, *Genesis*, 274.
2. Parry, *Old Testament Story*, 136.
3. Bechtel, "Shame," 36.

Introduction

narrative structure of the story, shows that the Dinah story was intended to explain that such a shameful and life-threatening event happened to Jacob, one to whom God had promised protection wherever he went, as a consequence of Jacob's failure to fulfill his vow to God in Bethel. According to the regulations of the vow institution this must be carried out in a place chosen by God (28:10–22).

Scope and Delimitation

The whole Jacob story (Genesis 25:19—37:1, according to the author's view of the narrative unit of the Jacob story) is an interwoven large story or narrative unit. However Genesis 28:10—35:15, giving special attention to the narrative role of Gen 28:10-22 within it, will be the main focus. Genesis 28:10-22 is a foundational passage of the narrative unit, because the promise made by God to Jacob and the vow made by Jacob to God in 28:10-22 raise an expectation of relevance, or a searching for cognitive effects, in the audience which will reach its final fulfilment in 35:1–15. Thus Gen 28:10-22 creates a topical or thematic context for the global and local coherence of the whole narrative. This helps the inferential processing of the rest of the episodes of the narrative unit in these chapters. Genesis 28:10—35:15 is seen as a *"votive narrative"* which concurs with the public representation of other similar votive narratives in the Old Testament (1 Samuel 1:10—2:11 and Judges 11:30–39).

Methodology

I provide a literary analysis of Genesis 28:10—35:15, employing relevance theory parameters (see section 1.5), recognizing the text as a literary document or discourse, but considering the "interdependence between the world of the text and the situation which produced it."[4] The biblical writers integrated theological, historical, and literary features in the texts.[5] However, as a translation-oriented reader, I will treat the biblical data as a literary document without giving much attention to the issues of the historical, redaction, and source criticism. Nevertheless, I will closely examine the situation in which the narrative was produced and the communicative intention of the communicator, which presumably reflects his

4. Hayas and Holladay, *Exegesis*, 68.
5. Ryken, *Guide to the Bible*, 16.

historical and theological view. Adam Jaworski and Nikalas Coupland make a remarkable note about this feature of a text: "Discourse is language use relative to social, political and cultural formation—it is language reflecting social order but also language shaping social order, and shaping individuals' interaction with society."[6]

My use of "literary document" is intended to denote the creative and artistic procedures of this narrative discourse-presentation employed by the narrator to make his communicative stimulus more salient.[7] This is in order to achieve his communicative intention, and must be distinguished from the imaginative art used in fiction. Besides, no dichotomy needs to be created between the intention of the author (author meaning) and text meaning, on the one hand, and reader meaning, on the other, because the reader interacts with the communicative intention of the author through the constraints of the textual stimulus provided.[8]

A synchronic approach to the text is presented. It is analyzed by employing relevance theory parameters, without much worry about the diachronic aspect of the text. However, since discourse is a context-dependent communication, the contributions of the historical and cultural context of the text will be examined closely for their contribution to the process of interpretation and translation here will be no description of detailed linguistic (formal) regularities by making charts of sentences and clauses in order to describe topics, comments, focuses, and other linguistic features of the narrative. Instead, the ostensive linguistic signals that are intended to help the reader infer communicative and informative intention are examined (see section 1.5). Wilson explains that in the right context a hearer can infer from the narrator's point of view some feature of the intended interpretation of the discourse.[9] Inferring is pervasive in communication because, as I mentioned earlier, discourse is a complex phenomenon, and one of its complexities is being decisively dependent on its immediate context and on the behavior or attitude of a speaker.[10]

Therefore, establishing the context of this utterance is crucial for the understanding of the speaker utterance and deducing appropriate premises and conclusion(s) in order to achieve the cognitive effects exactly intended by the speaker. Consequently this literary analysis requires

6. Jaworski and Coupland, *Discourse Reader*, 3.
7. Powell, *Narrative Criticism*, 4; Alter, *Biblical Narrative*, 179.
8. Alter, *Biblical Narrative*, 179.
9. Wilson, "Metarepresentation," 429.
10. Blass, *Relevance Relations*.

Introduction

employing both a description and explanation of the utterances to explain the communicative intention of Jacob's vow to God and God's promise to Jacob at Bethel.

Secondly, this narrative is an institutional narrative. Charlotte Linde recommends the importance of analyzing institutional narratives within the context of the institutions "in which they are told" and the work the narratives were intended to do "in and for that institution."[11] This narrative unit will be analysed from the perspective of the institutions of the vow, the chosen people of Yahweh, the chosen place of worship (Bethel in this case), and the promised land of Canaan, which are the cognitive contexts in which the narrative was told from the point of view of relevance theory.

The main feature of the principle of relevance theory is maximization of the ever-increasing relevance of the human cognition in its operation of processing inputs of communicative stimulus until its search for cognitive effects is fulfilled.[12] More specifically, this is a way of examining the importance of the vow of Bethel for fostering the institution of the chosen place of worship (Bethel in this case) within the context of the chosen community of Yahweh, and within the contextual assumptions of the Promised Land. The expectations of relevance this same utterance raises include possible consequences for the failed vow. Relevance theory deals with the speaker, text/utterance, audience, and context of utterance holistically in the course of inferential processing of communications, and this is the model used.

It is worth noting that for translators a textual meaning is more than the meaning of the sum total of the discourse sentences. By interacting with a discourse, we go behind the text, to the communicator's world, but guided and constrained by the communicator's ostensive signals of the intended communication. The biblical text "allows the reader to penetrate the inner world of the biblical character, and reveals the emotional and psychological mindset which motivates them" to write the text.[13] Communicative meaning is always decisively based on the literary structure and sentences of a text which function as an ostensive communicative stimulus. To answer the question, "why did the narrator tell the story in this way in this particular context?," it will be necessary to examine, describe, and explain it from his/her point of view.

---

11. Linde, "Narrative," 532.

12. Sperber and Wilson, *Relevance*; Carston, *Thoughts and Utterances*; Blakemore, "Organization;" Gutt, *Translation*; Blass, *Relevance Relations*.

13. Levine, "Inner World," 307.

Reading and Translating Genesis 28:10—35:15 as a Votive Narrative

There is a third new approach for the close reading of the votive narrative of Jacob in general and of the Dinah story in particular. That there is a significant affinity between the Hadiyya culture and ancient Near East (ANE) culture can be shown by an empirical data analysis concerning the institutions of vow and marriage. Finn Rønne observes that there is an affinity between some Ethiopian and ANE cultures; and he specifically remarks about the region of South Ethiopia (which comprises the Hadiyya land) as follows:

> South Ethiopia may, in a way, be described as a border district and a meeting place, on the one hand, on African soil and, on the other, in an area which has been subject to influences since the distant past from the northern and eastern parts of present Ethiopia and thus from North Africa, the Middle East and the Mediterranean.[14]

This affinity suggests that understanding the Hadiyya vows will help us understand ANE vows and a comparison between them will be helpful. A comparative study of these two cultural worlds regarding the concept of vow and the episode of the Dinah story will show possible different interpretations of the vow and the Dinah story and elicit the role of the narrative for the moral, ethical, and religious value of those societies. The purpose will be to reconstruct contextual assumptions to help us interpret the literary data of the narrative, not to influence it. The understanding of the concept of vow among some other Ethiopian communities will also be considered. In other words, since discourse is totally dependent on the context of the utterance I suggest that the study of the concept of "vow" as understood in the ANE cultural context in the light of current Hadiyya culture will give an insight into the real-life context of ancient Israel and will throw some light on the interpretation and translation of the votive discourse of Jacob in general and the Dinah episode in particular. Other reliable ANE sources and helpful complementary models will also be considered.

The Hadiyya People

The major part of the Hadiyya people group live in southwestern Ethiopia around the town Hossana, about 230 kilometers south of the capital Addis Ababa, the capital city of Ethiopia. Linguistically the Hadiyya people

14. Rønne, "Kontinuitet og Forandring," 472.

Introduction

are categorized as the members of the Highland East Cushitic language family. Since 1992 the area has been known as the "Hadiyya Zone" for the administration purposes of the government of Ethiopia.

Hadiyya land extends as far as the Omo River on the west. Some Hadiyya people even live across the Omo River in the area called Bosha mixed with the Oromo people. On the east they are bordered by the Silt'i people who are Semitic, on the south by the Wolaitta people who are Omotic and on the north by the Gurage people who are also Semitic.[15]

According to the Ethnologue record of the 1998 census, the Hadiyya population is 927,933.[16] However, according to the National Central Statistical Agency's figure of 2005 the Hadiyya population is 1,506,623. There are four dialects of the Hadiyya language with relatively insignificant differences: Sooro Hadiyya, Leemo Hadiyya, Shaashoogo Hadiyya, and Badawaacho Hadiyya. The Badawaacho dialect is geographically separated from the other groups by the Kambaata, Alaaba, and Tembaro people and the speakers are in a physical contact with the Wolaitta language speakers to the south. So they experience linguistic influence from the Wolaitta people though their language status is not threatened so far.[17]

Historical records concerning the origin of the Hadiyya people are limited. Ernesta Ceruli in his survey noted that "the name Hadiyya is derived from that of the Muslim trading state and is spelt similarly in later Ethiopic chronicles."[18] However, there is not sufficient evidence that this name was borrowed from Muslim traders. On the other hand, some historical records indicate that Hadiyya was mentioned by some Arabic historiographers.[19]

The Hadiyya are a religious people who have different religious institutions. Traditional Hadiyya people used to worship for example trees, rivers, stones, mountains, and the sky (they thought that the blue sky is God himself). They also worshipped the sun and moon, by associating

---

15. There is another Hadiyya group in another district known as Woliso to the north of the Hadiyya people. In the early twentieth century this group used to speak the Hadiyya language; but now they have completely switched to the Oromo language. Sim, *Predicate Conjoining*, also noted that another Hadiyya group live in Bale Province and they also have completely switched to the Oromo language. For the purpose of this work I will focus only on the major Hadiyya group which lives around the Hossana (Waachamo) town.

16. Grimes, *Ethnologue*, 115.

17. For more information about the Hadiyya people see Sim, *Predicate Conjoining*, and Hankore, "Nominalization."

18. Ceruli, *People of South-West Ethiopia*, 118.

19 Braukämper, "The Correlation of Oral Tradition," 38.

them with the supreme God, and spirits. However, they do not worship animals. They also believe in some patronal spirits of family gods called *Jaara* which usually possess or indwell a subject (man or woman) who belongs to a particular family. Many families may have this family god *Jaara* who makes his subject prophesy, promise, or give warnings to the family and other clients. People go to such people for consultation. However the community does not build any particular permanent venue for them, although the diviners themselves may build a temporary shelter for divination ceremonies. Such divination practices are forbidden in Christian circles.

There was a particular family group called Anjamma believed to be rainmakers besides having other religious duties. They were consecrated as a special religious group and they received gifts for making rain. Other individuals like diviners *(boroodaano/kiiraano)*, and people with special knowledge *(hiraagaano)*, were very important figures in religious and social affairs.

Definition of Terms

Relevance theory is a communication theory which is based on a definition of relevance.[20] It recognizes that it is the mental faculty of the human being that draws inferences from people's behavior and enables them to communicate with each other.[21] Communicators exploit this cognitive capacity and do not say everything to their audience when communicating.

In terms of this theory, relevance is a phenomenon "which makes information worth processing for a human being"[22] particularly for the audience who presuppose that a speaker gives some unspoken guarantee to his audience that his utterance is worth processing. Such guarantees evoke a certain context, and the audience uses both guarantee and context to draw certain contextual implicatures.

There are two general principles of relevance: the *cognitive* principle that human cognition tends to be primed to maximize relevance, and the communicative principle that utterances and any ostensive communicative stimulus creates the expectation of optimal relevance in the audience.[23] The term "relevance" comprises a property of inputs, produced by the

---

20. See also Carston, *Thoughts and Utterances*, 12.
21. Gutt, *Translation*, 24.
22. Sperber and Wilson, *Relevance*, 46.
23. Gutt, *Translation*, 31; Wilson, "Metarepresentation," 419.

communicator for the cognitive processes of his audience. This input is analyzed by the audience inferentially "in terms of the notion of cognitive effects and processing effort."[24] When an utterance or any other ostensive stimulus (input) is processed by the cognitive process of the audience in a context of appropriate assumptions, it will result in the intended cognitive effects. For example, I intend my friend to open the window but I say to him "The room is suffocating because the windows are closed." And then my friend opens the window based on this utterance. My utterance has two propositions: "the room is suffocating" and "the windows are closed." The procedural marker "because" denotes that the cause of the suffocation is the closed windows. The literal propositional meaning of my utterance expresses a state of affairs in the world, which is a suffocating room because of the closed windows. However, my friend's action of opening the windows shows that he correctly drew the conclusion: "He requested that I open the windows" inferentially, which is the "implicature" or a cognitive effect, which I did not say explicitly. This example shows that our utterance comprises saying, asking, or commanding, but they are processed according to their relevance, not according to their propositional or literal sense.

As I mentioned above, human communication is geared to maximize relevance because we cannot process everything. We select and maximize relevance based on cost-benefit and cognitive effects are in direct proportion to the relevance of input: the greater the cognitive effects, the greater the relevance of the input; "the smaller the processing effort the greater the relevance of the input."[25] Since relevance is context dependent and there is a huge potential contextual resource in the human cognitive environment selection is inevitable.[26] The selection of the context includes keeping the processing effort to a minimum.[27] The expected benefit of this effort is described as a contextual effect or a contextual implicature. There are three kinds of contextual effects: drawing a new contextual implication, strengthening or confirming the existing assumption, and eliminating the existing assumption by contradicting.

Some technical terms are used in relevance theory. When reading it will be useful to refer to the how the key technical terms used are understood and these are given a brief definition in what follows.

24. Wilson, "Metarepresentation," 420.
25. Ibid., 420.
26. Allwood, "Meaning Potentials," 52.
27. Gutt, *Translation*, 28.

Context is a psychological construct. It is a dynamic and wholistic notion which is described as the "mutual cognitive environment" of the speaker and hearer rather than external and textual.[28] It comprises the speaker's and hearer's assumptions about the world. Thus the context of an utterance is a set of assumptions or premises employed by our mental processing device in order to interpret the utterance.[29] The cognitive environment of a person comprises a huge amount of information which includes "information derived from preceding utterances plus any cultural or other knowledge stored there—and further information that can be inferred from these two sources."[30] Any relevant stored information in the cognitive environment could be retrieved as the context of an utterance.[31] Therefore, sufficient clues must be provided by the speaker, in order to guide the hearer to choose the intended contextual assumptions from their cognitive environment which will help to avoid misunderstanding.

Interpretive resemblance refers to the shared meaning properties between the original and its companion which comprises implicatures, explicatures, and an interpretive use of a communicative stimulus of the original. Since all human communicators presume the inferential processing capacity of human cognition, not everything is literally expressed by the communicators to their audience. Thus an utterance is an interpretive expression of the speaker's thought not strictly a literal expression. Accordingly, only sufficient stimulus, optimally relevant or worth processing, is provided to the audience and the rest of the relevant linguistic propositional forms (explicatures) are reconstructed inferentially by the audience. If a representation is literal in an analytic sense (all the logical forms of thought and its representation) and all contextual implication (all what is intended to be conveyed) are the same then it is a limiting case.[32] Any descriptive representation of a thought has a propositional form and any propositional form of an expression has also a logical property. Hence, the propositional forms of an ostensive stimulus (companion of the speaker's original thought) share some logical properties with the propositional forms of the speaker's thought (which is the original one) and consequently they resemble each other. Such propositional forms are also constrained

---

28. Sperber and Wilson, *Relevance*, 39.
29. Gutt, *Translation*, 26.
30. Ibid., 27.
31. Ibid., 27.
32. Ibid., 41.

by linguistic forms such as procedurals (*so, after all, anyhow*, etc.) in order to direct the way an interpretation is processed.

The propositional forms of an utterance of a speaker share some, but not all, of the logical properties of the propositional forms of his thought because the "speaker is presumed to aim at optimal relevance not at literal truth" of thought expressed in an utterance.[33] Therefore, the resemblance between the propositional forms of speaker's thought and the propositional form(s) of his utterance is called interpretive resemblance.

Similarly, any utterance attributed to someone else's thought or utterance (reported speech) shares some logical properties (which comprise analytic implication or explicatures and contextual implication which the speaker intends to convey) with the original which makes them resemble each other.[34] Since reported speech re-uses or represents what someone has already represented it is described as a "representation of representation" or "metarepresentation."[35] The resemblance between the original and representation cannot be perceived as strictly literal or verbatim because it is a common experience that reporters do not exactly repeat the original utterance. Rather they report only optimally relevant logical and linguistic information which enables the audience engaged for the inferential processing to know if the utterance is worth the processing effort. Therefore, since the latter is not related to the former in a strictly literal fashion, but has "some logical properties in common" such as sharing all the logical and linguistic properties of the original speaker's thought and utterance, the resemblance between the original utterance and metarepresented (reported) utterance is called interpretive resemblance.[36] The speaker of such a representation could entertain it as a true thought or dissociate himself from it, simply representing it as someone else's thought, or he may show that he has a particular attitude toward it. In relevance theory such use is also described as *interpretive use*.[37] Relevance theory also explains *translation* (secondary communication) of an original work (primary communication) as an interpretive use. The translation resembles the original interpretively; the original being made to a second audience in a different context. Particularly all modern readers of the biblical text are secondary

---

33. Sperber and Wilson, *Relevance*, 233.
34. Gutt, *Translation*, 36–39.
35. Wilson, "Metarepresentation," 411.
36. Gutt, *Translation*, 36.
37. Ibid., 39.

audiences; thus the effort of reading it in its original context is more difficult. Hence it requires a contextual adjustment.[38]

Metarepresentation is described as an act of attributing one's utterance or any other public representation and thoughts to someone else's thought or utterance. Such attribution or metarepresentation can be marked in several ways. But the most common ones are employing the device of direct and indirect quotation markers (which also may differ from language to language). The reporter of the metarepresentation may show his attitude toward the original thought—for example, he may endorse it or dissociate himself from it. Making an adjustment to the contextual assumptions between the original and reported utterance might be essential in order to make the resemblance between them accurate, because utterances are context dependent.

An *echoic utterance* is a metarepresentation that uses someone else's thought or utterance interpretively to convey a certain attitude about the thought or utterance which is usually manifested in the interpreter's utterance. For example, according to the narrative representation of 2 Chronicles 18:1–27, the utterance of Prophet Micaiah: "Go up and triumph; they will be given into your hand" is an echoic metarepresentation. He ironically echoes what the other prophets said to the kings, and by this utterance he dissociates himself from the belief of the other prophets. His utterance shows that he has an attitude toward what they told to the kings: he does not believe that what they said is true; they are lying.

Ostension or *Ostensive behaviour* is intentional behavior of a communicator aimed at attracting the attention of his audience to a particular phenomenon.[39]

Ostensive inferential communication[40] is when a communicator produces a stimulus by the means of an utterance or by any other way through which he intends to make a set of assumptions[41] manifest or more

---

38. Gutt, *Translation*; Hill, *Communicating Context*; Sim, *Handbook for Translators*.

39. Sperber and Wilson, *Relevance*, 50.

40. See Sperber and Wilson, *Relevance*, 156–59.

41. It is very difficult to describe "meaning." However, relevance theory describes it as a "set of assumptions." According to relevance theory, the communicative intention is manifest by the means of ostensive stimulus employed by the communicator which could be an utterance or any other means. The informative intention is manifest through the communicative intention and "the content of the speaker's meaning is the set of assumptions ... embedded under the informative intention." When the informative intention of the communicator is made mutually manifest to both the communicator and his audience then transparency is achieved, which is perceived as a meaning (Wilson, "Metarepresentation," 424; Gutt, *Translation*, 24).

Introduction

manifest to the audience and to himself. The means of making a set of assumptions mutually manifest to both the communicator and his audience is described as "ostensive stimulus."[42] An ostensive stimulus aims to attract the audience's attention to the communicator's intentions. From the communicator's side communication is ostensive and from the hearer's side the ostension is inferential because the communicator does not say everything;[43] thus it is sometimes called ostensive inferential communication.[44] This effort is necessary in communication because communication involves two parties (communicator and audience) and ostensive communication can be successful only if the communicator's effort successfully attracts the audience to pay attention to the ostensive stimulus.[45]

Raising expectation of relevance is an ostensive act or behavior of a communicator with a tacit guarantee that his utterance or stimulus is relevant or worth processing.

A Contextual assumption is any assumption accessible through an utterance or a text employed by the communicator as a stimulus within a particular context to his audience. It is a logical premise formed from a stimulus in a particular context in order to draw a conclusion.

An implicature is a thought that the narrator or speaker intended the reader to come to by inference, it is not stated explicitly. Relevance theory describes such intended thoughts as implicatures or contextual effects.

There are two layers of intention: (1) the *informative intention*, which aims to make a certain set of assumptions manifest or more manifest to the audience; and (2) the *communicative intention*, which aims to make the informative intention mutually manifest by the means of an ostensive stimulus.[46]

Informative intention denotes that the intended communication will be accepted by the audience and it will influence their cognitive system such that they will eventually be ready to draw cognitive effects from

---

42. Wilson, "Metarepresentation," 423.

43. "A hearer following the relevance-theoretic comprehension procedure should consider interpretive hypothesis in order of accessibility. Having found an interpretation that satisfies his expectation of relevance, he should stop. The task of the speaker is to make the intended interpretation accessible enough to be picked out. Notice that the best way of doing this is not always to spell it out in full. In appropriate circumstances, the hearer may be able to infer some aspect of the intended interpretation with less effort than would be needed to decode it from a fully explicit prompt" (Wilson, "Metarepresentation," 429).

44. Sim, *Handbook for Translators*, vol. 1, 46–47.

45. Ibid., 52.

46. Sperber and Wilson, *Relevance*, 9–12; Wilson, "Metarepresentation," 423.

the utterance. Therefore, the communicator's informative intention is described as an intention aimed at modifying the cognitive environment of the audience.[47] Thus, the informative intention aims to make a set of assumptions of the communicator mutually manifest to both the communicator and his audience.[48]

Communicative intention is when the communicator shows that he wants to communicate and he is heard and understood. Thus, a communicative intention is an effort of making "mutually manifest to an audience and the communicator that the communicator has this informative intention."[49]

An *optimally relevant utterance* is one controlled by the principle of cost-benefit optimization. The effort of achieving intended benefits, which are positive changes to the audience's cognitive environment, presumes that the audience will be geared to look for an ostensive stimulus which is adequate and without unnecessary processing effort. Any effort or utterance that fulfils these requirements is said to be optimally relevant for the audience.[50]

A *commissive speech act* is employed in order to commit to a future course of action for example making promises.[51] This concept is not from relevance theory but is from speech act theory. But it is relevant to my research because it helps to explain the commissive speech act of the vow of Jacob. In the ancient Hebrew context נדר is much more than a simple act of making a promise as we shall see in chapter 4.

An *ad hoc concept* can be employed and interpreted differently. Depending on a different context it can be used in different times, in different places, and involving different things or people. The inferential conclusions achieved in such contexts through different premises and conclusions are geared by searching for relevance and are varied. Such mental processing is described as *ad hoc* processing. For example, if a husband says to his wife metaphorically and sincerely "you are my honey," on hearing this expression the wife perceives that in this particular context her husband excludes some logical or defining features of the encoded concept "honey" and narrows down to the feature of "sweetness" and at the same time he

47. Sperber and Wilson, *Relevance*, 58
48. Sim, *Handbook for Translators*, vol. 1, 46–47.
49. Ibid., 46–47; Sperber and Wilson, *Relevance*, 61.
50. Sim, *Handbook for Translators*, vol. 1, 52.
51. Levinson, *Pragmatics*, 240; Saeed, *Semantics*, 239f.; Austin, *Words*, 11, 151f., 157f.

broadens the logical or defining features of "sweetness" to cover his wife. There is no apparent semantic relationship whatsoever between "sweetness" and a "woman." However, searching for relevance (relevance-driven processing) for adequate contextual effects, human cognition creates a new meaning on an *ad hoc* basis by connecting both woman and sweetness by inference.[52]

Overview

Since the task of translation involves the process of interpretation before conveying the message into another language, in chapters 2 to 6, the communicative intention of the primary communication of Genesis 28:10—35:15 is viewed from the secondary audience's point of view. And then in chapter 7 I will conclude with remarks on possibly more effective ways of bringing out and conveying the communicative intention of the story in the process of translation (secondary communication).

The boundary of the Jacob story will be defined in chapter 2, which will function as background information for the main argument. In order to investigate the soundness of the hypothesis, the narrative context and structure of 25:19—35:15 will be closely examined, for evidence of the communicative intention of the narrator. The main points of this chapter will be addressed in the following way: firstly, defining the boundary of the Jacob story; secondly, defining the narrative structure of the narrative unit episode by episode in order to describe the role of Gen 28:10–22 for the process of interpreting the narrative unit and in order to explain the relevance of the Dinah story to the Jacob story.

Chapter 3 deals with the Hebrew concept of "vow" and establishes what aspects of the encyclopedic information of the contemporary audience will help us to access the contextual assumptions of the primary audience in this narrative. In order to achieve this objective I wish to examine the concept "vow" in the light of the Hadiyya concept of vow silet, and in terms of the ancient Near East cultural context, the Hebrew Scriptures, and ancient Israelite literature in order to describe or elicit the main encyclopedic entries in the cognitive environment of the original audience. At the end of the chapter, there is a brief comparison between the Hebrew and Hadiyya concept of vow. The discussion in this chapter will significantly assist the task of interpretation for the translation of the concept of vow and the whole narrative unit in which it occurs. Access to the contextual

---

52. Carston, *Thoughts and Utterances*, 349ff.

assumptions of the primary audience will play a very significant role in understanding and interpreting the discourse.

In chapter 4 there is a close examination of Genesis 28:10-22, in order to establish its role in the process of interpreting the narrative unit of 28:10—35:15. Thus, the utterances of God to Jacob and Jacob's vow to God in 28:10-22 will be treated as an abstract of the narrative unit because God's promise to Jacob and Jacob's votive plea to God in Bethel raise an expectation of relevance which functions as a topic or a common theme about which the whole discourse makes a meaningful coherence-relation. Therefore, in this chapter I will propose that the utterances in 28:10-22 will be treated as a base episode of the narrative unit because these are the utterances which raise an expectation of relevance in the audience and they will thus be primed to search for relevance in the following episodes until their expectation of relevance is fulfilled or the cognitive effects are achieved. The search for relevance is primed to see whether God has granted Jacob's votive plea. If so, did Jacob fulfill his vow to God? Why did the narrator include the Dinah story in Jacob's votive narrative? All these features will be explained from the narrator's point of view. Thus, the discussion of this chapter will explain why the utterance of the vow at Bethel is relevant to the interpretation of this narrative unit.

In chapter 5 there is an analysis of all the relevant passages of Genesis 29:1—33:20 in terms of the fulfillment of the vow of Bethel in order to explain the relevance of the Dinah story to the narrative of Jacob from the narrator's point of view. "Were the cognitive effects of the votive utterance of Jacob achieved?" In order to answer this question, all communicative clues /ostensive communicative stimuli used in the narrative are investigated in all the episodes in Genesis 29:1—33:20 to see how the expectations of relevance raised in 28:10-22 are fulfilled. Again, as the narrative discourse presented in chapters 29–33 is an evaluative one intended to fulfill the hearer's expectation of relevance (cognitive effects), raised in 28:10-22 the episodes of 29–33 will be treated as an evaluative narrative of the characters (God and Jacob) in terms of fulfilling the expectation of relevance raised in 28:10-22 and describe and explain any linguistic and contextual evidences available in the narrative in order to support this claim.

In chapter 6 the relevance of the Dinah episode to the votive narrative of Jacob is explained. It is also shown that the raised expectation of relevance caused by the utterance of the vow also includes the expectation of possible adverse consequences, if the vow were not to be fulfilled.

Introduction

Finally, chapter 7 will conclude the book with a brief general summary recapitulating the main supporting arguments for the interpretation and restating new insights. This will be followed by a brief outline of the implications of this interpretation of Genesis 28:10—35:15 for translation into a secondary communication, showing that Genesis 34 is a congruent part of the votive narrative.

2

Boundaries of the Jacob Story and Its Literary Structure

DISCOURSE IS A "COMPLEX cognitive and social phenomenon."[1] Therefore, interpreting and translating a discourse is primarily pragmatic, although it certainly involves syntactic and semantic analysis which are instruments used to express the speaker's or the writer's mental representation in order to achieve the communicative intention of the discourse.[2]

A discourse can be either oral or written and is organized by the principle of functional connectedness or coherence. Relevance theory explains discourse coherence as a way humans understand communication rather than as a textual feature.[3] Context and coherence are psychological phenomena which are usually exhibited by public representations in the linguistic organization of the discourse.[4] Accordingly, a dictionary of linguistics and phonetics defines the public representation aspect of the concept "coherence" of a discourse as follows:

> Coherence (n) ... refer[s] to the main principle of organization postulated to account for the underlying functional

---

1. Brown and Yule, *Discourse Analysis*, 271.
2. Ibid., 26.
3. Sperber and Wilson, *Relevance*, 289; Blass, *Relevance Relations*, 17–25.
4. According to relevance theory the context of utterance interpretation is part of the interlocutors' "beliefs and assumptions about the world" (Blakemore, "Organization," 18), or what is termed their *mutual cognitive environment* (Sperber and Wilson, *Relevance*, 39). More specifically, the context of an utterance is that part of the interlocutors' mutual cognitive environment which interacts with the utterance to provide a coherent interpretation of the utterance (Sperber and Wilson, *Relevance*, 15). Thus in terms of relevance theory, context and coherence are psychological, dynamic, and holistic notions rather than linguistic (See "context" in chapter 1).

connectedness or identity of a piece of spoken or written language (text, discourse). It involves the study of such factors as the language users' knowledge of the world, the inference they make, and the assumption they hold, and in particular of the way in which *coherent* communication is mediated through the use of speech acts.[5]

Thus interpreting a discourse involves describing the communicative function of a text in a given context, the assumed shared socio-cultural knowledge of the communicator and his audience, and "determining the inference to be made" in the process of interpreting and translating.[6] Therefore, it is crucial for the interpreters and translators of a discourse to recognize the organizing features of a discourse that contribute to its coherence so that they can be aware that every component of a discourse is a coherent building block. Hence, it is essential for us to describe the feature of coherence in the narrative unit of the Jacob story from the narrator's point of view by first defining its boundaries[7] stating its beginning and ending and describing its internal literary structure. This will help us to view the general contextual framework of the narrative, will unfold the meaning of the text and help translate it into other languages as a coherent unit.

After dealing with the probable textually signaled comprehensive theme of the Jacob story in particular and of the Genesis story in general; the development and structure of the Jacob story according to the theme will be shown episode by episode, making clear the role and relevance of the vow of Jacob in Bethel (28:20–22) and of the Dinah story (chap. 34) to the Jacob story.

Fishbane observes the importance of having the general framework of connectedness for the work of analyzing a particular narrative unit of the Jacob story when he says, "The episode of Jacob, his early life and trials, provide a rich context in which to study the patriarchal narratives in the book of Genesis."[8] Stanley D. Walters also supports this view when he says that Jacob's narrative has been "artfully arranged" around Jacob's return to

---

5. Crystal, *Dictionary*, 81.

6. Brown and Yule, *Discourse Analysis*, 225.

7. Many biblical scholars attempt to define the boundary of the Jacob cycle about which I am skeptical. Thus I prefer to define it as a narrative unit because the boundary issue is so fuzzy.

8. Fishbane, *Text and Texture*, 40.

the land of his fathers (Canaan) after his long stay in Padan Aram where he fled away to escape the revenge of his brother Esau.[9]

These remarks show that it is essential to describe the theme of the Jacob story in order to describe its boundary effectively. Every narrative unit of the book of Genesis is naturally connected to and distinct from others within the discourse-plot of the Genesis story, according to the episode(s) each narrative unit may comprise. However, it is not my intention to exhaust all the textual features of the narrative of Jacob.

Review of Other Works

Boundaries of the Jacob Story

Different scholars have proposed different boundaries for the Jacob story. Therefore, it is important to review the main views of the scholars about the boundary of the narrative unit of the Jacob story before proposing an alternative view. Each scholar attempts to establish the contextual framework (theme) of the patriarchal narrative which will guide her or him to interpret the textual data about the patriarchs as well as to decide the boundary of each patriarchal narrative. Some of their conclusions can be summarized briefly as follows. Of those who define the beginning of the boundary of the Jacob story as Genesis 25:19 or 25:21 a number of them have employed the genealogy and family criterion to decide.[10] Scholars such as von Rad, Fishbane, Wiseman, Westermann, Wenham, and Kissling use this criterion and describe Gen 25:19 as the beginning of the family story of patriarch Isaac.[11] George W. Coats also employs the theme *tolodoth* as a criterion for categorizing the patriarchal cycle and he describes Genesis 37:1 as the beginning of the Joseph story which is the *tolodot* (genealogy) of Jacob, thus beginning of the Jacob saga.[12]

David W. Cotter, however, uses the theme of "troubled family of the patriarchs, who were saved by God" in order to interpret the story of the patriarchs. Consequently he perceives the beginning of the family problem in the Jacob story as Genesis 37 and thus he describes 37:1 as

---

9. Walters, "Jacob Narrative," 599.
10. Gunkel, *Genesis*, 285 suggests 25:21.
11. Von Rad, *Genesis*; Fishbane, *Text and Texture*; Wiseman, *Ancient Records*; Westermann, *Genesis*; Wenham, *Genesis 16–50*; Kissling, *Genesis*.
12. Coats, *Genesis*. Generally, he describes Jacob story within the Isaac saga.

the beginning of the Jacob story.[13] Leon R. Kass suggests that the story of the book of Genesis teaches how understanding the threat in life and the human limit to overcome that threat leads one to seek the way to a greater life. Thus self-relying Jacob understood the danger to his life and his limits to overcome it which eventually led him to seek the greater way of life as presented beginning from Genesis 28.[14]

So the beginning of the Jacob story is not universally agreed and it varies depending on the scholar's contextual assumptions. Although it is very difficult to show that the other scholars' views are wrong the following evidence supports those scholars who propose the beginning of the Jacob narrative as Genesis 25:19. Firstly, the preceding narrative concludes the narrative of Ishmael, who is in the *tolodot* of Abraham in 25:18 which shows that the following narrative is a distinct unit. Secondly, the setting of the family story of the Isaac who is also in the *tolodot* of Abraham was introduced formally by the expression ואלה תולדת יצחק בן־אברהם "these are the descendants of Isaac the son of Abraham" (Gen 25:19). Thirdly, the story of the two brothers, Esau and Jacob, which is mainly marked for the conflict, immediately follows the introduction of the narrative of the family of Isaac and it was continuously intensified, as the story proceeds (Gen 25:22–26). However, it is worth noting that these evidences cannot be claimed as strong boundary markers because there is no clearly stated evidence provided by the narrative itself that the narrator was intending to make distinct boundaries within the story of the patriarchs. There is an even greater diversity in defining the ending boundary. Gunkel reads Gen 25:19—37:1 as the narrative which concerns Isaac, Jacob, and Esau.[15] Consequently he proposes 37:1 as the end of the story because it is here that the closing report of the narrative about Isaac, Esau and Jacob was provided. Similarly, Wiseman reads Genesis 25:19b—37:2a as a genealogical story of Esau and Jacob.[16] Consequently he proposes 37:2a as the closing verse of the story because it is from there that the story proceeds to the narrative of the family of Jacob rather than Esau and Jacob.

Cotter and Coats employ the death report of the patriarchs as a criterion for deciding the ending boundary of the patriarchal cycles. Therefore

13. Cotter, *Narrative and Poetry*, 79.
14. Kass, *Beginning*, 402.
15. Gunkel, *Genesis*.
16. Wiseman, *Ancient Records*, 69.

Reading and Translating Genesis 28:10—35:15 as a Votive Narrative

they propose Genesis chapter 50 as the end of the boundary of the Jacob story because it is in this chapter that the death of Jacob was reported.[17]

Gordon Wenham treats the Jacob story within the family history of Isaac, which he contrasts with the family history of Ishmael.[18] He argues that the narrative of the Jacob story which is presented within that of the family of Isaac covers Genesis 25:19—35:29 until the death of Isaac (who is the head of the family) was announced in 35:29.[19] Then he describes the narrative about Joseph, which is usually known as the "Joseph story" as the continuation of the Jacob story and thus describes it as the Jacob-Joseph story that "ends with the last words and death of Jacob" who is the head of the family.[20]

Fishbane reads Genesis 25:19—35:22 by searching for symmetrical binary pairs. Consequently he perceives 25:21–34 and 35:1–22 as a binary pair because 35:1–22 is a fulfillment of the divine oracle of Gen. 25:21–34. In addition he perceives the problem of child-bearing in the pregnancy of Rebekah in 25:19–21 as a symmetrical binary pair with the child-bearing problem of Rachel in Genesis 35:16–20, which resulted in her death. Thus Fishbane proposes Genesis 35:1–22 as the ending of the Jacob story because it is a denouement of the cycle which functions as a final conclusion of the *tolodot* of Isaac bringing the story to the final resolution.[21] Gerhard von Rad proposes Genesis chapter 50 as the ending of the Jacob story based on the criterion of the death report of the patriarch Jacob.[22] However, Westermann proposes 36:43 as the ending of the Jacob story because this is where the conflict between the two brothers culminated in the report of Esau's moving out of the Promised Land.[23] Kevin Walton reads the Jacob story in the context of Jacob's flight from Canaan and return to Canaan. Consequently he proposes 35:29 as the ending of the Jacob story because it reports Jacob's return to Canaan.[24]

Finally, Kass reads the Jacob story in the perspective of the human behavior of perceiving a possible danger or problem and recognizing the human limits to overcome it, which eventually will lead one to seek the

---

17. Cotter, *Narrative and Poetry*, 79; Coats, *Genesis*, 259–60.
18. Wenham, *Genesis 16–50*, 166.
19. Ibid., 168.
20. Ibid., 168.
21. Fishbane, *Text and Texture*, 46.
22. Von Rad, *Genesis*, 263–64.
23. Westermann, *Genesis*, 23, 407.
24. Walton, *Traveller Unknown*, 3.

way to a greater way of life. Since this behavior of Jacob was revealed in two incidents: strife with and overcoming his brother (chaps. 25–28) and facing the future leadership problem (chaps. 29–50) and finally addressing it in chapter 50; therefore, according to Kass, the ending of the Jacob story is Genesis 50.

The Preferred Solution

The above-mentioned variations in the boundary categorization of the Jacob story show that it is difficult to determine a fixed boundary of the patriarch's story because the proposed boundaries shift according to the perceived theme of the story. Kevin Walton remarks that there is a significant overlap of the patriarchal stories that makes difficult to make a fixed beginning and ending of the boundary of the Jacob story because the boundaries of the patriarchs' cycles overlap.[25] This is true even with the criterion of *tolodot,* which is supported by many scholars as a narrative boundary marker in the patriarchal story. This is because there is no clearly stated textual evidence showing that the narrator was intending to make a clear and distinct boundary for each patriarchal cycle. Moreover, the Jacob story shows that there is a significant overlap of the genealogy of Isaac, Esau, and Jacob within the same story. Why an overlap if the narrator was intended to make a distinct boundary for each patriarchal cycle?

The position taken here is that the traditionally called "Jacob cycle" is simply a narrative unit of the continuation of the patriarchal story. Gunkel remarks that the story presented in the book of Genesis in different narrative units can be termed as the whole history of the Israel's religion.[26] Surely, it seems that the narrator of Genesis has a religious motive focused on Yahweh and his people Israel. According to the narrative of the origin of the life in the paradise of Eden, the sin of humanity was so rampant that God found or saved only a remnant and then chose Abraham and established a new people for himself from Abraham.[27] Thus the narrator presents the creation story as a preamble to the patriarchal story, representing how the created people became so evil that God found only remnants from the line of Seth[28] who was the son of Adam (Gen 5:3) and

25. Walton, *Traveller Unknown,* 3.
26. Gunkel, *Genesis,* lxxxvi.
27. Gunkel, *Genesis,* 1.
28. Seth was not the only son of Adam, in fact he was one of the sons of Adam (Gen 5:4).

who was the ancestor of Noah, who was also the father of Shem. Shem was the ancestor of Eber,[29] and Eber was the ancestor of Abraham and his descendants such that they acquired their ethnic name "Hebrews" from Eber (Gen 10:21—11:24).[30]

Gunkel remarks that different narrative units of Abram and Lot are held together by the common clearly stated theme: how Abraham and Lot migrated from Padan Aram and how they arrived in Canaan and how their descendants became the heirs of their respective lands. This theme answers the question, "How did the people who name themselves after Abraham and Lot originate and come to these localities?"[31] Thus, Gunkel summarizes the patriarchal narrative of Genesis as a story of a family which is based on a basic theme how, "God chose this family in order to raise up the people of Israel from it" and how Yahweh's intervention and providence was active in the beginning of the people of Israel and in bringing them into the land of Canaan.[32]

Wenham and Gunkel suggest that the whole patriarchal narrative is a continuous story with different narrative units comprising an "ongoing account of the fulfillment of the promises made to Abraham and renewed to Isaac and indeed to Jacob just before he left the land of Canaan."[33] Thus this theme is pertinent to the content of Genesis. Accordingly, the narrative unit traditionally described as the Jacob cycle is the continuation and an integral part of the same theme or Genesis plot. The genealogy report of the patriarchs in this narrative unit is presumably employed as evidence to show that the descendants of the chosen line of Abraham and Isaac remain in the Promised Land in order to inherit the promise of Yahweh while the rest of the descendants of the patriarchs left it. Therefore, the phrase "Jacob cycle" has been abandoned and Genesis 25:19—37:1 is defined as a narrative unit in the continuing story of the patriarchs. Thus I concur with Gunkel that the ending of the narrative unit is Genesis 37:1. Presum-

---

29. Brand et al., *Bible Dictionary*, 735.

30. The ethnic name "Hebrew" is related to Eber, grandson of Shem and a progenitor of the Israelites (Hebrews). In this regard, the discourse structure of Genesis 10–11 is striking. In Genesis 10:21 Eber was introduced in a focused way as if the whole genealogy was organized around him and concerning him. In Genesis 11:16 he was referred to again up until his lineage came down to Terah, and then to Abraham. Thus the narrator puts Eber as a significant ancestor of Abraham (for the detailed discussions see my excursus on 'Hebrew' in Appendix 1).

31. Gunkel, *Genesis*, 159.

32. Ibid., 158.

33. Wenham, *Genesis 16–50*, 259.

ably the narrative of the Jacob story was intended to explain how and why Jacob and his descendants became the sole line of the promised seed of the Abrahamic covenant to inherit the promise of Yahweh contrasted with Esau and his descendants.[34] This intention becomes more apparent when the narrator concludes the narrative unit by reporting that Esau and his descendants were moved out of the Promised Land while Jacob and his descendants remained in the promised land as the chosen inheriting line (Gen 36:43—37:1).

Literary Structure of the Narrative Unit of Genesis 25:19—37:1

Different scholars read the narrative of the Jacob story in different perspectives, described as "themes." They have been divided into two general categories: genealogy-family and other diverse themes. Some points from previous sections will be repeated for the sake of clarity.

Literary Structure based on Genealogy and Family

There are many scholars who base their analysis of the literary structure of the passage on genealogy and family. Scholars such as George W. Coats, David W. Cotter, and Paul J. Kissling do not agree that Jacob story is part of the above mentioned larger narrative unit 25:19—37:1 or even recognize Gen 25:19—37:1 as part of the Jacob story.[35] In addition, some scholars

---

34. Walters, "Jacob Narrative," 599–600. Walters remarks that Jacob story is "bracketed at the beginning and end by the genealogies of the two sons who stand outside the lines of promise, Ishmael (25:12-18) and Esau (chap. 36), so that Jacob's role as the bearer of the promise is unmistakable."

35. A) Coats, *Genesis*, uses the theme *tolodoth* as a criterion for the categorizing the patriarchal cycle. He categorizes the Jacob story under the Isaac Saga; and then he describes the Gen 37:1—50:26 as "Jacob the Saga" which comprises different individual stories. Thus he describes the Jacob saga as the Joseph story which is the genealogy of Jacob. He employs the death report of the patriarchs as a criterion of closing of the narrative of each cycle and he categorizes the main story line of the Jacob saga as follows:

The Jacob story	37:1-36
The Judah-Tamar story	38:1-30
The continuation of the Joseph story	39:1—47:27
Jacob's death report	50:15-21
Recapitulation of the Joseph story denouncement	50:15-21
Joseph's death report	50:22-26

B) Cotter, *Narrative and Poetry*, who interprets the book of Genesis in the context of God's saving action, which is his theme, perceives the succession of the patriarchs

such as Walton, though they consider it as part of the Jacob story, do not organize a detailed literary structure of their readings of the story (see below). However, as we saw above several scholars recognize the Jacob story within this narrative unit and they perceive it as the genealogy and family narrative but they categorize the structure of the story diversely.

Gerhard von Rad categorizes the narrative structure in a more or less similar way to Wenham's, below in point 6.[36] But then, regarding the Jacob story, he claims that one must recognize that the Jacob story is located in the following narrative which is traditionally called the Joseph story. He argues that this view is supported by the textual evidence provided in 37:2: "This is the history of the family of Jacob" which is concluded by the death report of Jacob in Genesis 50.[37]

---

as a chosen family of God, which was troubled in different circumstances but saved by God. And then he categorizes the Jacob story within the scope of Genesis 37:1—50:26 around this theme. Consequently he describes the symmetrical plot structure of Genesis 37:1—50:26 in terms of the family strife as follows:

a. Joseph and the family strife he incites	37:1–36
a.' Judah and the family strife he incites	38:1–30
b. The descent and ascent of Joseph	39:1—41:57
b.' The descent of the brothers	42:1—47:27
c. Blessings: Joseph	47:28—48:22
c.' Blessings: all the brothers	49:1–28
d. The end for Jacob	49:29—50:14
d.' The end for Joseph	50:15–26

C) Paul J. Kissling describes Genesis 37:2—50:26 as the Jacob story based on the theme of genealogy (Kissling, *Genesis*, 25) and he categorizes the story according to the different episodes of the family story as follows (Kissling, *Genesis*, 44–48):

I. Internal Family Tensions Resulted in Joseph's Enslavement in Egypt	37:2–36
II. Judah's Story Begins Badly	38:1–30
III. Joseph Ends up a Slave and Prisoner in Egypt	39:1–23
IV. Joseph Interprets the Dreams of Pharaoh's Cup-Bearer and Baker	40:1–23
V. Joseph is elevated by Accurately Interpreting Pharaoh's Dreams	41:1–56
VI. The First Trip to Egypt Goes Badly	42:1–38
VII. On the Second Trip to Egypt Joseph Reveals Himself to his Brothers	43:1—45:28
VIII. Israel Moves to Egypt	46:1—47:27
IX. Israel's Final Day	47:28—49:32
X. Jacob Death, Mourning and Burial	49:33—50:14
XI. Final Reconciliation between Joseph and His Brothers	50:15–21
XII. Final Day of Joseph	50:22–26

36. Von Rad, *Genesis*, 264–342.

37. Ibid., 263–64.

Boundaries of the Jacob Story and Its Literary Structure

Fishbane, based on the same theme of genealogy, however, proposes the scope of the Jacob story as Genesis 25:19—35:22.[38] He categorizes the structure of the narrative in a chiastic or symmetrical spectrum of the genealogical organization as follows:

A Struggle in childbirth and birth right (25:19-34)

B Interlude; strife; deception; *berakhah*-blessing; covenant with foreigner: (ch. 26)

C Stealing of the blessing and flight from the land (27:1—28:9)

D Encounter with the divine (28:10-22)

E Internal cycle opens; arrival; Laban at border; deception; wages; (ch. 29) Rachel barren; Leah fertile (vv.1-24)

F Rachel fertile; Jacob increases the herds (ch. 30)

E' Internal cycle closes; departure; Laban at border; deception; wages (ch. 31)

D' Encounters with divine beings at sacred sites; near border; *berakhah* (ch. 32)

C' Deception planned; fear of Esau; *berakhah* gift returned; return to the land (ch. 33)

B' Interlude; strife; deception; covenant with foreigner (ch. 34)

A' Oracle fulfilled; Rachel struggles in childbirth; *berakhah*, death, resolution (35:1-22)

However, there are no clear textual or linguistic markers Fishbane employed to describe the above chiastic structure in order to avoid any conclusion based on the "eye of the beholder" or on the presupposed assumption of the reader.

John Skinner describes Genesis 25:19—36:43 as "the third division of the Book of Genesis . . . devoted exclusively to the biography of Jacob."[39] He categorizes the story as follows:

The birth of Esau and Jacob, and the transference of the Birthright	25:19-34
Isaac and the Philistines	26
How Jacob secured his father's blessing	27:1-45

---

38. Fishbane, *Text and Texture*, 40.

39. Skinner notes that chapters 26 and 36 are "misplaced appendixes to the history of Abraham and Edomite genealogies" respectively (Skinner, *Genesis*, 355).

Isaac's charge to Jacob	27:46—28:9
Jacob at Bethel	28:10-22
Jacob's marriage with Laban's daughters	29:1-30
The birth of Jacob's children	29:31—30:24
Jacob enriched at Laban's expense	30:25-43
Jacob's flight from Laban; their friendly parting	31:1—32:1
Jacob's measures for propitiating Esau;	32:2-21
his wrestling with the deity at Peniel	32:22-33
The meeting of the brothers; Jacob's march to Shechem	33
The outrage on Dinah	34
Jacob in Canaan	35

Wiseman describes the book of Genesis as a series of documents. He argues that the underlying "master key" of the compilation of the structure of the book of Genesis is genealogy.[40] As a result he describes and categorizes the narrative of Genesis 25:19b—37:2a generally as the genealogical stories of Esau and Jacob.[41]

Claus Westermann describes Gen 25:19—36:43 as the Jacob-Esau cycle.[42] He categorizes the narrative plot structure of the story around the theme of the family of Isaac which is marked by conflicts. He describes the family conflicts as super-ordinate and subordinate themes. He describes the super-ordinate theme as "what happened between brothers" (chaps. 25–36), which is the conflict between Jacob and Esau (chaps. 27–33) and he parallels it with the narrative about what happened between parents and children (chaps. 12–25). He describes the subordinate theme as one which comprises the conflict between Laban and Jacob (23–31), as well as the conflict between Rachel and Leah (29:31—30:24).[43]

Gordon Wenham divides the narrative of Jacob story into two phases which was split by the family history of Esau (36:1—37:1). The first phase of the Jacob story was represented within the family history of Isaac (25:19—35:29) which was concluded in 35:29 by the death report of Isaac. The second phase was represented within the Joseph story which was concluded by the death report of Jacob and Joseph (37:2—50:26). Thus

---

40. Wiseman, *Ancient Records*, 59.
41. Ibid., 69.
42. Westermann, *Genesis*, 23, 412.
43. Ibid., 407.

Boundaries of the Jacob Story and Its Literary Structure

Genesis chapter 50 is the ending of the Jacob story.[44] He categorizes the first phase of the Jacob story as follows:

First encounter of Jacob and Esau	25:19–34
Isaac and the Philistines	26:1–33
Jacob cheats Esau of his blessing	26:34—28:9
Jacob meets God at Bethel	28:10–22
Jacob arrives at Laban's house	29:1–14
Jacob marries Leah and Rachel	29:15–30
Birth of Jacob's sons	29:31—30:24
Jacob outwits Laban	30:25—31:1
Jacob leaves Laban	31:2—32:1 (31:25)
Jacob meets angels of God at Mahanaim	32:2–3
Jacob returns Esau's blessing	32:4—33:20
Dinah and the Hivites	34:1–31
Journey's end for Jacob and Isaac	35:1–29

Hermann Gunkel bases his assumption on "Yahweh's providence over Israel's beginning" which he describes as the motto of the story.[45] Then he employs the source and form critical methods and proposes the scope of the Jacob story as 25:21—37:1.[46] He describes the literary structure of the family story of Jacob as follows:

The Jacob-Esau Narratives. Part I. With Isaac	25:21—28:9
The Jacob-Laban Narrative	28:10—32:1
The Jacob-Esau Narrative Part II, associated with the divine manifestation	32:2—33:17
Jacob in Canaan, which comprises Esau's genealogy	33:18—35:22; 36:1—37:1.

In summary one can observe that even though the theme of genealogy and family could be used as the organizing framework of the story, the categorizing principle of the structure of the story can be diverse depending on the individual's reading of the story.

---

44. Wenham, *Genesis 16–50*, 168.

45. Gunkel, *Genesis*, 158.

46. Gunkel notes that Esau's genealogy of chapter 36 probably stems from an independent source (ibid., 285).

Reading and Translating Genesis 28:10—35:15 as a Votive Narrative

Literary Structure based on Various Themes

Yahweh's Faithfulness to His Covenant

Victor P. Hamilton describes Genesis 25:19—36:43 as "The Isaac/Jacob story," probably because of the overlapping nature of the narratives of both patriarchs (Isaac and Jacob) in these chapters.[47] He interprets Genesis 18–50 in terms of the thematic contextual framework of Yahweh's faithfulness to fulfill his promises and covenant "to those whom he has chosen." He categorizes the major plot structure of the Isaac/Jacob story as follows:

A. The birth of Esau and Jacob	25:19–26
B. Esau surrenders his birthright	25:27–34
C. Isaac and Abimelech	26:1–35
D. Jacob receives blessing through deception	27:1–45
E. Jacob meets God at Bethel	27:46:—28:22
F. Jacob meets Laban and Rachel	29:1–35
G. Jacob gains children and flocks	30:1–43
H. Jacob's flight from Laban	31:1–54
I. Encounters: Human and divine	32:1–33
J. Jacob is reconciled with Esau	33:1–20
K. The humbling of Dinah	34:1–31
L. From Shechem to Mamre via Bethel	35:1–29
M. Esauites and Edomites	36:1–43

Contrast between Divine and Human

Kevin Walton reads the story of Jacob by exploring "the contrast between divine and human," which is perceived as the paradox of divine presence and absence in the story of Jacob.[48] He claims that the harmony of the Jacob story is based on the theme of Jacob's flight and return, which was caused by the family conflict.[49] Consequently, he concludes that the scope of the Jacob story covers 25:19—35:29. However, he admits that "there is an overlap, and that the distinction is not complete." Thus, Walton categorizes the Isaac/Jacob story in terms of Jacob's flight and re-

---

47. Hamilton, *Genesis 18–50*, 173.
48. Walton, *Traveller Unknown*, 2.
49. Ibid., 2.

turn.[50] He considers the expression: "These are the descendants of . . ." as a beginning of the new section.[51] Then he views the literary structure of the Jacob story as follow: The divine presence in the life of Jacob (25:19-26), passages related to the issues between the presence and absence of God, and the human versus divine, showing that the divine plan will be accomplished in everything despite the deceptive nature of Jacob and his sons. The nature of Jacob and his children shows that "God's grace does not overcome human nature" (28:10-22; 34:1-35:29).[52] He argues that the story of Peniel shows the ambiguous nature of the divine presence in the life of Jacob. Divine working and human striving is contrasted. He remarks that although it is apparently implied that God is present in the life of Jacob yet it is indicated that there is still confusion about the presence of God as the things happening in his life show.[53] Probably the motive of the story is to correct the tendency or attempt of limiting God "to any predictable pattern" (32:23-33).[54] It shows that human beings cannot discern the divine will. Consequently they fail to act according to God's will. However, the divine will is fulfilled through human failing, even where families are torn apart and the father deceived (26:34—28:9).[55] God seems totally absent in the life of Jacob, which is contrary to his promise to Jacob in Bethel that Jacob was deceived by Laban and consequently he struggles for justice. However, at the end God proved that he is at work for Jacob actively (29:1—33:20).[56]

Seeking the Way to a Greater Way of Life

Leon R. Kass approaches the book of Genesis as a philosophical classic whose stories teach how "understanding the danger and accepting the limits of human power" helps to seek the way to a greater way of life. Thus, Kass reads the Jacob story in the perspective of the human behavior of perceiving a possible danger or problem and recognizing the human limits to overcome it which eventually will lead one to seek the way to a greater way of life. Thus he interprets Genesis 25-28, the first phase, as how Jacob

50. Ibid., 3.
51. Ibid., 11.
52. Ibid., 59, 215.
53. Ibid., 90, 93.
54. Ibid., 91.
55. Ibid., 124.
56. Ibid., 179.

perceived the danger of losing the birth-right and at the same time he was aware about his limits to overcome the danger which eventually led him to seek the way to a greater way of life.

Then he claims that the second phase of the narrative covers chapters 29–50 and it concerns the challenges of the leadership of the fast-growing family of Jacob. The family of Jacob became a great community, and consequently faced the danger of "disintegration within and of assimilation without."[57] Thus Jacob realizes the need of effective leadership to resolve the challenges of the perpetuation of the new nation. Therefore, first, he nurtures Joseph as a leader and then he replaces the leadership position of Joseph by Judah before his death.[58]

John Goldingay agrees with Kass' view of the second phase when he says that the basic driving motive of the patriarchal narrative is "the completing of the series of acts stretching from the call of Abraham to the giving of the land."[59] Leslie Brisman also concurs with Goldingay when he treats the Genesis story as a literature developed from different origins with distinct motifs and intentions. Thus he reads the narratives of patriarchs as a work fashioned in its most significant moments by literary art as well as theological and political motivations.[60] However, the challenge is how to decide the assumed deriving motivation or theme of the patriarchs' narratives because, as Westermann observes, scholars hardly agree about what the narratives of the patriarchs tell us.[61]

In summing up this review, it will be observed that there is similarity between the boundary description of Fishbane, Wenham, Hamilton, and Walton. These scholars, although they differ in terms of organizing the episodes of the narrative unit, show significant agreement in terms of boundary description of the same as the following synopsis shows:

57. Kass, *Beginning*, 510.
58. Ibid., 648.
59. Goldingay, "Patriarchs," 28.
60. Brisman, *Voice of Jacob*, xvii–xviii.
61. Westermann, *Promise*, 2.

Boundaries of the Jacob Story and Its Literary Structure

Fishbane
A. Struggle in Childbirth and birth right 25:19–34
B. Interlude; strife; deception; *berakhah*-blessing; covenant with foreigner: 26
C. Stealing of the blessing and flight from the land: 27:1—28:9
D. Encounter with the divine: 28:10–22
E. Internal cycle opens; arrival; Laban at border; deception; wages; (29) Rachel barren; Leah fertile (vv.1–24)
F. Rachel fertile; Jacob increases the herds 30
E' Internal cycle closes; departure; Laban at border; deception; wages 31
D' Encounters with divine beings at sacred sites; near border; *berakhah* 32
C' Deception planned; fear of Esau; *berakhah* gift returned; return to the land 33
B' Interlude; strife; deception; covenant with foreigner 34
A' Oracle fulfilled; Rachel struggles in childbirth; *berakhah*, death, resolution 35:1–22

Wenham
25:19:34: First encounter of Jacob and Esau
26:1–33: Isaac and the Philistines
26:34—28:9: Jacob cheats Esau of his blessing
28:10–22: Jacob meets God at Bethel
29:1–14: Jacob arrives at Laban's house
29:15–30: Jacob marries Leah and Rachel
29:31—30:24: Birth of Jacob's sons
30:25—31:1: Jacob outwits Laban
31:2—32:1 (31:25): Jacob leaves Laban
32:2–3: Jacob meets angels of God at Mahanaim
32:4—33:20: Jacob returns Esau's blessing
34:1–31: Dinah and the Hivites
35:1–29: Journey's end for Jacob and Isaac

Hamilton
A The birth of Esau and Jacob: 25:19–26
B Esau surrenders his birthright: 25:27–34
C Isaac and Abimelech: 26:1–35
D Jacob receives blessing through deception: 27:1–45
E Jacob meets God at Bethel: 27:46:—28:22
F Jacob meets Laban and Rachel: 29:1–35
G Jacob gains children and flocks: 30:1–43
H Jacob's flight from Laban: 31:1–54
I Encounters: Human and divine: 32:1–33
J Jacob is reconciled with Esau: 33:1–20
K The humbling of Dinah: 34:1–31
L From Shechem to Mamre via Bethel: 35:1–29
M Esauites and Edomites: 36:1–43

Reading and Translating Genesis 28:10—35:15 as a Votive Narrative

Walton
25:19–26: The divine presence in the life of Jacob
26:34—28:9: Divine will is fulfilled through human falling
28:10–22; 34:1–35:29: God's grace does not overcome human nature
29—33:20: God proves that he is at work for Jacob
32:23–33: Correcting the human tendency of limiting God

The Preferred Literary Analysis

The above discussion shows that categorizing or describing the literary structure of the Jacob story varies based on the thematic contextual framework or assumption one may have when he/she reads this text. Thus the commentators' criteria used to decide the boundary of the patriarchal narrative is relative, and as a result the boundary is indeterminate. More specifically it may not be appropriate to categorize the patriarchal narratives into different cycles, as many scholars attempted. They could simply be considered as a continuous narrative, of which Genesis 25:19—37:1 is a narrative unit.

Here the story of Jacob is treated as a narrative unit,[62] part of the continuing patriarchal story, devoted to explaining how one line of patriarchal descendants was chosen to inherit the promise of Yahweh and why that patriarchal line was chosen while other descendants of the patriarchs were excluded from the Promised Land as well as other promises of Yahweh.[63] Thus I concur with Fishbane who affirms this view as follows:

> The Jacob cycle is a series of episodes in the life of Jacob framed by the genealogical lists of the excluded sons, Ishmael and Esau. It is thus part of a larger patriarchal cycle of tolodot in the Book of Genesis, linking the earlier "*tolodot*-account of the creation of heaven and earth" and the ante- and postdiluvian genealogies with the list of Israelites opening the Book of Exodus (1:1–7).[64]

To conclude the discussion, Genesis 25:19—37:1 will here be considered as a narrative unit of the patriarchal story, employed to elucidate how and why Jacob and his descendants were chosen and how and why Esau and his descendants had to leave the promised land. It is a narrative unit which shows that Jacob the younger son of Isaac and his descendants

---

62. Narrative unit and Jacob story are used interchangeably
63. Kissling, *Genesis*, 415.
64. Fishbane, *Text and Texture*, 40.

became the heirs of the promise of Yahweh as contrasted to Esau, the older son of Isaac, and his descendants.

Contextual Framework of 25:19—37:1

The focus must now change to what makes this section a distinct narrative unit of the continuing patriarchal story.

Gillian Brown and George Yule note that a speaker or a writer of a discourse organizes each unit of a larger discourse strategically in order to influence the interpretation of his/her audience. Accordingly, he/she sets an element of the discourse around which "every clause, sentence, paragraph, episode, and discourse is organized" right at the beginning of the unit or discourse.[65] This narrative strategy is employed in Genesis 25:19-23, when the narrator says:

> The children struggled together within her; and she said, "If it is thus, why do I live?" So she went to inquire of the LORD. And the LORD said to her, "Two nations are in your womb, and two peoples, born of you, shall be divided; the one shall be stronger than the other, the elder shall serve the younger (25:22-23).

This abstract shows that the narrative unit is devoted to explaining why Esau and his descendants were excluded from inheriting the promised land. Accordingly, the narrative unit concludes by reporting Esau's and his descendants' moving out of Canaan to Seir or Edom (36:6) permanently (permanently because it seems that Esau used already to live in Seir as well as Canaan where his father lived Gen. 32:3) while Jacob and his descendants stayed there (37:1):

> Then Esau took his wives, his sons, his daughters, and all the members of his household, his cattle, all his livestock, and all the property he had acquired in the land of Canaan; and he moved to a land some distance from his brother Jacob. Jacob settled in the land where his father had lived as an alien, the land of Canaan.

Therefore, I presume that the whole stretch of this literary structure is a self-contained narrative unit probably intended to communicate the above mentioned one main point: explaining that God's covenant to the patriarchs to give the promised land to their descendants is limited only to one particular line of descendant(s) of Abraham and Isaac, excluding the

---

65. Brown and Yule, *Discourse Analysis*, 134, 148.

Reading and Translating Genesis 28:10—35:15 as a Votive Narrative

other descendants of the patriarchs, and how that promise was fulfilled by God's active guidance and involvement as manifested by choosing Jacob and his descendants.[66] Kevin Walton reflects this view when he says:

> On the one hand, Jacob is singled out by divine oracles as the one to receive the patriarchal blessing even before his birth, it is he who receives the name of Israel and is father of the twelve sons who become the twelve tribes, and he has the remarkable experience with God at Penuel.[67]

The descendants of Esau, the son of Isaac who was the promised child of Abraham, were equally entitled to inherit the promise of Yahweh as Jacob was because both of them were descendants of the promised son Isaac (Gen 25:21). In fact, Esau should have been the privileged inheritor of the promise, not Jacob, because since he was the first-born of Isaac he had the full birthright (Gen 25:25). But the story tells us that this was not the case—instead the descendants of Jacob became heirs of the Promised Land enjoying the privileges of inheritance. Leon R. Kass observes this view as follows:

> In each of the first two founding generations, the covenant of God with Abraham was successfully passed to one (the younger) of the founder's two sons—first Isaac, then Jacob—while the other son—first Ishmael then Esau—was cast to the side.[68]

In conclusion, the contextual framework or theme of the narrative unit of the Jacob story could be described as 'Jacob and his descendants as a chosen seed opposed to Esau and his descendants.' The following categorization of the literary structure of this narrative unit also shows this view more clearly.

The Literary Structure of Gen. 25:19—37:1 Based on the Theme "Jacob and His Descendants as the Chosen Seed"

Though the Jacob story is presented to show or explain how Jacob was appointed as a line of the promised descendant of the covenant made by God to Abraham and Isaac to inherit the Promised Land contrasted to other descendants of Abraham and Isaac this privilege is based on a

---

66. Kass, *Beginning*, 509; Wenham, *Genesis 16–50*, 168; Westermann, *Promise*, 2–30.

67. Walton, *Traveller Unknown*, 1.

68. Kass, *Beginning*, 509.

condition. That is, the realization of inheriting the covenant promises is dependent on Jacob's and his descendants' living up to the expected standard of the covenant of Yahweh; as he said to Abraham: "Any uncircumcised male who is not circumcised in the flesh of his foreskin shall be cut off from his people; he has broken my covenant" (Gen 17:14). Thus being faithful to the binding speech acts like covenant, vow, oath, and swearing are very crucial in the life of Jacob and his descendants in order to realize God's promises.

Though the organizing theme of the narrative is different, Wenham and Fishbane's sketch of the literary structure of this narrative unit of the Jacob story has been followed. The story line of the Jacob narrative unit according to this theme, episode by episode, can be described as follows: *Genesis 25:19—26:34:* Draws a contrast between Jacob the supplanter and Esau the natural heir. The narrative tells us that Jacob was singled out as a chosen seed of Isaac by God even before his birth (25:23). In order to explain this view the narrator tells us that the infants were struggling even in their mother's womb (25:22) and the oracle of God describes them as two nations and the elder will serve the younger (25:23). Thus, Jacob is presented as a promised seed of Isaac with whom God carries on his covenant to give the Promised Land to him and to his descendants. In Wenham's words this phenomenon "points forward to Jacob's domination of Esau, to Israel's subjugation of Edom."[69] The oracle of God started to be fulfilled when Esau sold his birthright by his own will (25:31–34). Thus Jacob acquired the birthright which was already prophesied even before his birth. Therefore, God's promises to Isaac to give the Promised Land to his seed in 26:3, 23–24 refers to Jacob by implication. The digression in 26:25–33 reflects one of the severe trials and tests which the patriarch experienced in the Promised Land.

Gen 27:1—28:9: Jacob receives a decisive blessing from his father Isaac by deceiving him, which seals him as a seed of the covenant to inherit the Promised Land. Jacob's cheating provokes Esau to anger so that he threatens to kill him. Consequently Jacob runs away to his uncle Laban to save his life as well as to get a wife.

Gen 28:10–15: After Jacob secured his position as a covenant seed (which was already confirmed by God even before he was born: Gen 25:23; Mal 1:2–3) by receiving the birthright and the blessing of Isaac, God reveals himself to Jacob at Bethel in a dream and confirms his covenant with him

---

69. Wenham, *Genesis 16–50*, 176.

while Isaac is still alive. This promise resembles the promises God made to Abraham and Isaac (Gen 13:14–17; 26:24). In contrast, God did not make such a promise to Esau, the elder son of Isaac. Thus the implicature is that Esau was excluded from inheriting the covenant promise and only Jacob and his descendants became the line of the covenant seed.

28:16-22: Jacob responds to the revelation of God and he makes an echoic vow at Bethel (which will be discussed later) while he is in distress. The vow is based on three conditions: if God keeps him safe in his journey to Padan Aram, if God gives him food to eat and clothes to wear, and if God brings him back safely to the land of his fathers.

29:1—33:16: God grants Jacob's plea that he give him relief from his distress:

1. God keeps him safe in his journey to Padan Aram (29:1–14)
2. God gives him wives (29:15–30)
3. God gives him children (29:31—30:24)
4. God blesses him with wealth (30:25–43)
5. God tells him to go back to Canaan, protects him from Laban and Esau on his way back to Canaan (31:1—33:16) and brings him back to the land of his fathers safely.

33:17-20: After arriving back to Canaan safely Jacob fails to fulfill his vow at Bethel. The failure of Jacob creates another expectation of relevance (adverse consequence): What adverse consequence did Jacob suffer as the result?

34:1-31: Jacob's negligence to fulfill his vow in Bethel results in a terrible adverse consequence.

1. Dinah is involved in an attempted abductive marriage by Shechem (34:1–11)
2. Jacob's children (Dinah's brothers) take revenge on the Shechemites killing all the Shechemite men (43:12–29)
3. Canaanites and Perizzites threaten revenge (34:30)
4. Consequently Jacob is confused and perplexed, presumably wondering why God did not protect him from this terrible event, which is a threat to his honor and which will also possibly result in terrible revenge from the people of the land and the possible death of all his descendants (30–31).

35:1: Amid his confusion, God reminds Jacob to go to Bethel and fulfill his vow.

35:2–15: Jacob responds to God and immediately goes to Bethel to fulfill his vow so that God's protection would resume. God appears to Jacob again and renews his covenant and confirms his promise to him as he did with Abraham and Isaac.

35:16–29: Jacob and his family continue living in Canaan and his deceased family members are buried where Sarah and Abraham were buried, which also functions as an authenticating sign of claiming the inheritance.

36:1–43: Esau and his descendants move out of Canaan (36:6–8) because he was already excluded from the Promised Land.

37:1: Reaffirms, as a conclusion, that on the contrary Jacob and his descendants continue living in the Promised Land.

It is worth noting that the above outline of the plot is provisional at this stage and it will be clarified in the subsequent chapters.

The Relevance of Jacob's Vow and the Dinah Story to the Jacob Narrative

The nature of Jacob's vow in Bethel has been observed by several scholars who consider Genesis 28:10–22 as an episode which has a central place in the Jacob story.[70] Thus although both the story of Jacob's encounter with God and his vow to God at Bethel appear making a self-contained narrative unit, both episodes are clearly connected to the preceding and following story of Jacob. This significantly strengthens and fosters the value of the sanctuary of God at Bethel which the primary audience already had in their cognitive environment.[71] Wenham rightly observes that the beginning and ending of this unit-story was clearly designed in a way to link the surrounding story, both preceding and following, "closing with Jacob's vow in vv. 20–22 which again looks back to his departure from home and forward to his eventual return."[72]

---

70. Pagolu, *Religion of the Patriarchs*, 158; Cartledge, *Vows*, 166; Gunkel, *Genesis*, 314; Dumbrell, "Role of Bethel," 68.

71. Wenham, *Genesis 16–50*, 220. See chapter four for a closer reading of Genesis 28:10–22

72. Ibid., 219.

Reading and Translating Genesis 28:10—35:15 as a Votive Narrative

The utterances in 28:10–15[73] have apparent interpretive resemblance with the promise Yahweh made to Abraham (12:2–3; 13:14–16) and to Isaac (26:2–4) showing that Jacob and his descendants are the divinely inaugurated sole line of the promised seed of Abraham entitled to inherit the promise of God to Abraham and Isaac, contrasted with Esau and his descendants.[74] Pagulo agrees with this view when he says that Gen 28:10–22 has a central place in the Jacob story and that it brings the theological aspect of the Jacob-Esau story to the forefront.[75]

The literary structure of this episode (Gen 28:10–22) shows that although it is clearly linked to the preceding and following narratives it is a distinct single unit. However, as Wenham notes, one may divide the story into two: Jacob's encounter with God in his dream and his response (10–17), and the vow of Jacob (20–22).[76] However, it is more natural to take it as a single unit which has three features: Jacob's encounter with God in a dream (10–15), his immediate response to the encounter as it was reflected by expressing his emotional feeling (16–19), and making his echoic vow (20–22). His vow is apparently echoic to 28:10–15.[77] It was an interpretive use of the thought of God which was represented by the utterance of God in 28:13–15.

When God spoke to Jacob he made the following six promises to him and his descendants: God promised to be with him and protect him, to give the promised land to him and his descendants, to make him and his descendants a blessing for all the families of the world, to multiply his descendants and to bring him back to the Promised Land. God also promised he would never leave him until he fulfills all that he has promised to him.

Similarly the echoic vow of Jacob contains the following plea represented by the conditional nature of the votive utterance: if God will be with me, if God protects me on my journey to Haran, if I return in peace to my father's house then: the Lord will be my God, the stone which I set as a pillar shall be the house of God and I shall give a tenth out of all God will give me. This votive utterance of Jacob shows that Jacob echoically or interpretively selected the thoughts of God that are relevant to the context of his distress and flight from the Promised Land without any clear idea

---

73. See my translation in appendix 2
74. Wenham, *Genesis 16–50*, 223.
75. Pagolu, *Religion of the Patriarchs*, 158.
76. Wenham, *Genesis 16–50*, 19.
77. Ibid., 219.

about his future fate. His vow shows that he was encouraged, and a positive emotion about the event was aroused by the promises of God to him in his dream. Thus he validated it, believed that God would fulfill what he promised and committed himself to express his gratitude to God in a particular way if he fulfills what he has just said. Similar echoic utterance continues to recur in the subsequent narratives: 31:3, 5, 42; 32:12–13; 35:1, 3, 13–15.

Thus this votive utterance raises an expectation as to whether Jacob's votive plea was granted and whether Jacob would fulfill his vow or not. Thus the votive utterance of Jacob raises an expectation of relevance which integrates the different componential parts of the narrative of the Jacob story in chapters 29—35:15. How this is achieved will be examined later. Cartledge accurately observes that one of the several functions of 28:10–22, which includes Jacob's votive utterance, is that it "integrates the components of the Jacob/Esau and Jacob/Laban cycles."[78]

It is argued that the writer of the story strategically put the vow of Jacob right at the beginning of this narrative unit as a 'staging' in order to represent his cognitive organization of the discourse in its linguistic or public organization.[79] Accordingly every linguistic resource goes around this staging (28:10—35:15) in order to achieve the intended cognitive effects.

Conclusion

In conclusion, the above analysis shows that 28:10—35:15 is a distinct narrative unit presented within the Jacob story of Gen 25:19—37:1. Therefore, the interpreters and translators of the Bible should treat Gen 25:19—37:1 as a coherent story within which the votive narrative of Jacob (28:10—35:15) is embedded. Hence, defining the relevance of the vow of Jacob in Bethel is crucial for defining the coherence of the narrative unit 28:10—35:15 and for the task of interpreting and translating it. The summary given above of the literary structure of the story shows that the vow of Jacob was made within the larger context of the story of Jacob because its immediate context, Genesis 28:10-17, which is in fact echoed in the utterance of Jacob's vow (28:20-22), is strongly linked to the preceding and following narrative of Jacob.[80]

78. Cartledge, *Vows*, 166.
79. Brown and Yule, *Discourse Analysis*, 148.
80. Cartledge, *Vows*, 166.

Reading and Translating Genesis 28:10—35:15 as a Votive Narrative

Genesis 28:10-22 is linked to the preceding narrative of Jacob because Jacob's votive utterance is echoic to the utterance of God to him in his dream.[81] Likewise, the utterance of God to Jacob in his dream is also linked to God's oracle to Rebekah in 25:23 as well as God's promise to Abraham in Genesis 12:1-3; 13:14-17 and to Isaac in 26:2-6. Similarly it is linked to the following story of Jacob because the fulfillment of this vow was referred to in key places: 31:3, 5, 42; 32:12-13; 35:1, 3, 13-15. Therefore, Genesis 28:10-22, beyond its linkage to the preceding and following story, functions as a framework for the narrative unit of Gen 28:10—35:1-15.

It is also crucial for the translator to understand the Hebrew concept נדר "vow" and its practice in its ancient Israelite context so that s/he may be able to understand what kind of expectation of relevance the votive utterance of Jacob creates or raises in the mind of the contemporary audience.

---

81. Its echoic aspect will be discussed in chapter 4.

3

The Concept of נדר "Vow" in the Hebrew Scriptures

Introduction

In the previous chapter Bible translators and interpreters were challenged to treat Genesis 28:10—35:15 as a narrative unit within the larger Jacob story and at the same time as a coherent part of it. They were also provoked to consider that Jacob's vow-making in Genesis 28:10-22, beyond its immediate linkage to the preceding and following story, functions as a framework for the whole narrative unit of Genesis 28:10—35:15. Hence, defining the relevance of the vow of Jacob in Bethel is crucial for defining the coherence of the larger narrative unit and for the task of interpreting and translating the Jacob story.

As a first step to demonstrating this it is now necessary to describe the concept נדר, which is usually translated into English as "vow." Understanding the concept of נדר in its ancient Near Eastern cultural context is crucially relevant before embarking on reading Genesis 28:10—35:15 because the narrator employed the נדר of Jacob in Bethel as the framework of his narrative presentation. It is necessary to establish whether there is an adverse consequence for the unfulfilled vow, in order to interpret the votive narrative of Jacob in general and Genesis 34 in particular. Understanding the Hebrew concept "vow" will help to explain how the vow-making of Jacob in Bethel functions as the framework of the narrative unit and how the Dinah story is a coherent part of this narrative unit, which will also be discussed in chapters 4, 5, and 6.

Reading and Translating Genesis 28:10—35:15 as a Votive Narrative

Being from a community which has an institution of the vow and actively practices it, I have observed to my surprise that the concept of the Hebrew "vow" is described as if it were the same concept as "oath." *The Encyclopedia of Judaica*,[1] *Theological Wordbook of the Old Testament*,[2] *The Encyclopedia of Religion*,[3] and *Encyclopedia of the Dead Sea Scrolls*[4] have all overlooked the need to make a clear distinction between the Hebrew concept נדר "vow" and other similar Hebrew concepts like "oath" and "covenant." However, the Hebrew vow is distinct from oath, covenant, swearing, and any other similar commissive speech acts of the ancient Hebrews.

The votive institution of the Hadiyya and other vow-conscious communities of Ethiopia may shed further light on the ancient Hebrew institution of the vow and the votive narratives of the Hebrew Scripture. The Horn of Africa, North Africa, and Near Eastern cultural areas have geographical, cultural, and linguistic links and they were culturally contiguous societies. Rønne observes this phenomenon when he notes that the Hadiyya and other neighboring ethnic groups might have experienced significant cultural influences from North Africa, the Middle East, and the Mediterranean since the distant past. He describes the area as follows:

> South Ethiopia may, in a way, be described as a border district and a meeting place, on the one hand on African soil and on the other in an area which has been subject to influence since the distant past from the northern and eastern parts of present Ethiopia and thus from North Africa, the Middle East and the Mediterranean.[5]

There is a close affinity between the Hadiyya concept of vow and the ANE concept of vow and, a comparative study of the current Hadiyya concept of vow and the ANE concept of vow will throw light on the Hebrew concept נדר and make the adverse consequences of an unfulfilled נדר "vow" clear. Examining the Hadiyya concept of vow for the reading of the Hebrew concept נדר "vow" will not change the Hebrew meaning.

---

1. Rabinowitz, "Vows," 227–28.
2. Coppes, "Make a Vow."
3. Klinger, "Vows," 303. Klinger claims that the distinction between vow and oaths is that "a vow is merely a personal promise, where as an oath is a promise made before some institutional authority." He even claims that the Hebrew vows are unconditional.
4. Schiffman, "Oaths and Vows."
5. Rønne, "Kontinuitet og Forandring," 472.

The Concept of נדר *'Vow' in the Hebrew Scriptures*

Encyclopedic information about a term and its use in particular contexts will help us to uncover the speaker-intended meaning so that the translator may be able to translate the meaning exactly as intended by the communicator for every use of the concept. S/he will be able to uncover the presupposed or assumed encyclopedic information of נדר ("vow") in the cognitive environment of the primary audience, to establish its conceptual distinctiveness or contrast with other similar concepts or speech acts like "oath," "covenant," and "curse" and to analyze and understand the communicative intention of the discourses in which it occurs. Roy Dilley rightly remarks that the lack of mutually shared knowledge of a key concept, which otherwise would trigger the salient feature of the text, could lead to misunderstanding or overlooking it.[6] Furthermore it will help us to choose the most relevant expression of the target community in order to achieve the highest interpretive resemblance in the translation process.

It was the Hadiyya concept of vow that triggered this study of the votive narrative of Jacob, so I will examine the Hadiyya concept of vow and establish its encyclopedic information in the cognitive environment of the Hadiyya people first. Secondly, the nature of Hebrew נדר in three literary corpora: in the ANE cultural context, in the Hebrew Scriptures, and in other relevant Israelite literature will be investigated. Thirdly, the distinctiveness of נדר compared to other similar Hebrew concepts will be shown in order to establish sufficient encyclopedic information on the concept נדר, which presumably was in the cognitive environment of the original audience. Finally a comparison of the conceptual range of vow in both ancient Hebrew and the current cognitive environment of the Hadiyya people will help choose appropriate expressions when translating.

The Hadiyya Concept of Vow

The Hadiyya concept of vow *"silet"* will be discussed with a view to interpreting the Hebrew concept נדר "vow" by comparison. This discussion will show that a vow-conscious society can sufficiently reconstruct the social institution of the Hebrew vow and studying such societies' concept of it will give us an opportunity to reconstruct votive utterances and votive narratives in their institutional frameworks It will also show that an unfulfilled vow is expected to result in adverse consequences.

Making a vow is common among the Hadiyya people among both followers of traditional religion and Christians, and it is popularly

---

6. Dilley, "Context," 16.

practiced in the community. The concept of "vow" is lexicalized as "*silet.*" However, so far there is not even a single written document found about the concept or about its practice among the Hadiyya people. Therefore, the writer saw a need to do research among the Hadiyya people and other relevant people groups in order to further understand *the peoples' concept* in their cognitive environment. Fifty people were interviewed at different venues and places among the Hadiyya people and elsewhere.

The interviewees include both men and women of different ages. The interviewees' geographical location included different parts of Ethiopia: Addis Ababa, Hadiyya, Central Shoa, Gondor, Gojam, Sidamo, Kambatta, and Wollo. Two Eritreans were also interviewed. The majority of the interviewees are from the Hadiyya people because in this research Hadiyya is taken as a single language community. The following are summaries of the interview responses.

There were fourteen questions about the Hadiyya concept of vow (see appendix 4) and then the interviewees responded to the questions as follows:[7]

All the interviewees, unanimously, said that while it is certainly possible to pray to God without making a vow, making a vow is the petitioner's commitment to express his thanks and appreciation to God in a particular way for granting her/his votive plea. The respondents were asked whether vow-making is intended to influence God. Except for two scholars, one from Eritrea and the other from Ethiopia, all the participants said that making a vow is not intended to influence God. Rather it is caused by the distress of the petitioner. It is a reflection of the emotion of the petitioner because of his distressing situation or problem. They indicated they need to bring gifts as a thanks giving if the deity rescues the petitioner from his distress. If the deity does not help, the vow maker is under no obligation to fulfill his vow.

All the interviewees were clear about to whom one makes a vow. They emphatically said that they never make a vow to another human being. A vow is *always* made by humans to a deity.[8] When they were asked when or in what circumstances people make a vow they unanimously responded that people make vow only when they are distressed because of specific problems.

---

7. The questions and their answers are restructured here but the content is retained exactly as the interviewees responded (see the full interview in appendix 4).

8. A vow could be made to deities like God, the angel Gebre'el, the angel Michael, family spirits, spirits which work through witchdoctors, etc.

Regarding where people make vows and where they fulfill their vows if a deity grants their votive plea, they responded that they can make a vow anywhere but they must fulfill their votive promise to the deity only in a place where they believe the deity resides.

The interviewees also said that they would fulfill their vow only if God answered their votive plea. When questioned as to what would happen if one failed to fulfill a vow, they emphatically responded that it is a bad thing not to fulfill one's vow; terrible things will happen as an adverse consequence. Several of the interviewees illustrated this by giving examples about their own experiences, when and how they make their vows and whether they fulfill their vows or not. One example from a middle aged man who described his own experience has been paraphrased as follows:

> Once I bought a goat and the goat was seriously sick, which distressed me a lot. So I made a vow to God saying: "God if you heal this goat and if it produces many young then I will give you one out of them as a thanks-giving." God healed the goat and eventually it produced so many goats. But I failed to fulfill my vow. Consequently God hit all the goats with the plague and all of them died. Thus I learned a lesson. It is not an obligation to make a vow but once it is made it is seriously binding.

The interviewees also responded that anybody can make a vow. They said that even a thief can make a vow to God saying: "God, if you give me success in my stealing I will give . . . to you."

They also responded that it is impossible to change their vows and that they never annul a vow once it is made; it is very binding. But they are obliged to fulfill their votive promises if and only if the deity answers their votive plea.

Finally, regarding whether there are some things which are not supposed to be offered as a vow offering they told me that they can offer anything. I was told that some people even offer lice, rats, walking on barefoot to the sanctuary of the deity, building a sanctuary for the deity, etc.

To summarize, the making of *silet* "vow" in Hadiyya is always perceived as a *conditional* commitment made by people to a deity. The context in which a *silet* is made is always distress—a person presents his plea to a deity in order to get relief from his distress, and commits himself to do something for a deity as an expression of his gratitude if the deity grants his votive plea. The cause of the distress can be anything: barrenness, war, poverty, sickness, examination, journey or travel, etc. The commitment is not binding if the deity does not grant his plea.

Reading and Translating Genesis 28:10—35:15 as a Votive Narrative

The Hadiyya votive institution is not legislated; rather it is an informal institution. However, within the informal institution the concept of vow is well understood in the community, covering the essentials of the concept, including the level of expectation on the human party for the granting of the conditions requested, and the need to promptly fulfill the commitment made.

A vow can be made anywhere. However, the place of fulfilling the vow must be in the church, or at the diviners' place, or at a tree or river or a mountain depending to whom the vow was made. The focus is on the deity, not on the location or a sanctuary. It is required that one must fulfill his vow exactly as he committed himself to the deity. Otherwise, it is expected that some kind of adverse consequence is inevitable if one fails to fulfill the vow.

Finally the concept *silet* in Hadiyya has the following encyclopedic information:

1. It is always made between man and deity addressed by a human to a deity.
2. It is always conditional.
3. It is made in the context of distress.
4. It must be fulfilled on condition that the deity has answered one's plea.
5. It can be made anywhere.
6. It must be fulfilled at the place perceived as where the deity resides.
7. Adverse consequences are expected if one fails to fulfill ones vow.
8. Once it is made it can never be changed to something else.
9. It is never annulled.
10. You can promise to do or give anything you want as a thanksgiving to the deity.
11. Anybody can make a *silet*.
12. It is not intended to influence the deity rather it is an expression of emotion of the petitioner and his commitment to express his gratitude to God in a particular way if his plea is granted.

The Concept of נדר "Vow" in Ancient Israelite Society

We have investigated the Hadiyya concept of vow in brief. Now let us investigate the ANE cultural context whether they had a similar institution of vowing and whether they conceived that the unfulfilled vow will result in adverse consequence. Since the Hebrew Scriptures were written in the ANE cultural context there is no doubt that the outcome of this investigation will throw significant light for the understanding of the biblical concept of vow; and it is more reliable light than the current Hadiyya concept of vow.

The Nature of נדר in the Ancient Near Eastern Context

This discussion concerns the nature of the concept נדר in the ancient Near Eastern context before the third century BCE. Tony Cartledge has done a remarkable work in examining the ancient Near Eastern culture regarding vow-making.[9] He examined Sumerian, Akkadian, Egyptian, Hittite, Ugaritic, Old Aramaic, Punic, and Neo-Punic texts and argued that נדר in the ancient Near Eastern cultural context was conditional, it was made only between God and man, it was done in the context of distress, serious adverse consequences were expected if one failed to fulfill the vow, and it served a similar function to the biblical vow in the life of the people. In this section I rely heavily on Cartledge's work.

Vows in Mesopotamia and its Culturally Contiguous Area

The broad geographical area of the Mesopotamia includes the region of the southwest Asia, eastern Syria, southeastern Turkey, and most of Iraq. This area was a center of ancient civilization whose culture influenced a wider geographical area including North Africa, as Edzard observes: "This area was a center of the ancient civilization whose cultural influence extended throughout the Middle East and as far as the Indus Valley, Egypt, and the Mediterranean."[10] It is therefore relevant to explore the concept of the vow in the ancient cultural environment of Mesopotamia and in those other related areas which are culturally influenced by Mesopotamia in order to get some insight about the concept of vow in the Hebrew Scriptures.

---

9. Cartledge, *Vows*.
10. Edzard, "Ancient Mesopotamia," 860.

Reading and Translating Genesis 28:10—35:15 as a Votive Narrative

Sumerian Vows

The literature resources we have access to so far about the Sumerian culture do not show that the concept of vow was lexicalized in the Sumerian language. However, it is observed that the Sumerians practiced the vow in its conditional nature. For example, people made petition to a deity for healing from an illness and they promised to do something in response to express their gratitude if the deity healed them.[11] The promise of the vow includes "material gifts, temple service, or more commonly, public praise."[12] The vow was made in the context of distress, only between deity and humans who wish to get out of distress. The fulfillment of the vow was held only in the temple.[13]

Babylonian and Assyrian Vows

The Babylonian and Assyrian language is a dialect of East Semitic called Akkadian. The concept "vow" was lexicalized as *ikribu*, which is not cognate to the Hebrew נדר. However, there is sufficient textual evidence which shows that the conditional vow making was extensively common among the Babylonians and Assyrians.[14] Vows were made only between a human and a god. The vow of promise, including material promises, was fulfilled on condition of the granting of the votive request. The request comprises relief from sickness and different kinds of distress.[15] The vows include singing songs of praise,[16] serving the deity in different ways like proclaiming his greatness,[17] and making an image as a votive offering and depositing it in the temple of the deity.[18] The praise has a public nature.

Most of such Babylonian and Assyrian prayers are similar to those in the Hebrew Psalms. For example, they promise to praise publicly on condition of a request being honoured. This is a promise of an abstract gift rather than a material gift,[19] but even so the fulfillment of the promise was

11. Cartledge, *Vows*, 75.
12. Ibid., 75.
13. Ibid., 75.
14. Oppenbeim, *Ancient Mesopotamia*, 26.
15. Cartledge, *Vows*, 77.
16. Ibid., 80–81.
17. Ibid., 82–83.
18. Leick, *Sex and Erotocism*, 94.
19. Cartledge, *Vows*, 85.

a serious matter and failure could lead to serious adverse consequences as Cartledge observes: "Failure to fulfill one's vows could lead to sickness or other troubles, and recovery was conditional on fulfilling the promised payment."[20] For example, some letters written by two women narrate that some family members were attacked by sickness and the whole family was in danger. The god Assur unleashed the demons to attack them because a person called Pushuken failed to fulfill his vow to him.[21] The location for the payment of the vow was the sanctuary/temple of the deity.[22]

In summary, the Assyro-Babylonian customary practice of vows as recorded by Cartledge is similar to that of the Hadiyya: it was conditional, it was taken in the context of prayer, the motivation of the vow was to seek relief from distress and the content of votive prayers could be the promise of public praises. The vow was binding—it must be fulfilled, the unfulfilled vow would result in adverse consequences, and the fulfillment of the vow should be in the place where they believe the deity resides.[23]

Egyptian Vows

Cartledge notes that there is no significant evidence in the Egyptian religious literature about the conditional vow compared with other ancient Near Eastern.[24] He presumes that this was because all the accessible written documents were from the kings who used to consider themselves as gods. Consequently vow-making is not expected from them, because vow-making naturally implies a petition from a distressed human being to his god for special favor and help. However, the few documents available from the common people show that conditional vow-making was practised.[25] The location for the fulfillment of the Egyptian vows was also the temple of the deities.[26]

---

20. Ibid., 86.
21. Ibid., 88.
22. Ibid., 90.
23. Oppenbeim, *Ancient Mesopotamia*, 242.
24. Cartledge, *Vows*, 99.
25. Ibid., 95.
26. Hoffmeier, "Egyptians," 284.

HITTITE VOWS

Unger notes that Hittites were non-Semitic people probably of Indo-European origin. Their language is categorized as one of the Indo-European language family. Hittites were one of the groups of inhabitants of the land of Canaan at the time of the Israelite's conquest of the land.[27] Thus ancient Israelites share the same cultural environment with the Hittites.

Hittite religious literature shows that conditional vow-making was extensively common in the Hittite culture,[28] and it was made in the context of prayer to get relief from distress.[29] The concept of vow is lexicalized as *malda*.[30] The fulfillment of the vow was considered as a joyful reason for celebrating with a feast.[31] The act of vow-making was so serious that it was believed that the failure to fulfill a vow would provoke the anger of gods and would result in punishment which was perceived by the Hittites as a reminder by gods to that the suppliant should fulfill the vow.[32] Making the promise and accomplishing the same was perceived as a demonstration of their confidence in the gods and thanksgiving to them for answering their requests.[33] Thus reciprocity is observed in the institution of vow. The location of the vow-making and its fulfillment was the temple of a god, and it should be done publicly.

UGARITIC VOWS

The Ugaritic literatures also show that vow-making was common in the Ugaritic culture. The concept of vow is lexicalized in the Hebrew cognate *ndr*. But the concept of *ndr* in Ugaritic is broader than the Hebrew concept of נדר because it comprises a vow of man to god, a vow of god to man, and even a serious promise of one king to another king (probably to the superior).[34] For example, the promise of the god El to King Keret (spelled also as Kirta) to give him children and the Ugaritic king's promise

---

27. Unger, *Bible Dictionary*, 576.
28. Bryce, *Life and Society*, 175.
29. Cartledge, *Vows*, 102.
30. Ibid., 100.
31. Ibid., 101.
32. Ibid., 103–5.
33. Ibid., 104, 107.
34. Ibid., 108, 112.

to another king were referred as *ndr*.³⁵ The pragmatic sense of the term נדר when it is used in relation to the human vow to deity is distinct from these. However, my main focus here is to show that the Hebrew concept נדר parallels with the other Ugaritic concept of vow as David Marcus rightly observes the similarity between the ancient Israelite's narrative vow and the Ugaritic narrative vows.³⁶ That it is conditional marked by the Hebrew cognate *hm* and it is made in the context of prayer motivated by desiring to get relief from one's deity from one's distress.³⁷ The causes of distress are various including enemy threat, lack of children, getting a wife, and a long journey.³⁸ For example, see the vow-making of the Keret, King of Habur (transcribed as Kirta)³⁹. The vow was presented in the poetry as follows:

> He there makes a vo[w, Ki]rta the Noble:
> "As Asherah of Tyrians lives,
> The Goddess of the Sidonians,
> If I take Huraya into my palace,
> And have the girl enter my court,
> Her two parts I'll make silver,
> Her third part I'll make gold!" ⁴⁰

The seriousness of the vow making is manifest in Ugaritic literature. For instance King Keret takes a vow for his successful journey to get his wife Huray.⁴¹ It is perceived that the king received from god what he requested: "sons of Kirta are as many as vowed; Huray's daughters are just as were vowed."⁴² But he failed to fulfill his vow which resulted in devastating

---

35. Ibid., 112, 122.
36. Marcus, *Jephthah*, 21.
37. Cartledge, *Vows*, 110–11.
38. Ibid., 117–18.
39. Since the original inscription was syllabic different people supply different forms of vowels.
40. Parker, *Narrative Poetry*, 19–20. The following is the Ugaritic transcription of the text:
tm yrd krt t
Iitt airt srm
Hm hry bty iqb
Asrb gimt hzry
Tnh kspm atn
W tltth hrsm
Ylk ym wtn
Tlt rb ym.
41. Cartledge, *Vows*, 108–9.
42. Parker, *Narrative Poetry*, 26.

consequences. It was perceived that the king was seriously ill because the goddess Asherah punished him for failing to fulfill his vow.[43] But when the King fulfilled his vow the god El brought healing to the ailing king by lifting the punishment.[44] Hendel compares the vow of King Keret and the vow of Jacob and observes similarity between the two stories except that he wrongly concludes that Keret was presented as failing to fulfill his vow while Jacob was presented as faithful to his vow.

In the Ugaritic concept the vow fulfillment was perceived as an occasion of joy or celebration and the location of taking and fulfilling the vow is the temple/shrine of god(s).[45]

Aramaic Vows

Aramaic literature also shows that the conditional vow to a deity was practised in Aramaic culture and the concept of vow was lexicalized by the Hebrew cognate *nzr*.[46] However, the evidences are limited and many of them are controversial. The nature of the vows was that the vow-making took place in the context of prayer and it was motivated by a distress. For instance, King Bar-Hadad made a vow to a god known as Melqart in the time of war.[47] Thus the vow was directed from human to a deity to get relief form the distress. The vow-making and fulfillment of the same was held in the sanctuary of the deity although the evidence is limited about this claim.[48]

Phoenician, Punic, and Neo-Punic Vows

Phoenician, Punic, and Neo-Punic texts provide an enormous corpus of votive literature. But Cartledge questions their relevance to the ancient Near Eastern cultural context because almost all of them are from the third, second and first century BCE and most of them are from Mediterranean and North African cultural environments.[49] However, the his-

---

43. Ibid., 27.
44. Cartledge, *Vows*, 114.
45. Ibid., 112.
46. Ibid., 127.
47. Ibid., 125–26.
48. Ibid., 125.
49. Ibid., 129.

torical documents indicate that the Phoenicians were Semitic people who migrated from the ancient Near East Mediterranean region and settled in North Africa and Western Spain.[50] Thus, there is no doubt that the migrants carried their culture along with them and gleaning their concept of vow will contribute toward this discussion.

Phoenician: The practice of conditional vow-making is common in the Phoenician cultures. The nature of a vow was that it was made in the context of prayer, it was motivated by distress desiring to get relief from a deity, and the promise of vow was to be fulfilled only when the deity granted the petition.[51] Fulfilling the vow was perceived as expressing one's gratitude to the deity for honoring the petitioner by answering his prayers. Therefore it should be a public celebration.[52]

Punic and Neo Punic: Punic refers to Carthage, a West Mediterranean Phoenician (Punic) city.[53] The Punic literatures also show that the conditional vow-making to gods was widely common, particularly to Baal-Shemaim. The concept of the vow was lexicalized by the Hebrew cognate *ndr*.[54] The nature of the vow was that it was made only between man and deity, and it was taken in the context of prayer, when the person who was in distress sought relief from a god.[55] A petitioner fulfilled his vow only when he received an answer from the god for his prayer. Fulfilling the vow was perceived as expressing one's gratitude to the deity and one's trust and request to the deity for continued blessing.[56] The location of the fulfilling of the vow must be in the sanctuary of the deity.

Summary of נדר in Ancient Near Eastern Cultural Context

The nature of the vow in the ancient Near Eastern Cultures could be summarized as follows.[57]

Conditional vow-making was a common cultural institution in all ancient Near Eastern societies. The tradition was most common among the Mesopotamians, Hittites, and the Phoenicio-Punic peoples.

50. Unger, *Bible Dictionary*, 1005–1006.
51. Cartledge, *Vows*, 130.
52. Ibid.
53. Crystal, *Encyclopedia*, 988.
54. Cartledge, *Vows*, 131.
55. Ibid., 133.
56. Ibid.
57. See also Cartledge, *Vows*, 134–36.

Except for a very few unusual examples in the context of Ugaritic vow-making all the vows in the ancient Near Eastern cultures were taken between humans and deity. Vow-making frequently took place in the temple of the deity and was almost always fulfilled in the temple of the deity.[58] Vow-making to a deity was taken in the context of prayer motivated by the personal or national distress seeking relief and blessing from the deity. Some of the causes of the distress are physical illness, desire for long life, war, long distance travel, and desire for wife and children.

It is implied by the texts that the fulfillment of the vow by the petitioner is perceived as an expression of gratitude, joy, and praise to the deity for granting one's request. So it was held as an event of public celebration in the temple as a sign of recognition of the deity's power and loving care for his people at the same time desiring and requesting for the continued blessing of the deity. Thus the relationship of the humans with their deity is apparent in the process of the vow-making. Hence, by nature the vow-making implies reciprocity between the deity and humans.

Finally most literature from the ancient Near Eastern cultures shows that vow making is a very serious matter. The petitioner must faithfully fulfill his vow without any delay. The failure to fulfill a vow will provoke a deity to wrath and may lead him or her to some adverse consequences.

Thus the examination of the ancient Near Eastern cultural context shows that their vow-making practice is in great affinity with the Hadiyya practice of the vow-making as well as with the ancient Israelites' practice of the vow-making which we are going to see in the following discussion.

The Nature of the נדר in the Hebrew Scriptures

The term נדר occurs thirty-one times in the Hebrew Scriptures in its verb form and fifty-nine times in its noun form.[59] It is mentioned for the first time in the Hebrew Scriptures in Genesis 28:20–22. The importance of the utterance of נדר in the ancient Israelite society is indisputable. This fact is exhibited by the Hebrew Scriptures and other ancient Israelite literatures, which will be examined and substantiated in the following discussion. Cartledge notes that in the Israelite tradition vow-making has been extensively practised throughout the history of the Israelites since the period of patriarchs.[60] At the very earliest phase of the process of inception of

---

58. Oppenbeim, *Ancient Mesopotamia*, 242.
59. Kohlenberger and Swanson, *Concordance*, 5616.
60. Cartledge, *Vows*, 11.

The Concept of נדר 'Vow' in the Hebrew Scriptures

national status journeying from Egypt to Canaan the Israelites practised making a corporate vow to God:[61]

> Then Israel made a vow to the LORD and said, "If you will indeed give this people into our hands, then we will utterly destroy their towns." The LORD listened to the voice of Israel, and handed over the Canaanites; and they utterly destroyed them and their towns; so the place was called Hormah. (Num 21:2–3)

Irrespective of their social and economic diversity every member of the society practiced vowing.[62] Significant numbers of the Jewish religious texts like the Talmud and Mishnah[63] also reflect this fact.[64]

One important question to be answered in relation to this discussion is the question of the intention of vow-making. In order to answer this question one needs to investigate the nature of the vow as presented in the Hebrew Scriptures in the ancient Near Eastern context. At the outset I presume that the Hebrew Scriptures exhibit some apparent features of this concept which will help us to describe the nature of נדר. In the following discussions, the different features of the נדר in the Hebrew Scriptures will be detailed and whether the essential nature of the concept נדר is consistent in different genres of the Hebrew Scriptures.

נדר Made Only between God and Humans.

One of the most important features of the concept נדר as presented in the Hebrew Scriptures is that in the ancient Israelite society vow-making only ever took place between God and humans.[65] Cartledge rightly observes this feature of נדר when he says "vows are usually motivated by some special

---

61. Cartledge, *Vows*, 12.
62. Berlinerblau, *Vow*, 166.
63. "Talmud is the work which embodies the mental labors of the ancient Jewish teaching during a period of about eight hundred years (from about 300 BCE to 500 CE) in expounding and developing the civil and religious law of the Bible . . . Talmud contains two distinct works: the mishnah, as the text and the gemara as a voluminous collection of commentaries and discussions on the text." (Mielziner, *Talmud*, 3). The Mishnah is "the authorized codification of the oral or unwritten law which, on the basis of the written law contained in the Pentateuch, developed during the second Temple and down to the end of the second century of the common era." (Mielziner, *Talmud*, 4).
64. Rabinowitz, "Vows," 227.
65. Skinner, *Genesis*, 379.

Reading and Translating Genesis 28:10—35:15 as a Votive Narrative

need and always directed toward God (never toward another person)."[66] He adds: "vow begins with a plea of humans for divine action, followed by a conditional promise of the worshipper's response."[67] Accordingly, all the uses of נדר in the Hebrew Scriptures show that נדר was a promise made by humans to God. The conclusion that vow-making takes place only between God and man, never between man and man is incontrovertible as all the available ninety references of the Hebrew Scriptures show this fact. It is exhibited in all three major genres of the Hebrew Scriptures: narrative, wisdom literatures and the books of the prophets. All the votive narratives show that in the ancient Israelite's vow-making was only between God and man. For example, see the vow-making of Jacob in Genesis 28:20–22. Similarly all the references to the נדר in the wisdom literatures (e.g., Prov 7:14; Ps 116:18; Eccl 5:4) and all the references in the prophets (Isa 19:21; Jer 44:25; Jonah 1:16; Mal 1:14; and Nah 1:16) show that vows are made only between the deity and humans.

נדר is Always Taken in the Context of Distress

It is evident that in the Hebrew Scriptures נדר is always taken in the context distress. All the utterances of the vow in the Hebrew Scriptures show that the vows are always motivated by distress and uttered to God in the context of calling upon the Lord for relief.[68] Cartledge notes that "vows are universally motivated by some sort of personal (usually) or national (occasionally) distress."[69] The cause of the distress could be sickness of oneself or one's relative, barrenness, rage of war, long journey, etc. For example, Hanna was so distressed by barrenness that she prayed and made a vow to God as follows:

> She was deeply distressed and prayed to the LORD, and wept bitterly. She made this vow: "O LORD of hosts, if only you will look on the misery of your servant, and remember me, and not forget your servant, but will give to your servant a male child, then I will set him before you as a nazirite until the day of his death. He shall drink neither wine nor intoxicants, and no razor shall touch his head." (1 Samuel 1:10–11)

---

66. Cartledge, *Vows*, 17.
67. Ibid., 16.
68. Wenham, *Genesis 16–50*, 224.
69. Cartledge, *Vows*, 135.

The importance of making a vow in such situation is that when a petitioner utters a vow to God in such a distressing situation she/he feels relieved because he has full confidence in God that he will hear his/her solemn request. This aspect was evident from the behavior of Hanna after she made the vow: "Then the woman went to her quarters, ate and drank with her husband, and her countenance was sad no longer" (1 Sam 1:18). Thus, the practice of vow reflects a good positive relationship between God and the petitioner.[70] This nature of the vow was evident in all the narratives concerning vows (Gen 28:20–22; Num 21: 2, Judg 11:30; 1 Sam 1:11; 2 Sam 15:7–8).

Psalm 132:2 also shows that distress is the context of the vow in wisdom literature. However, the utterances of the vow in the books of prophets do not clearly express this feature of the vow, presumably because the utterance of the prophets was more focused on criticizing and evaluating the behavior of the petitioners rather than in the narrative aspect of the vow (Jer 44:25; Mal 1:14).

נדר *as a Strictly Binding Utterance*

The Hebrew Scriptures attest that vow-making is a free will commitment and it is not a religious duty. Consequently not every member of the Israelite community is expected to make a vow (Deut 23:23). But once it is made it will become a seriously binding promise and it must be fulfilled promptly when God grants one's votive plea. In this regard the Hebrew Scriptures clearly state that נדר is a very serious binding utterance accompanied with some kind of sanction if one fails to fulfill the vow:

> When you vow a vow to God, do not delay paying it. . . . Do not let your mouth lead you into sin, and do not say before the messenger that it was a mistake; why should God be angry at your words, and destroy the work of your hands? (Eccl 5:4a, 6)

Similarly the Jewish Encyclopedia describes vow as "promise made under religious sanction" and such vows are so binding that a person is even expected to replace a gift promised but lost unlike the expectation for a free will offering.[71] This is an absolute obligation. An unfulfilled vow will result in serious adverse consequences for the human party because it will be a sin before God (Deut 23:21–23), which will provoke him to punish

---

70. Ibid., 136.
71. Lauterbach, "Vows," 451–52.

the petitioner: "why should God be angry at your voice, and destroy the work of your hands?" Likewise, as we will see below, the Mishnah, the Talmud, and the ancient Near Eastern cultural practice also provide sufficient evidence about the seriousness of the consequence of the neglected vow. But it is worth noting that the type of punishment is not stated as being of a particular kind.

Consequently, anything dedicated to God as a vow offering even including unclean animals becomes irreversibly holy to God (Lev 27:9–10). As a result a person who made a vow to dedicate himself or herself for the service of the Lord can only redeem himself/herself by paying a set amount, equal in value to his actual service; otherwise he cannot annul or abolish the vow (Lev 27:2–8). However, there will be no expected consequences for God if he does not answer what the petitioner asked him for.

Because of this, according to the Hebrew Scriptures, the chance of annulling the נדר is strictly limited. The votive legislation of the Hebrew Scriptures declares that a vow can be annulled only for very limited reasons. For example, women can take a vow as well as men. However, the father of a young girl with whom the girl is still living can make his daughter's vow void immediately he hears of it (Num 30:3–5). Similarly a woman's husband can also make a vow of his wife void immediately he hears of it. This also includes a vow of a woman who got married while her vow which she committed herself to before her marriage is still in force (Num 30:6–8, 10–15). But the vow of widows and divorced women are binding (Num 30:10).

The binding nature of the vow is evident in all the major genres of the Hebrew Scriptures. For instance, the vow narrative of Jephthah demonstrates the serious binding nature of the ancient Israelite's vow. Similarly the wisdom literature also demonstrates this same feature as it is exhibited by the advice of the wise man not to neglect to fulfill the vow in order to avoid the undesirable consequence (Eccl 5:6). Finally the prophets also presumably presupposed the mutually shared assumption of the ancient Israelites regarding the binding nature of the vow as it is demonstrated by the Prophet Malachi criticizing the behavior of the unfaithful petitioners (Mal 1:14).

נדר *is Always a Conditional Commitment.*

All the references to the vow in the Hebrew Scriptures show that all the utterances of the term נדר are absolutely conditional (. . . אִם־יִהְיֶה אֱלֹהִים "if

God . . . then . . ."). The petitioner, always motivated by some kind of distress, pleads to God seeking relief from his situation and takes a vow that s/he will express gratitude to God in a special way only if God honors him by answering his request.[72] Cartledge observes that this nature is clearly exhibited mainly in the narrative texts by "if . . . then" construction,[73] and Genesis 28:20–22 clearly demonstrates this:

20 וַיִּדַּר יַעֲקֹב נֶדֶר לֵאמֹר אִם־יִהְיֶה אֱלֹהִים עִמָּדִי וּשְׁמָרַנִי בַּדֶּרֶךְ הַזֶּה אֲשֶׁר אָנֹכִי הוֹלֵךְ וְנָתַן־לִי לֶחֶם לֶאֱכֹל וּבֶגֶד לִלְבֹּשׁ:

21 וְשַׁבְתִּי בְשָׁלוֹם אֶל־בֵּית אָבִי וְהָיָה יְהוָה לִי לֵאלֹהִים:

22 וְהָאֶבֶן הַזֹּאת אֲשֶׁר־שַׂמְתִּי מַצֵּבָה יִהְיֶה בֵּית אֱלֹהִים וְכֹל אֲשֶׁר תִּתֶּן־לִי עַשֵּׂר אֲעַשְּׂרֶנּוּ לָךְ

> Then Jacob made a vow, saying, "If God will be with me, and will keep me in this way that I go, and will give me bread to eat and clothing to wear, so that I come again to my father's house in peace, then the LORD shall be my God, and this stone, which I have set up for a pillar, shall be God's house; and of all that you give me I will surely give one tenth to you."

This vow exhibits four distinct features: the narrative introduction which comprises distress of the petitioner, the call upon God by direct address, protasis[74] (condition) of the vow introduced by אִם "if," and apodosis (the commitment of the petitioner).[75] The conditional statement of this vow (protasis) is introduced by אִם "if" with the imperfect verb: אם־יהיה "if he will be" with me, followed by three other requests: (a) ושמרני בדרך "keep me on this journey," (b) ללבש נתן־לי לאכל להם "give me bread to eat and clothes to wear," and (c) אל־בית אבי ושבתי בשלום "will return in peace to my father's house," and all of them are perfect verbs prefixed with the vav consecutive. The apodosis (commitment) is introduced or begins with perfect verb: והיה יהוה לי לאלהימ "YHWH will be my God" and followed by two other promises both of them expressed by the imperfect verbs.

However, it is worth noting that this empirical examination showed that pragmatically the construction of the conditional clause (protasis) does not imply that the petitioner doubts the ability of God to answer his request. It was unthinkable for the ancient Israelites that God was unable

---

72. De Vaux, *Life and Institution*, 465.
73. Cartledge, *Vows*, 12.
74. I will be using protasis or antecedent and apodosis or consequent interchangeably throughout this work.
75. Cartledge, *Vows*, 145.

to supply what they requested. There is no evidence from the Hebrew Scriptures that they doubt God's ability. Therefore, we can conclude that the conditional clause (protasis) simply implies the solemn nature of the request that the petitioner puts his trust in God believing that only God can give relief to his distress, if he wills to do so, and he is bound to his vow only if God answers his petition.

One may wonder whether the apodosis (promise) was intended to influence or manipulate God or otherwise. Either the petitioner intended to influence God by his promise or it was intended to signal a strong ostensive commitment that a petitioner puts himself in to give praises and thanks to God if he answers his request. On the one hand, it is possible that the vow-making was intended to influence God. Cartledge also notes that the vow is intended to influence God when he says "one assumes that the deity also appreciates appeals by flattery or by the promise of gifts."[76] Pagolu agrees with Cartledge when he says that the prayer in Jacob's vow was used as an inducement.[77]

However, it is difficult to believe that the ancient Israelites perceived God as a deity who could be manipulated by gifts and that they created the behavior of the vow to manipulate him. De Vaux notes that the purpose of the vow in the ancient Israel was intended "to add force to a prayer by making a kind of contract with God" rather than manipulating him.[78] In any case this view would need further clear evidence from the texts that the vow-making was intended to influence God. It is more appropriate to argue that the fundamental intention behind fulfilling a vow is to express the emotion of thankfulness, satisfaction, joy, and happiness resulting from God's act of giving relief from distress by answering the request. Presumably accompanying such praise with a particular kind of physical gesture is intended to express the magnitude of deep emotional response of praise to God for what he has done. There is an evidence that it was a custom for the ancient Israelites not to appear empty handed on occasions of celebration: ולא יראה את־פני יהוה ריקם "they shall not appear before the LORD empty-handed" (Exod 34:20; Deut 16:16). Probably it was intrinsic for the petitioners to promise to God in advance to appear before him with some kind of gift as a gesture on such an emotional occasion of thanksgiving.

---

76. Ibid., 30.
77. Pagolu, *Religion of the Patriarchs*, 134.
78. De Vaux, *Life and Institution*, 465.

The Concept of נדר *'Vow' in the Hebrew Scriptures*

Some scholars argue that some vows like Nazirite vows are not conditional.[79] There are indeed various types of vows in the Hebrew Scriptures: with various fulfillments such as an offering, abstaining, dedicating one's self to God, words of praises, etc. We may categorize them into three types of vows as they appear in the Hebrew Scriptures each with some distinct features:[80]

A *nedarim vow* is making a promise to do something for God on receiving a solemnly requested blessing from God. Sometimes this type of vow is described as a positive vow (Gen 28:20; 1 Sam 1:11, 21–23).

A *herem vow* is making a vow to utterly destroy enemies with their property without taking any spoil of them (Num 21:2), and

A *nazirite vow* offers total devotion or separation of oneself to the Lord as holy/sacred (Num 6:1–21). Usually the last two are described as the vows of abstinence. Such vows of self-deprivation are described as *neder issar* "promise of prohibition or deprivation."[81]

Some scholars categorize the vows into two: negative vows, negative in the sense of abstinence "from something which is otherwise permitted," and positive vows, which are sometimes described as performing something for God.[82] However, I suggest that positive and negative are not appropriate categories because any vow involves some kind of self-deprivation. For example, if a person takes a vow to offer a sheep eventually he will lose his sheep which is a kind of self-deprivation. Cartledge also points out this issue in his discussion.[83] Therefore, categorizing them in terms of negative and positive vows does not seem an appropriate alternative.[84] Rather it is more appropriate to describe them simply as "different types of votive objects" (dedicating one's self to God, abstinence, praise or a gift for God) all conditional on the action of God to relieve distress.[85]

As mentioned above in this section some scholars suspect there is a conditional feature of the Nazirite vow of Numbers chapter 6 compared with the life-long Nazirite separation, like Samson's in Judges 13. They argue that according to the legislation of the vow in Numbers 6, the Nazirite

79. De Vaux, *Life and Institution*, 466.
80. Rabinowitz, "Vows," 227.
81. Lauterbach, "Vows," 452.
82. Ibid., 451–52; Rabinowitz, "Vows," 227.
83. Cartledge, *Vows*, 72.
84. Ibid., 71.
85. Ibid., 71–72.

separation of devotion is only for the time being. On the contrary, a lifelong devotion/separation of Samson which is also called Nazirite (Judg 13:3–5) is not a נדר at all. Rather, it was a life-long separation for the particular purpose of God.[86] If it were a Nazirite vow he wouldn't defile himself by having contact with the dead body (Num 6:6–7) as he did in Judges 14:19. Besides, the narrative shows that he was not born as a result of vow either. Thus, all Nazirite separations are not votive separations. Therefore, the story of Samson is not valid evidence against the conditional nature of the Nazirite vow, because the Samson's case does not meet the requirements of the legislation of Numbers 6.[87] Thus as Cartledge argues, the Nazirite vows of Num 6 are all conditional vows.[88]

The conditional feature of the vow is evidently shown mainly in the narrative genre of the Hebrew Scriptures and is marked by the linguistic construction of protasis and apodosis. The other three major genres of the Hebrew scripture: legislation, wisdom literature, and prophets do not explicitly mark this feature because of the nature of their communicative intention about the institution of נדר. The wisdom literature, which includes Ecclesiastes and Proverbs, focuses mainly on giving advice about the fulfillment of the vow, not on the linguistic form of the vow. Psalms focuses on making a vow in poetic songs, focusing on the religious commitment of the vow rather than on its linguistic form (Ps 56:2). Similarly the prophets focus on criticizing or evaluating the behavior of the petitioner in relation to the institution of vow and so they do not bother to exhibit the linguistic form of the conditional nature of the vow. The torahic legislation literature also focuses on giving guidance and instructions regarding the social institution of the vow without bothering about the linguistic form of it. Nevertheless, I argue that the conditional feature of the ancient Israelite vow is implied in all Hebrew literature. They did not bother to represent the linguistic conditional form presumably because they presuppose that the conditional nature of the vow making is mutually shared knowledge. Thus the real linguistic conditional form of votive utterance manifests in the actual vow making event, which is usually represented in the narrative literature.

---

86. See ibid., 18–23.
87. Chepey, *Nazirites*, 4.
88. Cartledge, *Vows*, 23.

The Concept of נדר 'Vow' in the Hebrew Scriptures

Making a נדר Raises Strong Expectations of Relevance

One can easily detect that Hebrew vows raise expectations.[89] If vow-making is always a conditional promise which will take place in the future after the time of utterance it will create high expectations of relevance in both God and the petitioner, immediately when it is uttered.[90] On the one hand, the vow-maker will consciously expect and wait for the answer to his prayer from God. On the other hand, it is perceived that when God answers the prayer of the petitioner he will also await the prompt fulfillment of the votive pledge.

> When you vow a vow to God, do not delay paying it. ... Do not let your mouth lead you into sin, and do not say before the messenger that it was a mistake; why should God be angry at your words, and destroy the work of your hands? (Eccl. 5:4a, 6)

All the genres of the Hebrew Scriptures with references to vow-making demonstrate that the vow raises expectation in both deity and man.

Fulfilling the נדר was Perceived as Praise to God

In the Hebrew Scriptures the fulfilling of a נדר was considered as praise to God. There is reciprocity in the biblical vows: God grants one's solemn prayer and a person who receives the answer expresses his gratitude to God and praises God by fulfilling his vow. Reciprocity between God and

---

89. In this chapter and elsewhere I use two different expressions: "raises expectations" and "raises expectation of relevance" in relation to the concept *neder*. It is worth noting that these two expressions are distinct. The expression "raises expectations" is all about the cognitive principle of relevance. That is, knowing about the institution of the vow makes one watch to see (1) if it is granted (2) if the vow maker has fulfilled his votive commitment. That is what we observe will arise from our cognitive expectation within the framework of the votive institution, and is not necessarily communicated. However, the expression "raises expectations of relevance" denotes what is intentionally communicated. Hence, since we are being told the votive narrative of Jacob by the narrator in Genesis 28:10—35:15, the communicative principle of relevance is apparently involved. Thus, the presumption of relevance is involved in this votive narrative. That is, the narrator warrants us to hold a presumption that the story will be relevant in terms of having cognitive effects for his readers as they process his public presentation. Therefore, my use of the expression "raises expectations," apart from the context of this story, within the context of mutually shared knowledge of the votive institution is employed from the perspective of the cognitive principle, not from the perspective of the communicative principle.

90. This feature will be shown in my discussion of the votive narrative of Jacob in chapter 4.

Reading and Translating Genesis 28:10—35:15 as a Votive Narrative

man is evident in all genres of the Hebrew Scriptures: (Lev 7:16; Gen 28:20-22; Num 21:2-3, Ps 22:25; Job 22:27; Nah 1:15/MT 2:1).

The fulfilling of a vow was perceived as a joyful response of a petitioner for what God has done. Apparently it is an event of celebration and rejoicing for the faithfulness of God. Hence, fulfilling a vow always follows the good deeds of God according to one's solemn plea and it was perceived as a public joyous occasion (Ps 116:14, 17-18; 61:8; Num 21:1-3). The fact that the Vow-offering should be eaten on the first or second day shows that it is similar to the peace offering which is an offering of rejoicing. It also shows a continued trust in God as well as one's love for God:[91]

> Look! On the mountains the feet of one who brings good tidings, who proclaims peace! Celebrate your festivals, O Judah, fulfill your vows, for never again shall the wicked invade you; they are utterly cut off. (Nah 2:1)

However, the Hebrew Scriptures remind petitioners not to make unacceptable votive commitments. There are explicitly stated unacceptable נדר: anything abomination to God (Deut 23:18, 19), anything which are already belongs to God such as the firstborn of an animal and a tithe (Lev 27:26, 28), and a vow-offering offered by a person with a wicked heart (Ps 66:18; Prov 7:14). The things are referred as an abomination to God as is income derived from prostitution in the same passage.

Location and Time of Fulfillment

According to the Hebrew Scriptures the fulfilling of the נדר must be at the sanctuary of God or a place chosen by God because one of the legislative requirements for the fulfilling of a vow is that it must be done at the chosen place of God as stated in Deuteronomy 12:26: "But the holy things which are due from you, and your votive offerings, you shall take, and you shall go to the place which the LORD will choose." Both narrative and poetic vows explicitly demonstrate that the vow was fulfilled in the sanctuary of the deity: 1 Sam 1:24; Ps 66:13. However, the books of the prophets do not explicitly state the sanctuary as a place of the fulfillment of the vow, presumably because they presupposed that it was a mutually shared contextual assumption.

The Hebrew Scriptures are not specific about the time of the fulfilling of the vow. But the legislation of the נדר implies that the expected time of

---

91. Coppes, "Make a Vow," 558.

fulfilling of the נדר must be promptly after receiving the answer from God for the votive plea (Deut 23:21–23/MT 23:22–24). Similarly, the words of wisdom in Ecclesiastes 5:4 implies that the time of fulfilling a vow should be immediately after God has answered what a petitioner solemnly has requested for: "When you vow a vow to God, do not delay paying it; for he has no pleasure in fools. Pay what you vow" (Eccl 5:4). One can imagine that there is a good reason for such recommendation. When God responds to one's plea and gives relief from the distress it will definitely raise the emotion of excitement of relief, satisfaction, happiness, and joy in the petitioner which will eventually create a strong feeling of thankfulness to God. If the fulfilling of the vow delays for too long the emotion of excitement will die out. Therefore, I presume that the expected time of fulfilling the votive promise is promptly after receiving the answer for the plea. However, sometimes it may legitimately be delayed. For example, Jephthah delayed for two months (Judg 11:37), and Hanna delayed until the boy was weaned (1 Sam 1:21–22).

Synopsis of the Discussion according to the Four main Genres of the Hebrew Scriptures

The above discussion, besides describing the concept of נדר in the Hebrew Scriptures, attempted to answer the question whether the concept of נדר remained the same throughout Israelite history as well as in different genres of the Hebrew Scriptures. The major conceptual features of נדר which were evaluated with this in mind have been: its conditional nature, the nature of utterance directed only to God and never to man, taken always in the context of distress, and to be fulfilled in the sanctuary of the Lord. It is a serious utterance with the implication that there will be serious adverse consequences for failing to fulfill the vow. Another way of evaluating this feature, although it is very simplistic, would have been to go through all the different references of the occurrence of the term נדר in different genres of the Hebrew Scriptures and exegete them. However, I didn't do that because it is not my intention to do exegesis on every occurrence of the term נדר in the Hebrew Scriptures, unless a passage shows a different interpretation opposed to the above-mentioned major characteristics of נדר. In the following three sections I will recapitulate the three major genres of the Hebrew Scriptures: narrative/history, Torah, and wisdom literatures as summary statements.

Reading and Translating Genesis 28:10—35:15 as a Votive Narrative

נדר in the Narratives

The main narrative or historical books of the Hebrew Scriptures comprise all the historical books from the book of Joshua to Esther. There are eleven references to נדר in these historical books: five in verbal form and six in nominal form. But the five narrative vows presented in the Hebrew Scriptures are found both in the Torah and the historical books (Gen 28:20–22; Num 21:2; Judg 11:30–31; 1 Sam 1:11; and 2 Sam 15:8) and all of them exhibit the essential nature of the Israelite vow. One of the most referred narratives of a vow in the historical books is the vow of Hannah in the book of 1 Samuel:

> She was deeply distressed and prayed to the LORD, and wept bitterly. She made this vow: "O LORD of hosts, if only you will look on the misery of your servant, and remember me, and not forget your servant, but will give to your servant a male child, then I will set him before you as a Nazirite until the day of his death. He shall drink neither wine nor intoxicants, and no razor shall touch his head" (1 Sam 1:10–11)

Unlike the vow of Jacob, the protasis (condition) of Hannah's vow begins with a combination of infinitive absolute and imperfect verbs: אִם־ ראה and followed by two perfect verbs both prefixed with vav consecutive. On the other hand, the apodosis (commitment) is expressed by the perfect verb which is also prefixed with the vav consecutive. However, both utterances of the vow clearly demonstrate the expected nature of the narrative vow: narrative introduction of the vow, calling upon God, protasis (condition) of the vow, and apodosis (commitment of the petitioner).[92] Thus like other narrative vows, Hannah's vow also clearly demonstrates the essential nature of the נדר, "vow": it is conditional, it is made by a human to God, and it is taken in the context of distress. Thus, these features of the vow were perceived in the cognitive environment of the people of Israel in that particular social and cultural context.

נדר in the Torahic Legislation

Except for the Bethel story of נדר in Genesis 28:20–22 and the vow of Israel in Numbers 21:1–3, most of the references about נדר in Torah are legislations about the Israelites' institution of the vow. Making legislation about such social institution is usually intended to prevent or to control

---

92. Cartledge, *Vows*, 145.

misuse, abuse, or mischief, and to clarify unclear cases, which could be described as case law. Hence, making legislation for such institutions tends to be later action based on the reflection on the practice of the institution, particularly when problems turn up. Probably the same is true with the legislation of the ancient Israelites' votive institution.

Therefore, the combined reading of the legislation of the institution of vow in Leviticus 7:16; 22:21; 27:2; Numbers 15:3, 8; 30:3–4; and Deuteronomy 12:26; 23:21–23 shows that the vows presuppose the same encyclopedic information as the narrative texts about vows. Thus, the above mentioned major characteristics of נדר were well understood in the cognitive environment of the ancient Israelites when they encountered the legislation concerning the vow. The legislative references explicitly indicate that the form of נדר was conditional, it was uttered only to God, it was made in the context of distress, it should be fulfilled promptly, and a failure to fulfill the vow will result in adverse consequences. In addition, the encoding of the custom of נדר in the legislation of Torah shows that the practice of vow in the ancient Israel was common.

נדר IN PSALMS AND WISDOM BOOKS

In this discussion the wisdom literature comprises Job, Proverbs, Ecclesiastes, and Song of Solomon. Wisdom literature is distinguished from Psalms in this discussion because while the wisdom literature has reflections on making a vow, Psalms focuses on the vow as religious commitment.

The wisdom books are advisory, particularly cautionary, to those who make the vow. Thus the use of נדר in wisdom literature is a reflection on the concept of the vow and its use. All of the references about נדר in the wisdom literature are found in Ecclesiastes. Ecclesiastes 5:4–6 clearly implies that the above major characteristics of the נדר were also perceived in the cognitive environment of the ancient Israelites:

> When you make a vow to God, do not delay fulfilling it; for he has no pleasure in fools. Fulfill what you vow. It is better that you should not vow than that you should vow and not fulfill it. Do not let your mouth lead you into sin, and do not say before the messenger that it was a mistake; why should God be angry at your words, and destroy the work of your hands? (Eccl 5:4–6)

Reading and Translating Genesis 28:10—35:15 as a Votive Narrative

Some scholars claim that the conditional nature of the vow was lost in the Psalms so that they become "more like simple promise."[93] This is mainly because the poetic genre does not present the literary structure of the utterance of the vows with protasis and apodosis. However, it is unrealistic to expect the same linguistic structure in both narrative and poetic genres. In the narrative genres the story is told by the reporter. The intention is to tell what the participant(s) did and said. On the contrary, the Psalms are songs and they are intended to express the singer's religious commitment directly, in some cases without necessarily including the lexeme נדר. Thus the Psalmists are focused on their religious commitments rather than on linguistic form. In some cases of votive Psalms נדר is verbally mentioned (Pss 61:5–8; 116:14, 18) while in other cases it is not verbally mentioned at all, particularly in the Psalms of lament. Nevertheless, the fact is that the votive utterances are evident. For example, the following utterance is a votive utterance without using the lexeme נדר:

Deliver my soul from the sword, my life from the power of the dog!

Save me from the mouth of the lion! . . .

> I will tell of your name to my brothers and sisters; in the midst of the congregation I will praise you (Ps 22:21–23 RSV)

In this votive utterance, the linguistic conditional form is absent. However it is clear that the expression "*Deliver my soul from the sword, my life from the power of the dog! Save me from the mouth of the lions*" stands as protasis (conditional) while "*I will tell of your name to my brothers and sisters; in the midst of the congregation I will praise you*" stands as apodosis. If it were in the narrative form it would have been something like the following: *If* you deliver my soul from the sword, my life from the power of the dog, and save me from the mouth of the lion, *then* I will tell of your name to my brothers and sisters; in the midst of the congregation I will praise your name.

The linguistic conditional form of the vow is absent in the votive Psalms more likely because of the fact that it is not narrated, but is being enacted in song to God. However, despite the absence of the linguistic markers of the votive utterance, the essential features of the נדר: distress, calling upon God for help, protasis (conditional feature), and apodosis (commitment) are evident in the above Psalm of lament.[94] The votive

---

93. De Vaux, *Religious Institution*, 466.
94. For full discussion see Cartledge, *Vows*, 150–60.

The Concept of נדר 'Vow' in the Hebrew Scriptures

commitment of the Psalmist is described as praises; which may or may not be accompanied by other material gifts (Pss 61:5–8; 115:14, 18).

נדר IN THE PROPHETS

There are eleven uses of נדר in all the prophets: six in nominal form and five in verb form. In Jeremiah 44:25 and Malachi 1:14 it is used in the context of criticizing the people of Israel for the wrong use of the vow. The prophets criticize the behavior of the vow-making people, but never criticize the institution of vow and its practice at all. The rest of the references to נדר are found in Isaiah 19:21; Jonah 1:16; 2:10; Nahum 1:15/2:1 and are used positively. Hence, all the representations of vows in the books of prophets clearly show that the concept of נדר was an utterance of humans only to God, never to other humans, and thus consistent with vows in other genres.

Summary of נדר in the Hebrew Scriptures

To conclude this discussion, all references of the Hebrew Scriptures presuppose that the essential nature of the concept נדר was consistently mutually shared knowledge among the ancient Israelites, even in their different contexts.[95] This mutually shared knowledge of the nature of נדר includes the following features:

1. It is a promise made by humans to the deity: vow making takes place only between God and humans.

2. In essence it is made in the context of distress, calling upon God for help.

3. Making a vow is a free will commitment and to make it is not a religious duty (Deut 23:21–23).[96] Not every member of the Jewish community is expected to make a vow (Deut 23:23). But once it is made it is binding; it must be fulfilled. Otherwise it will be sin (Deut 23:21–23).

4. Vow-making is strictly conditional. It is perceived as a give-and-take action between God and human which shows a positive relationship between God and the individual: God answering one's solemn request and a person expressing his gratitude and praises by fulfilling

---

95. Cartledge, *Vows*, 50.
96. Coppes, "Make a Vow," 558.

his vow (Lev 7:16; Gen 28:20–22; Num 21:2–3; Ps 22:25; Job 22:27). Thus, individuals are in full control on deciding the type of their vows, not the religious leaders.

5. A vow can be an offering, abstaining, committing one's life to serve the deity, etc.

6. One can make a vow to dedicate a person or himself/herself to the Lord. But if this vow is too difficult to fulfill because of some serious reason a person can be redeemed by paying a set amount, equal in value to his actual commitment. In Leviticus such a vow is linguistically marked as *yapla-neder* יפלא נדר "make a difficult vow" (Lev 27:2) probably to denote a sense of extraordinary or difficult nature of such commitment (Lev 27:2–8). The term פלא occurs in the hiphil and pi'el verb forms collocating with God or humans. On the one hand, when its hiphil form collocates with God it denotes the wonderful, incomprehensible, and unusual thing which is beyond human capacity caused to happen by God (Gen 18:14). On the other hand, when this same form collocates with humans it denotes something beyond human capability to make happen (Deut 17:8).[97] Note that the verb is in the hiphil form. Thus in this context it denotes the sense of making a vow that is too difficult to fulfill. Hence, probably this regulation of valuation is aimed to avoid the possible tragic effect of unwise or rash vows like the one concerning Jephthah's daughter.[98] However, it cannot be seen as a change of the original commitment, but as a substitute because a vow cannot be changed.[99]

7. Vow-making is an utterance which creates strong expectations of relevance on both parts—human and divine.

8. Fulfilling of a vow was perceived as a response to what God has done and a celebration and rejoicing for the faithfulness of God. Thus fulfilling a vow always followed God's good deeds according to one's solemn prayer and it was considered as a joy (Pss 116:14, 17–18; 61:8; Num 21:1–3). The fact that the vow-offering should be eaten on the first or second day shows that it is similar to the peace offering which is an offering of rejoicing.

9. The place of fulfilling a vow must be at the chosen place by God (Deut 12:6, 11)

---

97. Hamilton, "Shebuha," 723.
98. Cartledge, *Vows*, 52.
99. Ibid., 33.

The Concept of נדר 'Vow' in the Hebrew Scriptures

10. The time of fulfilling a vow should be immediately after God has granted what a person solemnly requested (Gen 28:20–22)
11. If the utterance was made by a married women or unmarried girl only her husband or her father, respectively, can annul it. This also must be done immediately when they hear of it, otherwise it is binding.
12. A vow offering cannot include anything that is an abomination to God (Deut 23:18) or anything which already belongs to God (Lev 27:26).
13. Anything dedicated to God as a vow offering, even including unclean animals, becomes holy to God (Lev 27:9–10).
14. If there is wickedness in the heart of a person who makes a vow, his vow will not be accepted by God (Ps 66:18; Prov 7:14).

The Nature of נדר in Other Literature of the Israelites

Gleaning other literatures of the ancient Israelites such as the Dead Sea Scrolls, the Talmud and the Book of Jubilee will also throw some light on the conceptual features of נדר mentioned in the Hebrew Scriptures. These literatures will now be explored.

Dead Sea scrolls

Joseph A. Fitzmyer documents some evidence from the Dead Sea Scrolls[100] that reveals that the נדר was practised during the second century BCE through first century CE.[101] Similarly the Dead Sea Scrolls of the Second Temple period state that any violation of the vow will lead to transgression and punishment.[102] Consequently, these sources discourage people from making a vow, on the assumption that they could violate the votive commitment, or strongly advises them not to delay to fulfill the vow because of its seriousness,[103] which is in the line with the advice of the Ecclesiastes 5:4–6.

---

100. The development of the Dead Sea Scrolls covers approximately 520 BCE to 70 AD (Unger, *Bible* Dictionary, 291).
101. Fitzmyer, *Responses*, 142. Fitzmyer fails to make clear distinction between oaths and נדר.
102. Schiffman, "Oaths and Vows," 621.
103. Ibid.

Reading and Translating Genesis 28:10—35:15 as a Votive Narrative

In addition the legislation (laws and rules) found in the Dead Sea scrolls named as the Damascus Documents declares that the fulfilling of the vows must be carried out even at the sacrifice of one's life as stipulated in the books of Torah.[104] However, the wisdom texts of the scrolls advise husbands to abolish all the vows of their wives, probably in order to avoid the adverse consequences of unfulfilled vows.[105]

Likewise the Temple Scroll also advises to avoid vow-making. However, it states that if it is uttered then it must be fulfilled. But if a father of a daughter who still lives with her father or a husband of a wife hears of it and wants to annul or abolish it he must do it on the same day he hears of it and then God will forgive the woman for not fulfilling her vow. If the annulment was not done on the same day then the father or the husband will be held accountable for the transgression.[106] Thus these evidences show that the legislative representation of the Dead Sea Scrolls about the נדר focus, just like most of the ancient Israelite literature,' mainly on the binding nature of the נדר. Schiffman also notes that early Christianity and Rabbinic Judaism also followed similar trends.[107] Thus these rules show that the concept of vow during the time of the writing of the Dead Sea Scrolls was consistent with the legislation of the Torah.

Talmud

Most of the Talmudic documents present the views of different Rabbis regarding the application and binding nature of the vow rather than discussing about its nature in detail.[108] For example the Talmud discusses questions like who can effect and declare the annulment of the vow;[109] that Gentiles cannot take the vow of a Nazirite;[110] that a vow offering should be something which is not already consecrated to the Lord;[111] that fulfilling a vow requires the inclusion of a drink offering and that one should fulfill exactly what he vowed.[112] Further, that the votive offering should be

104. Ibid., 622.
105. Ibid., 622.
106. Ibid., 622.
107. Ibid., 622–23.
108. Epstein, *Nezikin*, 562; *Moed*, 148, 212, 430, 560, 687, 804, 805.
109. Epstein, *Nezikin*, 495–96.
110. Epstein, *Kodashim*, 437.
111. Ibid., 497.
112. Ibid., 550, 554, 629, 632.

fulfilled in the sanctuary/Temple;[113] that husbands are authorised to annul the vows of their wives;[114] how to exempt a person from a votive obligation if he becomes so poor that he cannot afford to fulfill his vow;[115] that the consequences of a neglected or unfulfilled vow could be the death of one's wife or children;[116] how vows can be annulled on the Sabbath by a husband and the annulment of a vow can be postponed if this is necessary for the sake of the Sabbath;[117] the necessity of a qualified person to annul the vow of a Nazirite leper;[118] deciding the appropriate age of a child to take a vow or how to decide the process of fulfilling the previously taken vow of a sister-in-law who cohabited with a new husband by the law of levirate marriage;[119] that an illegitimate husband cannot annul a vow of a woman;[120] that a woman is expected to inform her prospective husband about her vow, otherwise she should be divorced and he cannot remarry her.[121] There is guidance regarding the duration of sexual abstinence because of a vow;[122] and the valuation of the vow of a hermaphrodite[123] (probably while the person is still with the parents).[124]

113. Ibid., 671.
114. Epstein, *Nezikin*, 556.
115. Ibid., 649.
116. Epstein, *Moed*, 148.
117. Ibid., 212, 803.
118. Epstein, *Nashim*, 18.
119. Lauterbach, "Vows," 452; Epstein, *Nashim*, 728, 781.
120. Epstein, *Nashim*, 593.
121. Ibid., 453, 467.
122. Ibid., 369.
123. The term "hermaphrodite" refers to a person who has both female and male sexual organs. The Jewish Rabbis gave attention to this physical character of a person in relation to vow-making because according to Leviticus 27 the valuation of the vow depends on the sex and age of the vow maker. According to the Talmudic view a hermaphrodite above twenty years is considered as a male (Epstein, *Moed*, 687–88). This is probably because the ancient Israelite society was a male superiority oriented society so that the hermaphrodites at this age may be consciously inclined to opt to be identified as males rather than females. But this decision does not solve the questions about the hermaphrodites below age twenty in relation to the vow. For instance, we have seen that the legislation of the vow declares that a father can make a vow of his daughter, who still lives with him, void. Similarly a husband can make his wife's vow void including her vows before she got married. The question in this regard is that whether the hermaphrodite before age twenty should be treated as a male or female? Most likely the parents may opt to treat them as females because it gives them a chance to annul their vows.
124. Epstein, *Moed*, 687.

Reading and Translating Genesis 28:10—35:15 as a Votive Narrative

In summary, like the Dead Sea Scrolls the Talmud also advises one to avoid vow-making in order to avoid the adverse consequences of the neglected vow. One of the Rabbis says: "Children die as a punishment for [unfulfilled] vows."[125]

However, one needs to read the Talmudic description of vow cautiously because it is evident that Talmud also fails to make a clear distinction between oath and vow. For example, an oath of a sales-woman for her husband: "May all the produce of the world be forbidden to me if I misappropriated any of your goods or money" was described as נדר "vow,"[126] although it is rather an oath, from my point of view.

Book of Jubilees

The book of Jubilees claims that the content of its message is a revelation given by God to Moses "through the medium of an angel . . . and contains a history divided up into jubilee period of forty-nine years, from the creation to the coming of the Moses."[127] Although the authority and accuracy of the narration of the book of the Jubilee is questionable, the narrator relates that when Jacob came back to Canaan he told his father Isaac about his vow in Bethel and requested him to go to Bethel with him to participate in the celebration to fulfill his vow. But Isaac declined to go with him because he was very old. However, he warned Jacob not to neglect his vow and urged him to fulfill it. Then Jacob went to Bethel and celebrated the fulfillment of his vow and "he rejoiced and blessed the God of his fathers, Abraham and Isaac."[128] This story shows that the book of Jubilee also, as the Talmud and Dead Sea Scrolls, emphasizes the obligation of fulfilling the vow.[129]

Summary of נדר in other Israelite literature

In summary, besides the Hebrew Scriptures, other literatures of the ancient Israelites also presuppose the consistency of, or at least the essential nature of the נדר, throughout the different historical and social

---

125. Ibid., 148.
126. Epstein, *Nashim*, 547
127. Charles, *Jubilees*, vii.
128. Ibid., 161.
129. Ibid.

contexts of the ancient Israelites according to the teaching of Torah about נדר.¹³⁰ The evidence from other literatures of the ancient Israelites (apart from some cases in the Talmud) show that the vow was always made only between God and man, it is taken in the context of distress, and it is seriously binding. Besides, the attempt of the religious leaders to legislate the institution of the vow based on the Torah shows that it was a popularly practised custom. These literatures show unanimously that the adverse consequence of neglecting to fulfill a vow will result in a punishment by God. Finally, they also show that the expected location of fulfilling the vow must be the sanctuary or place chosen by God.

Distinctiveness and Contrast of נדר with Other Similar Hebrew Concepts

Coppes and Cartledge observe that unlike other similar concepts, vow-making implies a conditional solemn utterance of commitment only directed to God in the context of calling upon him for relief in the time of distress. Coppes says: "The biblical "vow" is always to deity, never a promise between man and man."¹³¹ Cartledge also concurs with Coppes' view when he says: "In the Hebrew Bible one may swear to another person, but may vow only to God."¹³² He adds:

> [V]ow *must* [emphasis mine] always be understood as taking place within the context of prayer, in an address to God. In Biblical usage, *vows are always conditional promises to God, to be fulfilled only when and if God answers the petitioner's request.*¹³³

The three Hebrew concepts that are similar to נדר (noun) "vow" (Gen 28:20) are ברית (noun) "covenant" (Gen 17:2), שבועה (noun) "oath" (Gen 26:3) and אלה (noun) "swearing" (1 Sam 14:24). Except ברית, which requires an auxiliary verb כרת the rest occur both as noun and verb in the Hebrew Scriptures. Basically they all denote binding speech acts of the ancient Hebrew language. However, each of them has its own distinct conceptual nuance which makes them contrast with one another, though the differences are very subtle. It is beyond the scope of this work to discuss

---

130. Cartledge, *Vows*, 71.
131. Coppes, "Make a Vow," 557.
132. Cartledge, *Vows*, 12.
133. Ibid.

the differences between them in detail. However, I will give very brief description of each concept at the risk of simplifying.

אלה *Swearing*

The concept אלה does not constitute or establish any kind of binding agreement, but it accompanies a constitutive commissive speech act like covenant and oaths. It functions as an instrument to strengthen/reinforce other commissive speech acts or it may be employed to reinforce some serious utterances like witnessing, to show that the witness is telling the truth. Usually oaths and covenants, which constitute a solemn agreement are accompanied by אלה, marking that the one who takes an oath or covenant was making a true and binding utterance (Ruth 1:17; 1 Sam 20:13). Sometimes אלה can be uttered by raising hand or putting hand under the thigh (Dan 12:7; Gen 14:22; 24:2–3). אלה implies the utterance of verbal swearing or invoking the name of God or a greater authority or highly valued person or things, in the process of making an oath and covenant. It involves two parties and implies consequences for breaking the oath or covenant.[134] Because of its instrumental nature it is used in the sense of invoking some kind of horrifying event in swearing if one is not faithful to his oath. It could be employed as "If I . . .then let what happened to people of Judah . . . also happen to me!" (Jer 44:12). It is also used to show a conviction that the one uttering אלה is telling the truth thus such swearing is employed in public witnessing (1 Kgs 8:31; Prov 29:24; Lev 5:1). In the case of public witnessing, אלה functions as a means of determining the truth when there is no other alternative to prove it.

שבועה *Oath*

The concept שבועה has a constitutive nature. Once it is uttered, it constitutes or makes and establishes an agreement which must be done or must happen. Thus it implies the general act of making a sacred commitment which may include performing some kind of physical gesture like slaughtering an animal as well as a verbal act of swearing (אלה) in order to signal one's unbreakable sacred commitment to perform something faithfully or not to perform it.[135] Because of its constitutive nature or sense, it is

---

134. Scott, "Alah."
135. Cartledge, *Vows*, 15–16; Hamilton, "Shebuha," 904.

employed as a sacred commitment between one person and another (Gen 21:22–31; 24:28), or it could be a sacred commitment of God to humans (Gen 26:3), or it could be an utterance made by a person to bind himself by an oath (Isa 45:23). In this regard the use of the Niphal stem in שבועה denotes the reflexive sense of "binding oneself by an oath."[136] The utterance of an oath comprises, as stated above, the act of swearing (אלה) by invoking another person "tacitly and mutually assumed to be greater or more precious than the one making the oath,"[137] or some kind of horrifying event (Jer 44:26); one may even swear by invoking one's wife, one's child, heaven, earth, and other things more valued than one's self. Thus, when God makes such an oath he invokes himself because there is no one greater than he (Heb 6:13).

ברית Covenant

Another very important concept or constitutive utterance, very similar to שבועה, and often mentioned in the Hebrew Scriptures is ברית. The basic concept of the term ברית is that it is a treaty for creating strong relationships apart from blood relationship between nations (Josh 9:14), between individuals (Gen 31:44–47; 1 Sam 18:3), between people and a king (1 Chr 11:3), and between God and humans (Gen 15:18). Usually the process of establishing a ברית is accompanied by some kind of physical gestures, animal sacrifices, and binding solemn utterances of speech act (אלה) which will imply blessing for faithfully keeping it and punishment for breaking it.[138]

One may wonder whether the above concepts could be interpreted generally as a concept of promise. It is worth noting that there is no specific lexical term in Hebrew for "promise." The common normal promises are communicated simply by declarative utterances which are introduced by דבר "say."[139] Although the above concepts are basically promises or commissive speech acts they are apparently strongly binding types of promises which imply serious adverse consequences for violating them. Thus it is evident that the Hebrew language makes a distinction between the normal utterance of promises and other binding commitments. Hence the ancient Israelite society perceived that there were social institutions

---

136. Hamilton, "Shebuha," 899.
137. Ibid., 904.
138. Smick, "Berit."
139. Cartledge, *Vows*, 14.

of vow-making, swearing, oath-making, and covenant-making; but there was no institution for simple promising.

The semantic relationship of these entities could be demonstrated by hyponymy, which denotes a semantic relation of inclusion.[140] Thus in Hebrew covenant, oath, swearing, and vow are hyponyms of the binding utterance of commitments or commissive speech acts as the following diagram shows:

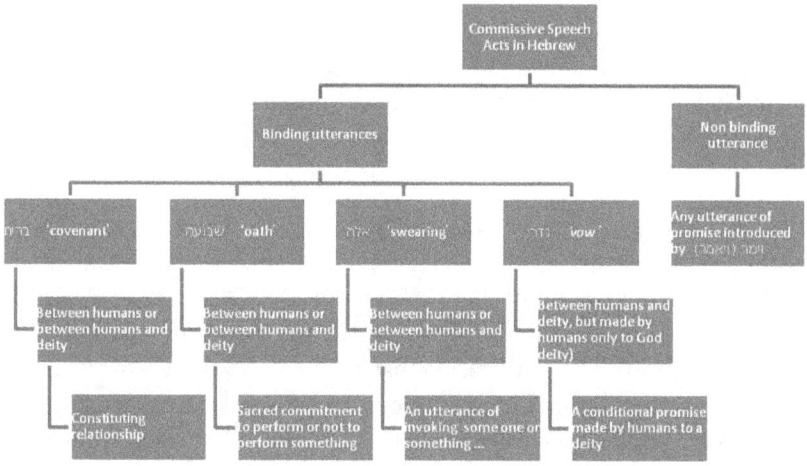

The semantic relationships between ברית "covenant," שבועה "oath," אלה "swearing," and נדר "vow" can also be shown in a chart:

	ברית "covenant"	שבועה "oath"	אלה "swearing"	נדר "vow"
Between humans or between humans and deity	+	+	+	−
Between humans and deity only, but made by humans, only to God	−	−	−	+
Function	Constituting relationship	Sacred commitment to perform or not to perform something	An utterance of invoking on some one or something	A conditional promise made by humans to a deity

140. Saeed, *Semantics*, 68–70.

The Concept of נדר 'Vow' in the Hebrew Scriptures

Thus, the nature of the biblical vow (נדר) makes it distinct from these other similar concepts.

Summary of the Comparison

The above discussion shows that unlike נדר all these speech acts or utterances involve swearing, but נדר does not involve swearing. However, violating anyone of these commissive speech acts will inevitably result in severe consequence. Besides, except for נדר, which is essentially made between humans and deity, all these utterances comprise a commitment between human parties as well as with the deity, and they are not intrinsically conditional, while נדר is essentially conditional.[141] Finally unlike the utterance of נדר they are not made in the context of distress.[142] Thus, our investigation of the ancient Israelite's worldview about the concept נדר clearly shows that נדר was distinct from oath and other similar Hebrew concepts.

Commissive Speech Acts and their Adverse Consequences

If one breaks the above discussed binding utterances: שבועה, אל, and ברית the consequence will be ארר "curse," which is always a terrible negative effect; a condemnation resulteding from violating God's law (Gen 3:14; Deut 27:15–26). Thus as a speech act, ארר is an utterance of denouncing or adjuration or invoking bad fortune upon another person or people or even things, and it does not necessarily involve two parties.

As I already noted above it is an essential feature of these that being unfaithful to them will result in adverse consequences. The following are some examples of the warnings about the adverse consequences of the failed binding utterances.

---

141. However, contrary to the above summary discussion, the description of Lawrence H. Schiffman on the Hebrew lexemes—נדר "vow," שבועה, "oath," and אלה "swear" in his article to the encyclopedia of the Dead Sea Scrolls implies that the Hebrew term נדר has the same concept as שבועה, "oath," and אלה "swearing" (Schiffman, "Oaths and Vows," 621).

142. Cartledge, *Vows*, 25.

Reading and Translating Genesis 28:10—35:15 as a Votive Narrative

THE CONSEQUENCES OF BREAKING BINDING UTTERANCES:

Oaths: When Jonathan broke the oath which his father made for all the Israelites—even though, he was not even aware of it—God refused to be with them to give them victory in fighting. Consequently the Israelites had to withdrew from fighting (1 Sam 14:24-46). Also the Gibeonite people deceived the Israelites so that they made an oath not to attack them. When the Israelites knew that they were deceived they did not dare to attack them because they were afraid of the adverse consequence of breaking the oath (Josh 9:20). Furthermore when King Saul violated the oath and mistreated and killed the Gibeonites, the whole land was punished by three years of drought. But when the violation was restituted by killing seven family members of Saul, the normal rains resumed (2 Sam 21:1-14).

Swearing: The people of Israel were warned not to make an oath in deception and swear falsely, otherwise they will be responsible for such an utterance (Lev 19:12)

Vow: The Israelites were warned that any unfulfilled vow will make one guilty before God (Deut 23:22-23; Num 30:2[MT 3]-15).

Covenant: Breaking a covenant will bring a curse (Lev 26:15-16; Gen 17:14)

Comparison of the Conceptual Range of נדר and Hadiyya Concepts of *Silet*

Comparing both the Hebrew and Hadiyya concepts of vow at this stage will help us to see the difference and similarity between them which will also have a significant implication for the choice and decision making in the translation process.

The Hebrew concept of vow נדר	*The Hadiyya concept of vow silet*
It is a promise made by humans only to God.	It is always made between man and a deity.
Vow is usually made in the place chosen by God.	Vow can be made anywhere.
In essence it is a plea to God for relief when one is in distress.	It is made in the context of distress.
It is always conditional.	It is always conditional.

The Concept of נדר 'Vow' in the Hebrew Scriptures

The fulfilling of a vow always followed (but not everyone fulfilled their vow) God's good deeds granted according to one's solemn plea and it was considered as a joy.	It must be fulfilled on condition that the deity has answered one's plea.
Making a vow is a free will commitment and to make it is not a religious duty.	Making a vow is a free will commitment and to make it is not a religious duty.
A vow offering cannot include anything which is an abomination to God or anything which already belongs to God.	You can vow anything you want to give as thanksgiving to the deity.
A vow can be an offering, an abstaining, committing one's life to serve the deity etc.	A vow can be an offering, an abstaining, committing one's life to serve the deity, walking barefoot, etc.
The place of fulfilling a vow must be at the place chosen by God.	It must be fulfilled at the place perceived as where the deity resides.
The time of fulfilling a vow should be immediately after God has answered what a person solemnly requested.	The time of fulfilling a vow should be immediately after the deity has answered what a person solemnly requested.
Adverse consequences are expected if one fails to fulfill one's vow.	Adverse consequences are expected if one fails to fulfill his vow.
Once it is made it is never changed to something else.	Once it is made never changed to something else.
If the utterance of a vow was made by a married women or unmarried girl only her husband or her father, respectively, can annul it, which also should be done immediately when they hear of it; otherwise it is binding.	It is never annulled.
If there is wickedness in the heart of a person who brings a vow-offering his/her offering will not be acceptable.	Anybody can make a vow.
A vow is not intended to influence the deity, rather it is an expression of emotion of the petitioner and his commitment to express his gratitude to God in a particular way if his plea is answered.	A vow is not intended to influence the deity rather it is an expression of emotion of the petitioner and his commitment to express his gratitude to God in a particular way if his plea is answered.
A vow shows a positive relationship and trust between the petitioner and God.	A vow shows a positive relationship and trust between the petitioner and God.

Reading and Translating Genesis 28:10—35:15 as a Votive Narrative

Anything dedicated to God as a vow offering, even including unclean animals, becomes holy to God.	Anything dedicated to God as a vow offering becomes holy to God, but they do not make a categorization between unclean and clean animals.
A person can make a vow to dedicate himself or herself to the Lord, and in such case a person can redeem himself by paying a set amount, equal in value to his actual service of vow.	

Based on the above comparison we can draw the following contrast between the Hadiyya concept of *silet* and Hebrew concept of נדר:

1. The Hadiyya culture does not have legislation concerning vow making, but the Hebrew culture does. The Hebrew worldview has an implication of fear of vow-making because of the adverse consequences of neglecting a vow, so that they make legislation concerning vow-making. The Hadiyya worldview also has the fear of adverse consequences of neglecting a vow intrinsically, but they do not have explicit legislation concerning it.

2. The Hebrew view is that if there is wickedness in the heart of a person who brings a vow-offering his offering will not be acceptable. But the Hadiyya does not have such view.

3. In the Hebrew view, if the utterance of a vow was made by a married women or unmarried girl, her husband or her father, respectively, can annul it, which also should be done immediately when they hear of it. But Hadiyya do not have such regulation.

4. The Hebrew legislation explicitly states things which cannot be given to God as a votive offering: anything which is an abomination to God and anything which already belongs to God cannot be offered. The Hadiyya view implies the petitioner should offer something of value, but does not state what things cannot be included.

5. According to the Hebrew view, if a person made a vow to dedicate himself or herself to the Lord, he/she can redeem himself/herself by paying a set amount, equal in value to his actual service of vow. But this practice is not known among the Hadiyya people.

The above comparison shows that the concept of vow held in ancient Israel and that held by the Hadiyya people is basically similar except for a few differences which are mainly based on the legislation of the institution. This similarity implies that in appropriate circumstances the current Hadiyya

The Concept of נדר *'Vow' in the Hebrew Scriptures*

people can easily reconstruct the Hebrew concept of vow, which makes translation easier.

Conclusion

In conclusion, the Assyro-Babylonian custom of vow-making, and that of other related areas, and of the Hadiyya are similar to their Hebrew counterpart: it is conditional, it is made in the context of prayer because of distress, the motivation of the vow-making is to seek relief from distress, the content of votive prayers is the promise of public praises in a particular manner, the vow is binding—it must be fulfilled, and the fulfillment of the vow should be in the place where the deity resides,[143] and all vows in all these cultures, that are unfulfilled, have adverse consequences. The similarity of this concept between the Hadiyya and some other Ethiopian cultures and the ANE cultures is not accidental because there is a linguistic link,[144] a geographical link, and probably there was also a historical-cultural diffusion among them during ancient times.

As the discussion of this chapter shows, the essence of the biblical vow can be described as a human commissive speech act of solemn commitment directed only to God in the context of distress seeking to get relief from God. It is a conventionalized utterance, operating within a social institution and gives rise to conventional contextual assumptions and the expectation of the grant of a desirable outcome from God, with an obligation to fulfilling the votive commitment made to God. A further expectation of adverse consequences is raised if the votive commitment remains unfulfilled.

נדר is a conditional solemn promise to God by humans which will be fulfilled only if God honors the petitioner's plea by granting it. The commitment is given to respond to the deity in a specified way. This nature of the biblical vow sets it off in contrast with oath, covenant and other similar concepts and commissive speech acts.

Finally, based on all the arguments of this chapter it can be claimed that the Hebrew concept נדר has the following encyclopedic information in the cognitive environment of the ancient Israelite society. The target audience's inferential process of interpretation within specific pragmatic contexts interacts with this encyclopedic information so that a particular relevant feature of the encyclopedic information would be mutually

---

143. Oppenbeim, *Ancient Mesopotamia*, 242.
144. Cushitic and Semitic are both in the Afro-Asiatic family.

manifest in terms of forming relevant contextual assumption(s) and cognitive effects:

1. It is a promise made by humans only to God: vow-making takes place only between God and humans.
2. In essence it is made in the context of prayer when one is in distress.
3. Making a vow to God was perceived as a reciprocal action between God and a human: God answers one's solemn prayer and one expresses one's gratitude and praises by fulfilling one's vow. Therefore the fulfilling of a vow was perceived as a response for what God has done and apparently it is a celebration and rejoicing in order to express gratitude to God.
4. Thus the fulfilling of a vow always followed God's good deeds according to one's solemn votive prayer and it was considered as a joy.
5. Making a vow is a free will commitment and to make it is not a religious duty. Therefore not every member of the Jewish community is expected to make a vow. But once it is made it is binding. Therefore, the uttered vow must be fulfilled. Otherwise it will be sin with a consequence of punishment which functions as a means of reminder. When it is fulfilled the normal situation of relationship between God and the petitioner will resume.
6. A vow can be an offering, an abstaining, committing one's life to serve the deity, etc.
7. The place of fulfilling a vow must be at the chosen place of God.
8. The time of fulfilling a vow should be immediately after God has answered what a person solemnly requested.
9. If the utterance of a vow was made by a married women or unmarried girl only her husband or her father, respectively, can annul it which also should be done immediately when they hear of it; otherwise it is binding.
10. A vow offering cannot include anything of abomination to God or anything which already belongs to God.
11. Anything dedicated to God as a vow offering, even including unclean animals, becomes holy to God.
12. A person can make a vow to dedicate himself or herself to the Lord. In such case a person can redeem himself by paying a set amount, equal in value to his actual service of vow.

13. If there is wickedness in the heart of a person who brings a vow-offering his offering will not be acceptable.
14. Vow shows positive relationship and trust between the petitioner and God.

4

Vow-Making of Jacob as a Metarepresentation

Introduction

IN CHAPTER 2 GENESIS 28:10—35:15 was represented as a distinct narrative unit of the Jacob story, and it was argued that the vow of Jacob (Gen 28:10–22) is employed by the narrator to function as a framework that gives coherence to the narrative unit. In chapter 3 the Hebrew concept of vow, which will help us to explore the relevance of the vow of Jacob in Bethel (28:10–22) for the narrative unit (28:10—35:1–15) from the narrator's point of view is described. In this chapter it will be shown how the vow-making of Jacob in Bethel functions as a framework for the narrative unit.

In interpreting the vow of Genesis 28:20–22 some principles of relevance theory are useful. Therefore, the nature of Jacob's vow and its contents are investigated by employing the relevance theoretic concept of metarepresentation. This approach seems helpful to examine the passage because of its explanation of echoic utterance; and its approach to interpreting the same from an inferential perspective comprehensively. Wilson says: "The formation and recognition of communicator's intention is central,"[1] and through hearing someone else's utterance or through reading a text we attempt to read some one else's mind inferentially in relation to what he/she said. Metarepresentation focuses on explaining the communicator's view when representing another person's words or thought.

---

1. Wilson, "Metarepresentation," 412.

Definition of Metarepresentation

The narrator of this story tells us that significant parts of his report were attributed to the thought of Jacob or God (13–15, 16–17, 20–22).

Deirdre Wilson discusses the depth and variety of the metarepresentational ability of the human mind deployed in linguistic communication and attempts to provide a pragmatic account for this ability. She notes that the metarepresentational ability helps humans to engage in inferential communication or comprehension. She defines metarepresentation as "a representation of a representation: a higher-order representation with a lower-order representation embedded within it."[2] It involves representing someone else's utterance or thought in one's own thought or attributed utterance of a speaker's thought) with a lower-order representation (representation of some one else's thought) embedded within it.[3]

Wilson provides an illustration to show how the lower-order representation is embedded within the higher order representation. The illustration is adapted here as follows:
Mary says to Peter: You are neglecting your job.
In understanding Mary's utterance, Peter might entertain a series of metarepresentations of this utterance as follows:

a. Mary said, "You are neglecting your job."

b. Mary said that I am neglecting my job.

c. Mary believes that I am neglecting my job.

d. Mary intends me to believe that I am neglecting my job.

e. Mary intends me to believe that she intends me to believe that I am neglecting my job.[4]

Thus, Wilson observes that in principle the process of metarepresentation in our mind is infinite. But she illustrates only up to the fourth-order metarepresentation of the utterance. For example, she illustrates that the fourth-order of Mary's utterance: *"You are neglecting your job"*[5] is *"Mary intends me to believe that she intends me to believe that I am neglecting my job"* which is complex enough.

---

2. Wilson, "Metarepresentation," 411.

3. Noh, *Metarepresentation*, 98; Wilson, "Metarepresentation," 411.

4. Wilson, "Metarepresentation," 412.

5. Wilson also illustrates that there are other higher-order representations observed in the human communication but are not attributed to someone else's utterance or thought. E.g., "Shut up" is rude (ibid., 413).

Wilson also notes that human language is full of metarepresentation which usually manifests in various ways in communication. She describes quotation (direct or indirect) as an utterance attributed to someone else's utterance or thought.[6] She also remarks that the Linguistic marking of a metarepresentation varies both in extent of explicitness and in the type of original representation they are used to represent, as the above illustration shows—direct quotation (*Mary said, "You are neglecting your job"*); indirect quotation (*Mary told me that I was not working hard enough*); mixture of indirect and direct quotation (*According to Mary I am "neglecting" my work*), free indirect quotation (*Mary was pretty rude to me. I am neglecting my job*). In addition, a representation of an abstract thought like "to say 'Sit down!' is impolite" is a non-attributive representation because it is not attributed to anybody's particular thought or utterance.[7]

She attempts to answer the following questions: What is the role of metarepresentation in identifying the content of the meaning of a speaker? How can one define the meaning of the speaker without getting into an infinite regress, which is requiring infinite metarepresentation for full transparency in communication? How can we reconcile the theoretical goal of transparency and the practical goal of psychological feasability? The answer is that although each metalevel representation is infinite in principle our inferential processing stops when the expectation of relevance is achieved because human communication is not geared to continue wasting one's effort if there is no further expectation of relevance.

Wilson also notes that the speaker's meaning is identical to the content of the set of assumptions embedded under the informative intention of the communicator which is made manifest by his ostensive stimulus.[8] The speaker's meaning of an utterance may also contain a metarepresentational component which is usually very rich and diverse.[9] As already noted the human mind has the ability to process these metarepresentational components and other different types of informational phenomena it perceives and makes a mental representation of them. It can also represent this representation to others in utterance and in other ways of public representation. The human mind can construct the books we read and the utterances of someone else we hear which are themselves representations of the thought of someone else and we can also represent them again to

---

6. Ibid., 413.
7. Ibid.
8. Ibid., 424.
9. Ibid.

Vow-Making of Jacob as a Metarepresentation

others.[10] Dan Sperber explains four main categories of metarepresentations as follows:[11]

1. Mental representation of mental representation; e.g., the thought "John believes that it will rain."
2. Mental representation of public representations; e.g., the thought "John said that it will rain."
3. Public representation of mental representation; e.g., the utterance "John believes that it will rain."
4. And public representation of public representations; e.g., the utterance "John said that it will rain."[12]

Thus, according to the representation argument, there is obvious regress in each metalevel.[13] Consequently, the requirement of the representation of each conflicting states in every metalevel, respectively, will create a complex representation structure or system.[14] So how can the human mind avoid the regress? Lehrer argues that it is avoided by exemplarization.[15] He argues that exemplarization is based on a quotation and disquotation (direct and indirect quotation) process. Humans generalize and exemplarize the experiences and sensations in their mind and convert the states of that experience or sensation into exemplaric representation (metarepresentation) which is similar to the quotation and disquotation process of metarepresentation. Quotation and disquotation is the referential process that our mind employs to convert the complex system of perceiving information, making a mental representation of it, and evaluating it, and it involves regress into exemplar. In Lehrer's words: "A process of quotation and disquotation yields a report on the content of our thoughts" rather than the complex system of regress. This is because the human mind employs quotation or disquotation in order to avoid the complex process of regress of representations at the metalevel.

Thus the tactic of quotation and disquotation is a "minimal report of meaning and content" of the complex process in our thought employed to resolve the problem of representational transparency. Exemplarization is the way that the inferential process of the mental capacity of the

---

10. See Sperber, "Introduction," 3; Noh, *Metarepresentation*, 1.
11. I have restructured the quote.
12. Sperber, "Introduction," 3.
13. Lehrer, "Metarepresentation," 299–310.
14. Sperber, "Introduction," 10; Lehrer, "Metarepresentation," 299–310.
15. Lehrer, "Metarepresentation," 305–6.

human mind works to communicate the complex metarepresentational process. Lehrer says: "Moreover thought about something is a matter of quotation and disquotation of some mental state in a similar loop of exemplarization."[16]

In summary, metarepresentation could be described as an act of attributing or representing one's utterance or any other public representation and thought to someone else's thought or utterance. Such attribution or metarepresentation can be marked in several ways. But the common ones are using direct and indirect quotation markers, which also differ from language to language.

The difference between direct and indirect quotation is that in direct quotation the saliency of shared property of linguistic expression between the attributed and reported utterance/text is high while in indirect quotation the saliency of the shared semantic or logical property is high.[17] For example:

Mary said, "You are neglecting your job"
Mary said that I am neglecting my job.

She calls this resemblance *metalinguistic* and *interpretive* respectively. In some uses of mixed quotation of both features we may observe that both the metalinguistic and interpretive resemblances are exploited. The quotations resemble the original, by sharing some properties of the original, and are not identical to the original.[18] Among the variety of resemblances, metarepresentations of thought are typically interpretive, which means resemblance in content by sharing the contextual implications. Metarepresentation accounts for all varieties of quotations including even the extended range of public, mental, and abstract features of quotations, so that the explanation would be more comprehensive.[19] Here "metarepresentation" will be used to denote an utterance which is attributed to the utterances and thoughts of someone else with some kind of attitude. Usually such utterances are marked linguistically.

Echoic Utterance and Metarepresentation

It has been argued that human communication involves interpretive representations (utterance attributed to someone else's thought or utterance)

---

16. Lehrer, "Metarepresentation," 305.
17. Wilson, "Metarepresentation," 426.
18. Ibid.
19. Ibid., 425.

more extensively than descriptive representations (representation of speaker's own thought).[20] The interpretive use of language also involves the case of utterances used to interpret someone else's utterance or thought rather than the speaker's own thought, which Eun-Ju Noh, among several others, explains in depth as "metarepresentation."[21] In the case of reported speech, such attributive use may be explicitly marked by expressions like "as so and so said . . ."

However, in other cases the speaker may not necessarily indicate or mark that he is using someone else's thought. One such tacit use is an echoic use. An echoic use is distinct from other interpretive uses of someone else's thought in that the speaker signals to the hearer that he has in mind both what someone has said, and that he has a certain attitude toward that thought. Echoic use "achieves relevance mainly by conveying the speaker's attitude to an attributed utterance or thought."[22] The attitude can be manifested as approval, disapproval, rebuke, rejection, amusement, skepticism, shock or surprise, happiness, etc.[23] When the interpretive use of someone else's thought achieves relevance in such a manner it is described as an echoic use. The three broad attitudes are endorsing it, questioning it, or dissociating from it.

However, at times such attitude(s) may be left implicit to be deduced from the context.[24] Therefore, the recovery of the intended implicature depends on three features: understanding the utterance as an echoic one, understanding the echoed thought itself, and recognizing and understanding the attitude of the speaker to the echoed thought.[25] I emphasise that the information conveyed by the speaker about his attitude to the thought echoed is crucial in recovering the echoic utterance and that this attitude is variable.[26]

In summary, in the process of understanding an echoic utterance, capturing the speaker's attitude to the attributed (metarepresented) utterance is crucial and that attitude "must be treated as part of the communicative

---

20. Sperber and Wilson, *Relevance*, 23, 239–42; Gutt, *Translation*, 41–42; Carston, *Thoughts and Utterances*, 158.
21. Noh, *Metarepresentation*.
22. Wilson, "Metarepresentation," 432.
23. Sperber and Wilson, *Relevance*, 238; Carston, *Thoughts and Utterances*, 298; Noh, *Metarepresentation*, 91–98.
24. Sperber and Wilson, *Relevance*, 237–42.
25. Ibid., 240.
26. Noh, *Metarepresentation*, 92.

content."[27] It is important to note that the echoic utterance might be linguistically explicit (metalinguistic) or interpretive. When the echoic utterances resemble the attributed thought metalinguistically, the form of the expressed attitude will resemble the original form of the echoed utterance. Otherwise the expressed attitude may be simply the content. In either case, some apparent attitudinal device might be employed.[28]

Conditionals and Metarepresentation

Noh argues that a metarepresentational approach accounts more comprehensively for the interpretation of conditionals than the traditional truth-functional approach (see appendix 5 about the truth-functional approach). This is because the truth-functional approach is not adequate to account for different features of the conditional expressions unless it is complemented with a pragmatic analysis.[29] More specifically, the traditional approach does not account for the non-basic conditionals (conditionals which do not denote logical cause and consequence like "if you do not eat you will die").[30]

Noh categorizes conditional utterances as metarepresentational utterances because the antecedents (protases) are used to represent another representation which they resemble in a particular context; "that is, to metarepresent an attributed utterance or thought."[31] She further observes that in some cases both antecedents and consequents (apodoses) may be used metarepresentationally (used to represent another representation) in which case the consequent may express the speaker's attitude to what is echoed in the antecedent.[32]

It is worth noting that the inferential processing aspect of the communication allows one to access the information assumed to be relevant, including the encyclopedic information of a certain concept in a given context, as well as the assumed mutually shared knowledge of the social institutions of the particular community. This phenomenon will be shown in the following discussions on the institution of vow in Jacob's votive narrative.

27. Wilson, "Metarepresentation," 431.
28. Ibid., 432.
29. Noh, *Metarepresentation*, 174–79.
30. Saeed, *Semantics*, 91–94.
31. Noh, *Metarepresentation*, 186.
32. Ibid., 205–8.

Vow-Making of Jacob as a Metarepresentation

The discussion of Genesis 28:10–22 in the following sections approaches the passage from the metarepresentational perspective and will show how the inferential processing allows one to access the encyclopedic entries of the cognitive environment of the hearers about the vow and the mutually shared knowledge of the votive institution of the vow-conscious society. In such a society, the narrator assumes that hearers or readers of the story will imagine these features for themselves.[33]

Reading Genesis 28:10–22 as a Story of Vow Making

Although many scholars have attempted to interpret Genesis 28:10–22 from the source critical point of view and collectively attributed the story to different sources (approaching the story diachronically), the approach to the story here is a synchronic one. Though giving careful attention to the historical and cultural context within which the events of the original story took place, it is not intended to discuss whether the narrator of the story in Genesis 28:10–22 is the original source or he intends to report a story which was represented to him by someone else. This is because it is difficult to prove whether the whole report of the Bethel story is descriptive or metarepresentational.

However, the narrator has explicitly attributed a significant portion of the episode to the words and thoughts of God, which were represented to Jacob in his dream, and it is Jacob' own echoic words and thoughts of the same words and thoughts of God, which we will examine in the following discussion in this chapter. Genesis 28:10–22 will be read as an episode of the vow-making of Jacob and explained from the metarepresentational perspective, so that we can understand the informative and communicative intention of the narrator, and describe and explain his attitude in his echoic utterances better.

Close Reading of the passage

Setting of the Story (vv 10–11)

10 וַיֵּצֵא יַעֲקֹב מִבְּאֵר שָׁבַע וַיֵּלֶךְ חָרָנָה׃
11 וַיִּפְגַּע בַּמָּקוֹם וַיָּלֶן שָׁם כִּי־בָא הַשֶּׁמֶשׁ וַיִּקַּח מֵאַבְנֵי הַמָּקוֹם וַיָּשֶׂם מְרַאֲשֹׁתָיו וַיִּשְׁכַּב בַּמָּקוֹם הַהוּא

---

33. Carston, *Thoughts and Utterances*, 349–59.

Reading and Translating Genesis 28:10—35:15 as a Votive Narrative

> Jacob left Beer-sheba and went toward Haran. He came to a certain place and stayed there for the night, because the sun had set. Taking one of the stones of the place, he put it under his head and lay down in that place. (10–11)

Narrative criticism (and also discourse analysis) deal with setting under four general features: temporal setting, spatial/locational setting, social setting (the occasion in which a story is set), and the character(s) or participants of the story. The temporal setting of the event in this passage is "when he reached certain place"; the spatial setting is "certain place/Bethel"; the social setting, the occasion in which the story is set, is Jacob's running away from Beersheba in order to escape the death-threat of Esau; and the main characters of the story are God and Jacob.

The narrator does not formally introduce the main characters or participants (God and Jacob) in the setting, because the story is continued from the preceding episode. This episode is a continuation of the Jacob story,[34] which represents the contention between Jacob and Esau and their descendants, though this phenomenon is not explicitly marked in the setting by any anaphoric linguistic signal because Jacob, the main character is already on-stage; and God is a frequent, but intermittent character in the patriarchal narratives.

The event's setting is that Jacob, instructed by his parents, Isaac and Rebekah, had set off to Haran (28:1–5, 10). Rebekah had two reasons for sending him off to Haran: to protect him from the revenge of his brother Esau and to get a wife for him from her brother Laban. Isaac seems to have had only one objective: getting a wife for Jacob from his original family.[35] In this regard it is strange that he sends his son empty-handed without supplying him with any engagement gifts as his father Abraham had done for him (Gen 24:10). Thus unlike Isaac's negotiator, who went with extensive gifts for his prospective wife Rebekah (Gen 24:52–53), Jacob went empty handed to get his wife from Laban, his uncle. Leon R. Kass argues that that was because Jacob was self-reliant person, and this behavior was corrected by his dream showing that the intelligence of the human being is imperfect and one cannot be self-reliant.[36] But on the other hand, one may argue that probably it was not culturally appropriate for a young man to negotiate for his prospective wife himself. Probably that was why Isaac did not go with the servant of Abraham to negotiate for his prospective

---

34. It is the story of Jacob because he is the main protagonist of the story.
35. Speiser, *Genesis*, 215.
36. Kass, *Beginning*, 413.

Vow-Making of Jacob as a Metarepresentation

wife although he was a mature person in age; forty years old (Gen 25:20). Thus, we can argue that presumably the main reason of Jacob's journey to Paddan Aram was to avoid the revenge of Esau. It was because of the tension between him and his brother Esau that he was forced to flee for safety.

The location of the story provided in verse 11 is significant for reading it as a votive narrative. The narrator tells us that Jacob reached a certain place (which was later called Bethel) and he slept there the whole night under the stars in spite of the fact that there was a possibility of being attacked by the wild animals of that region (Gen 37:33). It is not clear what kind of protection he expected when he slept in Bethel. When we think of other biblical stories about long distance travelers, it is strange that this verse tells us Jacob spent that particular night under the open sky rather than seeking a host. Wenham suggests that he might have been far from human habitation, not comfortable to spend the night with a host because of his family estrangement, or simply that the event was guided by God's providence which "overruled the traditional custom of finding lodging in someone's house."[37] However, it is possible that Jacob went to Bethel seeking God's guidance about his future, as people in some cultures like my own used to do. When they were perplexed about the location of their permanent settlement they seek divine discernment by lying down on the land which they feel will be their permanent habitat. Probably Jacob consciously slept in Bethel, perceiving it as a sacred place (see the following discussion on Bethel), seeking a revelation of God for his life as was the custom in ancient Near Eastern culture.[38] Whether this was the reason or not staying the whole night, perhaps alone, under the stars must have been an anxious experience for Jacob, who was a mild man תם (*tam*[39]) who always stayed near home (25:27).

The distance between Beersheba and Paddan Aram[40] is about 500 miles/800km.[41] Consequently, Jacob's trip to Haran probably took him about two weeks or more (if he was able to make 50km a day). Bethel is about 112km from Beersheba, according to Morris; but 85 km according to Ferris and Butler.[42] Thus he must have spent one or two nights at differ-

37. Wenham, *Genesis 16–50*, 221.
38. Pagolu, *Religion of the Patriarchs*, 162.
39. The semantic sense of the lexeme *tam* could be understood as "complete" or "perfect," or as "innocent and simple" (BDB 1070b). In this context the sense of innocent and simple is preferable.
40. I use Haran and Paddan Aram interchangeably.
41. Morris, *Genesis Record*, 446.
42. Ibid., 446; Ferris, "Hebron," 107; Butler, *Old Testament*, 116.

ent places before he got to Bethel and several nights before he got to Padan Aram. However, the narrator focuses on this particular night Jacob spent in Bethel because the event that happened that night was relevant to his narrative.

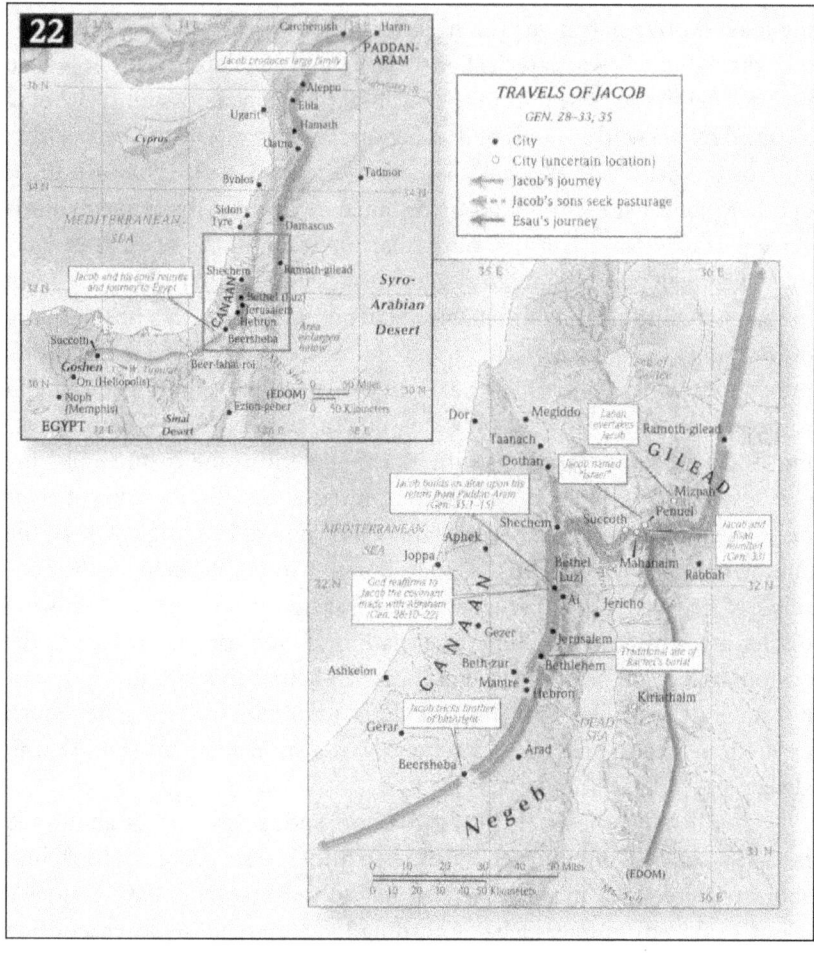

This map is taken from the Bible Atlas Access Foundation 2007 edited by Zaine Ridling. Reproduced by permission.

The referent "place" where the event took place is in focus in that it is mentioned three times in this verse.[43] Leslie Brisman thinks that:

> The place "maqom" can be just an ordinary place, but it can also mean "special place" or "religious site" perhaps evoking

43. Wenham, *Genesis 16–50*, 221.

specifically the place Abraham saw as the appointed one for the "aqeda." ... The expression "Jacob reached a certain place" has a special connotation of encounter.[44]

Pagolu argues that the narrator's focus on Bethel in Genesis 28:10–22 aims to consciously disassociate himself from the view that Bethel was a sacred site before this story.[45] His argument is based on Jacob's exclamation: אָכֵן יֵשׁ יְהוָה בַּמָּקוֹם הַזֶּה וְאָנֹכִי לֹא יָדָעְתִּי "I realized that the LORD is in this place—and/but I did not know it!" (Gen 28:16). However, it is difficult to concur with Pagolu and believe that Jacob was not aware that this place was where his grandfather Abraham had erected an altar.[46] The narrator of the Bethel story of Genesis 28:10–22 and of the Genesis narrative artfully sets the context of the place which was named "Bethel" by Jacob, according to the Bethel story of Genesis 28. It was at Bethel that God confirmed to Abraham that he will give the land to his descendants, when he migrated from Mesopotamia to Canaan. There Abraham built his first altar and called upon the name of the Lord (Gen 12:7–8).[47] It was to Bethel[48] that Abraham returned from Egypt and built an altar (13:3–4). It was here that God made the promise of expanding the descendants of Abraham to East and West, and to North and South (13:14–17). It was in that same place that Jacob now spent the night. God revealed himself to Jacob and affirmed that he would fulfill the Abrahamic covenant through him and his descendants.[49] It was here that Jacob made a vow to God. It was to Bethel that God instructed him to go from Shechem to fulfill his vow (35:1). It was here that Jacob built an altar to fulfill his vow and named the place "Bethel" changing it from Luz (Gen 35:6–7, 14–15). It was here that God appeared again to Jacob and fulfilled his dream at Peniel by changing his name from Jacob to Israel, when he returned back from Aram (35:9–10) and blessed him to multiply his descendants and confirmed the Abrahamic covenant and

44. Brisman, *Voice of Jacob*, 73.
45. Pagolu, *Religion of the Patriarchs*, 161ff.
46. Skinner, *Genesis*, 376.
47. Gunkel, *Genesis*, 158.
48. When Absalom, son of David, planned a conspiracy to overthrow his father he lied by saying: "Please let me go to Hebron and pay the vow that I have made to the LORD. For your servant made a vow while I lived at Geshur in Aram: If the LORD will indeed bring me back to Jerusalem, then I will worship the LORD in Hebron" (2 Sam 15:7–8) probably he was referring to Bethel loosely because Bethel was a place of worship in Hebron.
49. Wenham, *Genesis 16–50*, 223.

promise to him and to them (35:11–13).[50] Bethel was possibly a most prominent cultic place of Canaanites even before the early stage of the Israelite history.[51] Thus, probably Jacob knew about the place but he did not expect such a vivid experience of the presence of God at that place.

Bethel, therefore, was a place of worship from the time of patriarchs to Judges, until it was defiled by Jeroboam I who erected a golden calf there (1 Kgs 12:29–33). Bethel was highly respected for its patriarchal connections.[52] The tombs which have been excavated in the immediate surrounding area of Bethel also show that "the site was holy ground, even in patriarchal times."[53] Some scholars believe that the name "Bethel" refers to a pre-Israelite deity.[54] However, this view is very difficult to believe, because in the Israelite context, it refers to the place of worship, not to the deity himself, as Amos clearly refers to Bethel as "a place of worship" (Amos 3:14).

Fokkelman also observes the significance of Bethel in Jacob's journey when he says that the narrative representation of the episode of Genesis 28:10–22 shows that "only Bethel is essential in Jacob's journey."[55] Thus, presumably this votive narrative was designed to foster the concept of the binding nature of the vow, the location of Bethel as a very significant cultic place during the time of the Patriarchs, chosen by God, and to represent Jacob as a most appropriate and important patriarch figure next to Abraham. Consequently this episode is deliberately crafted to function as a running link throughout the literary structure of the preceding and following story of Jacob, which will be shown in the following discussions in this chapter.

Finally, before moving on to investigate whether the expectation of relevance raised by the votive utterance of Jacob in Bethel was fulfilled in the following narratives, it is worth noting that we need to observe the above-mentioned repetition of some ostensive features of the Jacob story, particularly the repetition employed by using the strategy of the repetition of direct reference to Bethel.

50. Even according to the later ancient Israelite history, it was in Bethel that the Ark of the covenant was kept during the time of judges and people inquired of the Lord seeking direction from him (Judg 20:26–28; 21:1–4). It was in Bethel that Deborah and Samuel judged the people of Israel (Judg 4:5; 1 Sam 7:16).

51. Kilpatrick, "Aaron," 41; Taylor, "The Asherah," 49.

52. Dumbrell, "Role of Bethel," 65.

53. Ibid., 65.

54. Ibid., 67.

55. Fokkelman, *Narrative Art*, 47.

Vow-Making of Jacob as a Metarepresentation

One can observe that the referring expression to "Bethel" was repeated six times explicitly in an extraordinary way: "he came to a certain place and he stayed there" (v. 11); "the Lord is in this place and I did not know it" (v. 16); "how awesome is this place" (v. 17); "this is none other than the house of God" (17); "this is the gate of heaven" (v. 17); and finally "he named that place Bethel" (v. 19). The communicative strategy of this ostensive repetition of Bethel in this episode cannot be defined by purely linguistic and semantic parameters, because the expected "effects of repetition on utterance interpretation are by no means constant."[56] The relevance theoretic parameters explain that the repetition of an expression is employed with the assumption of achieving certain optimal relevance which the communicator has aimed at.[57] Consequently the inferential process of the repetition differs based on the contextual assumptions of each utterance.

In this particular context the repetition of "Bethel" in various forms is aimed at achieving the relevance of a strong confirmation or strengthening of the existing assumption about the chosen place of God, as opposed to any other cultic places in general and Shechem in particular.[58] It shows that in the process of his mental representation of the chosen place of God in this context the narrator vividly remembered Bethel from his own cognitive environment and also the institutions of vow fulfilling only in a chosen place of God. He also has the confidence that his hearers can imagine this phenomenon for themselves because it is a mutually shared knowledge.

Jacob's Encounter with God in His Dream: Preamble to his Vow Making (vv. 12–15)

The major part of 28:12–22 contains the narrator's metarepresented report of the utterance of God and Jacob, so these verses are read from the metarepresentational point of view and what God said to Jacob in his dream and Jacob's response to what God said to him are focused on.

---

56. Sperber and Wilson, *Relevance*, 219.
57. Ibid., 220.
58. This view will be discussed in chapters 5 and 6.

Reading and Translating Genesis 28:10—35:15 as a Votive Narrative

The Dream (vv. 12–13a)

12 וַיַּחֲלֹם וְהִנֵּה סֻלָּם מֻצָּב אַרְצָה וְרֹאשׁוֹ מַגִּיעַ הַשָּׁמָיְמָה וְהִנֵּה מַלְאֲכֵי אֱלֹהִים

עֹלִים וְיֹרְדִים בּוֹ:

13a הִנֵּה יְהוָה נִצָּב עָלָיו

> 12 And he dreamed that there was a ladder set up on the earth, the top of it reaching to heaven; and the angels of God were ascending and descending on it. 13a And the LORD stood beside him...

We observe that in this passage (vv. 12–13a) the narrator interpretively represents Jacob's verbal representation of what he saw in his dream as a free indirect quotation. If this story was not verbally represented by Jacob himself, there is no way the narrator could access Jacob's mental representation of what he saw in his dream. Hence, this section is the beginning of the metarepresentation of Genesis 28:10–22.

The passage states that a ladder[59] was set on the earth whose top reached heaven and the angels of God were ascending and descending on it. God was standing by him and spoke to him.[60]

An interpretation problem occurs in the clause: יהוה נצב עליו "the Lord was standing on it/beside him" in verse 13a. There are two translation problems in this phrase: What does the deictic pronoun marker ו, suffixed to עלי, refer to? Is it referring to the ladder or to Jacob? What is the precise denotation of the preposition עליו—standing on it or standing beside him? Obviously, these are not fully separable issues. Thus, the main interpretation problem is how to interpret the expression נצב עליו יהיה?: This could mean that the Lord was standing on the ladder,[61] or that

---

59. This referring expression (*sulam*) "ladder" has been interpreted in different ways (Oblath, "To Sleep," 117–25). Thus, the referent of the referring expression / *sulam/* is controversial. The four suggested possible interpretations are ramp, stairway, enclosed chamber (or tunnel), or ladder. According to the theological word book of the Old Testament (Patterson, "Sulam") and BDB 699b–700 the root of /*sulam*/ is /*sala'l*/ which has the following derivatives: *selah*→ lift up, exalt; *solilah*→ mount; *sullam* → ladder; *mesillah/masulul* →highway (Patterson, "Sulam"). The Amharic cognate, which is one of the semitic languages of Ethiopia, is also *masalaal* "ladder." Therefore, I suggest that in this context ladder seems the most preferable sense. This ladder was a means set by God (implied subject of נצב "standing") to connect the heaven and earth so that the angels ascend and descend on it.

60. Wenham, *Genesis 16–50*, 221.

61. Ibid., 222.

the Lord was standing beside Jacob.⁶² Some translations like Rashi and JPS Hebrew-English TANAKH, interpret it as God standing beside Jacob while other translations like NIV and NRSV interpret it as "God was standing on the ladder."

In my opinion translating this expression as "beside him" seems preferable for the following two reasons: 1. The BDB dictionary states that when עליו collocates with עמד and נצב, it means idiomatically "stand by some one" (Gen 18:2), or standing by a superior as a servants (עליו להתאפק לכל הנצבים ולא־יכל יוסף Gen 45:1), or of persons surrounding a judge (Exod 18:13–14). Obviously, this expression is different from the literal meaning: 'stand on/over.'⁶³ Then this idiomatic sense "stand by some one" becomes more relevant when one is sitting down. For example, Abraham looked up from his sitting position: וישא עיניו וירא והנה שלשה אנשים נצבים עליו "he looked up and saw three men standing near him" (Gen 18:2). This sense fits the textual context because Jacob was presented in a lying position while he saw the dream (v. 1).

This phenomenon of divine presence beside Jacob has a significant contextual implication to Jacob himself in his mental representation of the event and to the later readers of Genesis. It denotes that the God of his fathers now has chosen Jacob to be the next patriarch—that he is with him. We can presume that the standing of Yahweh, the God of the patriarchs Abraham and Isaac, beside Jacob while he was in such distress brings him a very special encouragement, which was evident in the divine commissive speech act to Jacob in verses 13–15. The response of Jacob is reflected in his echoic vow in verses 20–22.

METAREPRESENTATION IN THE DREAM (VV 13B–15)

13 וַיֹּאמַר אֲנִי יְהוָה אֱלֹהֵי אַבְרָהָם אָבִיךָ וֵאלֹהֵי יִצְחָק הָאָרֶץ אֲשֶׁר אַתָּה שֹׁכֵב עָלֶיהָ לְךָ אֶתְּנֶנָּה וּלְזַרְעֶךָ: . . .

14 וְהָיָה זַרְעֲךָ כַּעֲפַר הָאָרֶץ וּפָרַצְתָּ יָמָּה וָקֵדְמָה וְצָפֹנָה וָנֶגְבָּה וְנִבְרֲכוּ בְךָ כָּל־מִשְׁפְּחֹת הָאֲדָמָה וּבְזַרְעֶךָ:

15 וְהִנֵּה אָנֹכִי עִמָּךְ וּשְׁמַרְתִּיךָ בְּכֹל אֲשֶׁר־תֵּלֵךְ וַהֲשִׁבֹתִיךָ אֶל־הָאֲדָמָה הַזֹּאת כִּי לֹא אֶעֱזָבְךָ עַד אֲשֶׁר אִם־עָשִׂיתִי אֵת אֲשֶׁר־דִּבַּרְתִּי לָךְ:

13 And the LORD ... said, "I am the LORD, the God of Abraham your father and the God of Isaac; the land on which you lie

---

62. Westermann, *Promise*, 455; Gunkel, *Genesis*, 310; Driver, *Genesis*, 265.
63. BDB 756.

Reading and Translating Genesis 28:10—35:15 as a Votive Narrative

I will give to you and to your offspring; 14 and your offspring shall be like the dust of the earth, and you shall spread abroad to the west and to the east and to the north and to the south; and all the families of the earth shall be blessed in you and in your offspring. 15 Know that I am with you and will keep you wherever you go, and will bring you back to this land; for I will not leave you until I have done what I have promised you."

In the preceding section we saw that the narrator metarepresented Jacob's verbal representation of what he saw in his dream as a free indirect quotation. In this section we observe that the narrator apparently attributes his representation to utterances of God or Jacob by marking them by the action-verb phrases like ויאמר "he said" (vv. 13, 16, 17), את־שם המקום ויקרא "he called/named that place" (v. 19) וידר יעקב נדר לאמר "Jacob made a vow by saying" (v. 20). However, it is worth noting that the linguistically marked metarepresentation (particularly direct quotes) in this passage might not necessarily be identical to the original utterance of God or Jacob, but presumably resembles the content of the original utterance or thought interpretively.

In addition, Follingstad and Sim describe the Hebrew linguistic particles והנה and כי as a linguistic device employed to mark metarepresentation.[64] Their work on these particles would lend further linguistic support for metarepresentation in this passage and their arguments provide the detailed linguistic support for the reading of והנה here. והנה is used three times in this passage: twice in verse 12 and once in verse 13a. Follingstad shows that the pragmatic function of והנה is deictic.[65] Thus, the first three והנה in verses 12 and 13 shift the deictic viewpoint from the narrator to Jacob and mark the metarepresentation of Jacob's visual and perceptual experience in his dream about God standing beside him, the ladder reaching to heaven, the angels descending and ascending on the ladder, thus giving climax and emphasis on Jacob's extraordinary experience of encountering God.

---

64. See Follingstad, *Deictic Viewpoint*, and Sim, "Language in Genesis," for a greater detail.

65. Follingstad, *Deictic Viewpoint*, 510–19. The dictionary of linguistics and phonetics describes that "deixis" is a term used in linguistic theory to subsume the linguistic features which refer directly to the personal (e.g., he/she), temporal (e.g., now/then), locational (e.g., here/there), and demonstrative (e.g., this/that) characteristics in a particular situation within which an utterance takes place. Thus the meaning of such words is relative to the situation of utterance. Such words are described as deictic words (Crystal, *Dictionary*, 127).

Vow-Making of Jacob as a Metarepresentation

However, the fourth והנה in verse 15 shifts the deictic viewpoint to the speaker-hearer context: God (speaker) and Jacob (hearer). Thus והנה used by the speaker (God) in order to mark that he (God) has new important pragmatic information for Jacob and intends to charge Jacob to give careful attention to the information. It signals that God intends to focus Jacob's attention so that he should fully understand what God is going to say to him and believe that God will be with him, will protect him, and will fulfill everything he said to him. Hence, there is a difficulty in explaining about the apparent metarepresentation marked by והנה in verse 15. Since this utterance is attributed to God, whose words or thoughts and on what occasion would God be metarepresenting? If we presume that God metarepresented Jacob's thought, then how can we prove this hypothesis?

In verses 13–15 the narrator reports what God said to Jacob in his dream and in verses 16–22 he reports Jacob's response. The major part of verses 13b–22 contains the narrator's metarepresented report of the commissive speech act of God and Jacob's response to it. This response is a commissive speech act to God: a votive response (20–22) to what God had promised him (13–15). It is also represented as a metarepresentation of God's promise to him in verses 13–15. That is why it is appropriate and comprehensive if these verses are read from the metarepresentational perspective.

As we discussed above, the initial part of Jacob's dream (vv. 12–13a) does not employ an explicit linguistic marker for the metarepresentation. This shows the "variety of metarepresentational abilities" human beings can deploy in linguistic communication.[66] The representation of God's words within Jacob's dream in verses 13b–15 is an overt metarepresentatation in the form of a reported utterance of God. The linguistic device used to mark this is ויאמר "and he said" (v. 13). Wilson notes that if a metarepresentation is marked by a linguistic device like this it could be categorized as "higher-order metarepresentation."[67]

The expression: "I am the LORD God of your father Abraham and God of Isaac" (v. 13) is introduced for the first time here and it is artfully designed to recapture the allusion about the promises God made to Abraham and Isaac previously (12:7; 13:14–16; 15:18; 17:8; 24:7; 26:24) and designates Jacob as the next patriarch of the people of Israel.

---

66. Wilson, "Metarepresentation," 411.
67. Ibid., 427.

Reading and Translating Genesis 28:10—35:15 as a Votive Narrative

יהוה "LORD":[68] The significance of the use of this referring expression for God in this context is meant to invoke a set of assumptions about God. These assumptions were communicated by using this name in the previous narratives of Genesis particularly in the context of the covenant between God and Abraham and Isaac. It is a self introduction of God.[69] As Zimmerli further states, the name of Yahweh gives access to a possible set of contextual implications including: God reveals himself with a covenant and remains faithful to it, he is an actor in historical experience; the God revealed is a speaking God and his voice reshapes the world; he is an inscrutably sovereign God; the revealed God is known always as a judging and saving God; his revelation is not a matter of assumption, rather it is a matter of life and death.[70] When the name "Yahweh" is invoked by God himself it designates the faithfulness of God to his covenant; hence it is similar to swearing.[71] It usually denotes God's encounter with human beings to comfort and encourage them with his promises in a time of frustration and discouragement, which is relevant to the situation of Jacob.[72] He is the one who led Abraham out of Ur (Gen 15:7); he is the God of Isaac (Gen 26:24); now he reveals himself as the God of Jacob at Bethel. Thus, the self-introduction of God, by the name "Yahweh," triggers this set of assumptions and consequently connects the votive narrative of Bethel to the previous narratives about Abraham and Isaac.[73]

Jacob is presented as the next one chosen by God to fulfill his covenant to Abraham and Isaac through him and his descendants rather than his brother Esau and his descendants.[74] The expression "the God of Abraham your father and the God of Isaac" is used to show that the same God who made a covenant with Abraham and Isaac is now confirming the

---

68. Although endless critical speculations about the origin and meaning of YHWH can be made, the etymology of this name is questionable and no one is sure about its original pronounciation. Therefore, in this discussion, I wish to discuss the possible contextual assumption provoked by the use of this name rather than describing its semantic sense.

69. Zimmerli, *I Am Yahweh*, 4.

70. Ibid., xv, 7.

71. Ibid., 11.

72. Ibid., 14.

73. Wenham, *Genesis 16–50*, 222–23.

74. Genesis 35:23–29; 37:1—50:14 narrates that Jacob and his family lived in Canaan and died and was buried in Canaan on the same burial site where the ancestors were buried which also denotes the significance of inheritance while Esau and his family moved out of the Canaan which signals that Esau was excluded from the covenant promise.

covenant with Jacob, which incorporates him as the true line of the promised seed.[75] This seems to be a very important implicature of this narrative.

The expression "the land on which you are lying" is a synecdoche used to refer the whole land of Canaan, not only the place he was lying on. Thus the message communicated to Jacob in 28:13b–14 is exactly parallel with the message previously communicated to Abraham in Genesis 12:3 and 13:14–16:

> And all the clans/families of the earth shall be blessed/shall bless themselves by you and your descendants (Gen 12:3). The LORD said to Abram, . . . "Raise your eyes now, and look from the place where you are, northward and southward and eastward and westward; for all the land that you see I will give to you and to your offspring forever. I will make your offspring like the dust of the earth; so that if one can count the dust of the earth, your offspring also can be counted. (Gen 13:14–16)

The interpretive resemblance between the two is of such a high degree that some expressions are verbatim. Wenham demonstrates the parallelism between these two passages as follows:

28:14: נברכו בך כל־משפחת האדמה ובזרעך "And all the clans/families of the earth shall be blessed/shall bless themselves by you and your descendants"

12:3: ונברכו בך כל משפחת "And all the clans/families of the earth shall be blessed/shall bless themselves by you"

28:13 הארץ אשר אתה שכב עליה לך אתננה ולזרעך "The land on which you are lying I shall give to you and your descendants."

13:15 את־כל הארץ אשר אתה ראה לך אתננה ולזרעך "The whole land which you see I shall give to you and your descendants for ever."

28:14 והיה זרעך כעפר הארץ "Your descendants will be like the dust of the earth."

13:16 ושמתי את־זרעך כעפר הארץ "I shall make your descendants like the dust of the earth."

28:14 ופרצת ימה וקדמה וצפנה ונגבה "You will spread westward and eastward, northward and southward."

---

75. Wenham, *Genesis 16–50*, 222.

Reading and Translating Genesis 28:10—35:15 as a Votive Narrative

13:14 וראה ... צפנה ונגבה וקדמה וימה "Look ... northward and southward, and eastward and westward."[76]

Similarly the message communicated to Jacob in 28:13b–15 is parallel with the message communicated to Isaac in Genesis 26:3–4 because there is a significant resemblance between them:

26:3 לך ולזרעך אתן את־כל־הארצת "To you and to your descendants I will give all these lands."

28:13 הארץ אשר אתה שכב עליה לך אתננה ולזרעך "The land on which you are lying I shall give to you and your descendants."

26:3 ואהיה עמך "I will be with you."

28:15 עמך ושמרתיך בכל אשר הלך אנכי "I am with you and will keep you wherever you go."

26:4 והרביתי את־זרעך ככוכבי השמים "I will make your offspring as numerous as the stars of heaven."

28:14 והיה זרעך כעפר הארץ "Your descendants will be like the dust of the earth"

26:4 והתברכו בזרעך כל גויי הארץ "All the nations of the earth shall gain blessing for themselves through your offspring."

28:14: נברכו בך כל־משפחת האדמה ובזרעך "And all the clans/families of the earth shall be blessed/shall bless themselves by you and your descendants."

    Finally, we observe that the Lord concludes his words to Jacob with a strong commissive speech act, giving him the promise of ultimate protection wherever he goes: "I am with you and will keep you wherever you go, and will bring you back to this land; for I will not leave you until I have done what I have promised you" (v. 15). This utterance is a very strong commissive speech act because God makes a binding commitment to Jacob as to a future course of action. He promises to be with him wherever he goes and to protect him, and he will bring him back to the Promised Land. In Wenham's words "Whatever unexpected turns Jacob's career may take, the Lord will be with him, saving him from disaster and ensuring the ultimate triumph of what he had promised."[77]

---

    76. Ibid., 222–23.
    77. Ibid., 223.

Vow-Making of Jacob as a Metarepresentation

Consequently, the commissive speech acts that God to Jacob in Genesis 28:13–15 shows explicit interpretive resemblance with the commissive speech act of God made to Abraham (12:1–3; 13:14–17) and to Isaac (26:3–4). Thus the optimal relevance of this utterance as already noted above, is that it is intended to explain the inauguration of Jacob as the sole line of the promised seed entitled to inherit the Abrahamic covenant of the promise, in contrast to Esau.

The communicative strategy of the repetition of the Abrahamic covenant to Jacob by allusion in this episode is expected to achieve the extra contextual effect of relevance, communicating something different from what the hearer would have thought otherwise.[78] The repetition emphatically dismisses the existing assumption of the birthright of Esau to inherit the promise of covenant, and, on the contrary, emphatically introduces Jacob as a sole heir, dismissing the assumption that he cannot be, thereby adding new/further contextual implicatures. Thus, this public representation of repetition shows the speaker's or the narrator's mental representation of the Abrahamic covenant and God's intentional choice of one particular line of the descendants of Abraham and Isaac, which evidently resulted from the inferential interaction of memories in his cognitive environment. He also assumes that his audience also will imagine this for themselves because this contextual assumption is mutually shared knowledge.

Jacob might have entertained a series of metarepresentations of the utterances of God in his mind. Let us take one of the utterances of God—the clause "I will bring you back to this land" to illustrate this phenomenon:

a. God said to me: "I will bring you back to this land."

b. God said that he will bring me back to this land.

c. God intends/plans to bring me back to this land.

d. God intends me to believe that he will bring me back to this land.

e. God intends me to believe that he intends me to believe that he will bring me back to this land.

Jacob's Echoic Response to His Dream (vv. 16–17)

Verses 16–17 concern Jacob's spontaneous response to the unique experience of his dream in Bethel:

78. Sperber and Wilson, *Relevance*, 220–21.

16 וַיִּיקַץ יַעֲקֹב מִשְּׁנָתוֹ וַיֹּאמֶר אָכֵן יֵשׁ יְהוָה בַּמָּקוֹם הַזֶּה וְאָנֹכִי לֹא יָדָעְתִּי:

17 וַיִּירָא וַיֹּאמַר מַה־נּוֹרָא הַמָּקוֹם הַזֶּה אֵין זֶה כִּי אִם־בֵּית אֱלֹהִים וְזֶה שַׁעַר הַשָּׁמָיִם:

> 16 Then Jacob woke from his sleep and said, "Surely the LORD is in this place—and I did not know it!" 17 And he was afraid, and said, "How awesome is this place! This is none other than the house of God, and this is the gate of heaven."

The narrator explicitly attributes the utterances of verses 16 and 17 to Jacob by employing a linguistic device ויאמר "and he said." It seems that Jacob's first awaking from his sleep occurred because of the shock caused by the awesome nature of his dream as it was expressed by his utterance of exclamation: "Surely the LORD is in this place—and I did not know it!" (v. 16). And he was so afraid that he said: "How awesome is this place! This is none other than the house of God. And this is the gate of the heaven" (v. 17). The context shows that Jacob was not talking to anybody in that particular situation because the text implies that there was nobody with him. Therefore, we can describe this expression as a representation of his own thoughts, perhaps uttered aloud.

The first sentence in verse 17 is an exclamative expression which represents his emotion and surprise when he stumbled on the fact that God was there.[79] On the other hand, relevance theory claims that exclamative utterances are metarepresentational.[80] However, Wilson notes that in terms of relevance theory if an exclamative expression is a non-attributive or non-echoic utterance then it has to be treated as a representation of desirable thoughts or desirable information of the speaker himself.[81] She would interpret Jacob's exclamative utterance in this context as signalling his own sudden realization of the fact that Yahweh was there. Hence, Jacob's exclamative utterance in this context could be perceived as showing Jacob's emotional response to God's very encouraging promises. The adverbial expression אכן, translated as "surely" by NRSV, marks Jacob's

---

79. In terms of speech act theory and the classification of the sentence function the term "exclamation" is used to refer any emotional utterance (Crystal, *Encyclopedia*, 169; Sperber and Wilson, *Relevance*, 244). However, in terms of the principle of relevance, which works on the basis of inference about getting the communicator's informative intention, exclamatives should be comprehended interpretively depending on the shared contextual assumptions (Sperber and Wilson, *Relevance*, 254). Thus, in this case the first accessible assumption could be that the presence of God in Bethel was a surprise to Jacob.

80. Noh, *Metarepresentation*, 99.

81. Wilson, "Metarepresentation," 437.

verbal representation of the surprise he felt when he suddenly became conscious of Yahweh's presence in Bethel.

Wenham explains that according to the ancient thought of the Near East, heaven refers to the house/dwelling place of the divine.[82] Hence the expression "the gate of the heaven" identifies Bethel as a place which directly leads one to the divine presence. Note that all the three sentences used by the narrator at this time are carefully crafted repetitions in order to magnify the significance of Bethel: certainly the Lord is present in this place; how fearful/awesome is this place; this is none other than the house of God; this is the gate of heaven.[83] Apart from the clause "how fearful/awesome is this place," the rest of Jacob's utterances say the same thing in different ways. This repetition achieves the relevance of strong confirmation or strengthening of the existing assumption about the chosen place of God (cognitive effect). Thus Jacob and the narrator too perceive Bethel as a unique sacred/holy place because of the divine presence there. Westermann observes this phenomenon when he says: "What is described here is a phenomenon of religion as a whole."[84] Consequently, Jacob referred the place as the house of God, which usually, in the later cultic practice of Israelites, is used to refer to the temple or sanctuary (Jdg 18:31; 1Chr 4:48; Ezra 1:4; Neh 6:10; Ps 42:4; Eccl 5:1; Dan 1:2).

The Vow Making of Jacob and Its Echoic Nature (vv. 18–22)

The second response of Jacob to his dream is presented in 18–22 and it has two phases. The first phase is presented in verses 18–19 and is largely narrative. In verse 18 we are told that Jacob woke up and took the stone[85] which was under his head and set it up as a pillar and poured oil on it as an expression of his reaction to the experience of his dream:

18 וַיַּשְׁכֵּם יַעֲקֹב בַּבֹּקֶר וַיִּקַּח אֶת־הָאֶבֶן אֲשֶׁר־שָׂם מְרַאֲשֹׁתָיו וַיָּשֶׂם אֹתָהּ
מַצֵּבָה וַיִּצֹק שֶׁמֶן עַל־רֹאשָׁהּ:

> 18 So Jacob rose early in the morning, and he took the stone that he had put under his head and set it up for a pillar and poured oil on the top of it.

---

82. Wenham, *Genesis 16–50*, 223.
83. Fokkelman, *Narrative Art*, 49.
84. Westermann, *Promise*, 456.
85. It is worth noting to observe that the stone which was under his head must have been a large stone because it was sufficient to be erected as an altar (he poured oil on it which shows that probably he also intended it be an altar) or memorial.

Reading and Translating Genesis 28:10—35:15 as a Votive Narrative

A key question to ask here is that: why did Jacob erect the pillar? Different answers have been proposed to this question. The practice of erecting stones as a pillar may have different functions in the ancient Near East culture: as a memorial to the dead, as a witness to the solemn agreement of treaty, as a victory memorial, as a cultic action, and as a boundary stone.[86] In addition, Gunkel notes that the veneration of stones by anointing oil shows the belief of ancient people as "feeding the god resident in the stone."[87] Similarly Pagolu also observes from different ancient literatures that there was a well-accepted notion that certain stones were perceived as indwelt by deities and were therefore holy stones.[88] However, he remarks that there is no implication that Jacob believed that God actually dwelt in the stone or that he worshiped it as a deity.[89] Moreover, anointing the stone by pouring oil implies making both the stone and the place it is erected as sacred cultic objects for God, who revealed himself to Jacob. This seems to be a stronger implication of the text than feeding the deity dwelling in that particular stone.[90] The name "Bethel" given by Jacob to this place in verse 19 also reinforces this notion:[91]

19 וַיִּקְרָא אֶת־שֵׁם־הַמָּקוֹם הַהוּא בֵּית־אֵל וְאוּלָם לוּז שֵׁם־הָעִיר לָרִאשֹׁנָה׃

19 He called that place Bethel; but the name of the city was Luz at the first.

Wenham notes that a stone inscription discovered in that region refers to the whole place as "Bethel" which means house of gods.[92] Jacob's utterance of the name also shows that he designated that particular stone as well as the place where it was erected as the dwelling place of God.[93] The first reference shows the inhabitants' consciousness of the presence of god(s) in that area while the second (Jacob's naming) shows his consciousness of the presence of God in that particular spot. He changes its name from "Luz" to "Bethel" (v. 19) in order to represent this phenomenon in its proper name. Pagolu notes that possibly Jacob's erecting the stone was a cultic

---

86. Westermann, *Promise*, 223; Gunkel, *Genesis*, 311–12; Pagolu, *Religion of the Patriarchs*, 147.
87. Gunkel, *Genesis*, 312.
88. Pagolu, *Religion of the Patriarchs*, 136.
89. Ibid., 174.
90. Ibid., 162–64.
91. Ibid., 162.
92. Wenham, *Genesis 16–50*, 224.
93. Ibid.

Vow-Making of Jacob as a Metarepresentation

action intended "to mark the immanence of the deity" in Bethel.⁹⁴ Thus, there is oblique mention of two metarepresentations here, both performative speech acts of naming. Therefore, we can conclude that presumably what Jacob intended to do by erecting the pillar in Bethel shows that he recognizes Bethel as a sanctuary of God and commits himself to worship God in Bethel.⁹⁵

The second part of Jacob's response metarepresents his words at that time: Jacob made a vow to God (vv. 20–22). Some scholars like Westermann consider the vow of Jacob in 20–22 as a secondary element. For example Westermann considers verses 10–12 and 16–19 as the main narrative and verses 13–15, and 20–22 as a later expansion of the old narrative.⁹⁶ However, I suggest that this conclusion could be disputed based on two pieces of evidence: grammatical or syntactic evidence and pragmatic evidence of the contextual assumptions of vow making.

In terms of grammatical evidence we observe that the Hebrew narrative feature of vav consecutive shows the sequential order of the event. The vav consecutive (suffix ו) is used at the beginning of both juxtaposed paragraphs with the imperfect verb (WAYYIQTOL): it begins with וישכם in וישכם יעקב "Jacob rose" and ends with ויקרא in ויקרא את־שם־המקום ההוא בת־אל, "and he called the name of the place Bethel" in the preceding clause, (Gen 28:19). Then next clause begins with the imperfect verb (WAYYIQTOL) וידר in וידר יעקב נדר "and Jacob made a vow," in the following clause (28:20) which shows the consecutive feature of the event line.

Regarding the role of vav consecutive in terms of the juxtaposed clause relationship in the ancient Hebrew narrative, there are two different constructions of vav consecutive which have two distinct semantic forces: relative force and coordinative or copulative force.⁹⁷ When vav consecutive is employed to signal relative force, the following or second *vav* preffixed to the verb will signal that the second verb is in relative relationship with the preceding one which is also preffixed with *vav,* thus the second one could be translated as "then. . . ."⁹⁸

Similarly, in terms of the role of *vav* consecutive at the relation of the paragraph level the analysis of Roy L. Heller shows that if two paragraphs

---

94. Pagolu, *Religion of the Patriarchs*, 150.
95. Ibid., 170.
96. Westermann, *Promise*, 452–53, 458.
97. Kelley, *Biblical Hebrew*, 145; Waltke and O'Connor, *Hebrew Syntax*, 519ff.
98. Waltke and O'Connor, *Hebrew Syntax*, 519ff.

Reading and Translating Genesis 28:10—35:15 as a Votive Narrative

are juxtaposed in a narrative and are tied together they are marked by the *WAYYIQTOL* verb construction in most cases. He explains:

> A corresponding initial *WAYYIQTOL* clause tied to a *WAYYIQTOL* chain, therefore, usually stands at the beginning of paragraphs whose preceding paragraph is terminally explicitly marked; likewise, a terminal *WAYYIQTOL* clause tied to a preceding *WAYYIQTOL* chain, stands at the end of paragraphs whose following paragraph is initially explicitly marked. ...These externally marked paragraphs are bounded by the final clause of preceding paragraph or the initial clause of following paragraph. The corresponding *WAYYIQTOL* clause either begins or concludes the *WAYYIQTOL* chains which comprise the paragraph in which they are found.[99]

This feature is apparent in these two juxtaposed paragraphs of this narrative: Jacob's setting out from Beersheba (28:10) (preceding paragraph) and Jacob's setting off to go to Padan Aram וישׂא יעקב רגליו׳ "Jacob raised his feet" (29:1) (following paragraph).[100]

Secondly, they are bound cognitively because of the contextual assumption that a vow is always made first (usually but not always in a sanctuary of the deity) and then vow-granting follows. Therefore, it follows that Jacob makes the vow at that place he designated as the house of God (vv. 20–22) which qualifies it as a powerfully valid binding votive utterance. Most importantly, this feature highlights that it must be here (Bethel) that he must fulfill his vow, not in any other place, when he returns to Canaan. And then the narrator proceeds narrating about the vow–granting according to the natural order of votive narratives beginning at (29:1). Thus, this public representation shows that this votive utterance meets the expected contextual assumptions of vow making and vow granting which will be discussed in the following chapters. Hence, these two paragraphs are bound together both grammatically and pragmatically or cognitively.

---

99. Heller, *Narrative Structure*, 440.

100. When I say paragraph, I am talking about the physical textual break represented as in the MT. The Hebrew scripture does not make a paragraph break between the events of setting up the altar which was concluded by changing the name of the place (18–19) and making a vow (20–22). Rather it treats 28:10–22 as one unit paragraph. However, in terms of pragmatic feature of a paragraph, it has been noted that what constitutes a paragraph is a particular central content about which the paragraph talks (Waltke and O'Connor, *Hebrew Syntax*, 633). Thus, although it is subjective, one may consider vv. 18–19 and 20–22 as talking about two distinct central ideas, thus constituting two consecutive paragraphs.

Vow-Making of Jacob as a Metarepresentation

The votive utterance of Jacob functions as a framework of this narrative unit and it is crucially relevant for the interpretation of the whole narrative unit. There are four pieces of evidence for this claim: this particular vow is mentioned again and again at key or strategic points of the narrative of the Jacob story (31:13; 35:1–3, 7). Jacob's votive utterance in verses 20–22 is strongly echoic when compared to Yahweh's utterance to him in the dream (28:10–15):

- I will multiply your descendants like the dust and they shall spread to the west and to the east, and to north and to the south of Canaan
- I will give the land on which you are lying to you and to your descendants
- Your descendants will be a blessing for all the families of the earth
- I will be with you and protect you and not forsake you
- I will bring you back to this land

In responding, Jacob then says in his vow:

20 וַיִּדַּר יַעֲקֹב נֶדֶר לֵאמֹר אִם־יִהְיֶה אֱלֹהִים עִמָּדִי וּשְׁמָרַנִי בַּדֶּרֶךְ הַזֶּה אֲשֶׁר אָנֹכִי הוֹלֵךְ וְנָתַן־לִי לֶחֶם לֶאֱכֹל וּבֶגֶד לִלְבֹּשׁ:

21 וְשַׁבְתִּי בְשָׁלוֹם אֶל־בֵּית אָבִי וְהָיָה יְהוָה לִי לֵאלֹהִים:

22 וְהָאֶבֶן הַזֹּאת אֲשֶׁר־שַׂמְתִּי מַצֵּבָה יִהְיֶה בֵּית אֱלֹהִים וְכֹל אֲשֶׁר תִּתֶּן־לִי עַשֵּׂר אֲעַשְּׂרֶנּוּ לָךְ:

> 20 Then Jacob made a vow, saying, "If God will be with me, and will keep me in this way that I go, and will give me bread to eat and clothing to wear, 21 so that I come again to my father's house in peace, then the LORD shall be my God, 22 and this stone, which I have set up for a pillar, shall be God's house; and of all that you give me I will surely give one tenth to you."

The second phase of Jacob's response to his dream (his votive utterance) is marked by metalinguistic device ויידר יעקב נדר לאמר "he made a vow by saying" in order to show the narrator's metarepresentation of Jacob's utterance. Similarly his votive utterance in verses 20–22 manifests an echoic feature to the utterance of God in his dream in that it resembles God's attributed utterance or thought significantly. The narrator's representation of the vow of Jacob resembles his representation of the utterance of God to Jacob in his dream. Consequently the conditionals of Jacob's vow are not descriptive utterances. Rather, they are metarepresentations.[101]

---

101. Noh, *Metarepresentation*, 205–8.

Reading and Translating Genesis 28:10—35:15 as a Votive Narrative

The vow can be broken into the following constituent parts:

Protases (conditions):
אם "If"[102]

- You will be with me and protect me in this journey
- You give me food to eat and clothes to wear
- I return back to my father's house in peace

Apodoses (commitments)[103]:
Then

- You shall be my God
- This stone which I set as a pillar shall be the house of God
- I shall give you a tenth of all you will give me

First of all, the conditional statement marker, אם "if," in a votive narrative does not denote doubt; rather it is a natural form when making a vow. In addition, in the votive utterance of Jacob, the conditional clauses do not encode a causal-consequential link between the antecedent and consequent because the truth value of the antecedent is not a sufficient condition for the truth value of the consequent. The truth value of this conditional expression is open. Consequently, the truth value of the conditional expression of granting Jacob's votive plea shows a commitment of the vow maker and not a strict logic. This is because the vow making, in every vow-practicing society, is based on a social institution, not on logic. If the vow is fulfilled it is over. But if it is not fulfilled it will raise further expectations.

Therefore, in order to comprehend this utterance a truth-functional analysis must be complemented by a pragmatic approach.[104] We agree that

---

102. We observe that the Hebrew conditional marker אם occurs only with the first condition אִם־יִהְיֶה אֱלֹהִים עִמָּדִי וּשְׁמָרַנִי בַּדֶּרֶךְ הַזֶּה אֲשֶׁר אָנֹכִי הוֹלֵךְ. However, we should note that it is intended to cover all the three conditions because the following two conditions are connected to the first condition by ו (vav consecutive)—thus one initial אם covers three conditional protases.

103. The end of the protases (conditions) as a semantic unit and the beginning of the apodoses is marked by the disjunctive accent marker *atnah* (֑) which is deployed under בת־אבי in verse 21 (Scott, *Simplified Guide*, 25f, 27).

104. According to the truth-functional description of the conditionals, if God does not grant Jacob's plea then Jacob is not obliged to fulfill his vow. But if God grants Jacob's plea and then Jacob fails to fulfill his promise to God then Jacob's claim is false; that is all according to logic. Thus the truth-functional analysis cannot adequately account for the institutional contextual implications of the serious consequence of the conditionals of Genesis 28:20–22 because these utterances are based on mutually

Vow-Making of Jacob as a Metarepresentation

there is a general implication of condition and consequence, but it cannot be explained by the truth-functional analysis. Hence, a metarepresentational approach (which is based on inferences of interpretive resemblance) accounts more comprehensively for the analysis of the conditionals in Jacob's vow because Jacob's vow has varied deeper implications which are left to the hearer to infer due to language indeterminacy. Those contextual implications are mutually shared knowledge that the writer assumes the readers can imagine for themselves.

When we say that Jacob's vow is "echoic" we mean Jacob first interpreted the utterance of God in his dream so that when he made this utterance God's utterance was in his mind and he had an attitude about it. The relevance theoretic explanation of echoic utterances broadly notes that an echoic utterance either endorses the original, or disassociates from it, or questions it.[105] The attitude of Jacob toward the utterance of God cannot be doubt/questioning or disassociating because the conditional clause of the votive utterance does not mark a doubt or disassociation.[106] Jacob's attitude in this context was of approval or endorsement.[107] Thus, Jacob's votive response signals his encouragement through what God has said to him in his dream, because a votive utterance is a binding commitment of thanksgiving to a deity on condition of his granting vow. This feature of Jacob's votive utterance makes it crucially relevant for the interpretation of the following episodes of Jacob's votive narrative. Cartledge also observes the echoic nature of Jacob's vow when he says that Jacob made the vow to God in order to bind Yahweh to his commissive utterance for him. But he also suggests that this is because Jacob distrusted God and so he wanted to intensify it in a vow.[108] However, Cartledge's discussion falls short in terms of developing this view further within the framework of the votive narrative and institution of the vow. In addition, in the ancient Israelite context, a vow is made in the context of distress, usually in the sanctuary, and it must be fulfilled in the sanctuary, if a deity answers his plea.[109]

All these criteria of vow making were met in the vow making of Jacob: he was in distress because Esau threatened to kill him and he was

shared knowledge of the votive institution of the community than truth-functional semantics of cause and consequent

105. Sperber and Wilson, *Relevance*, 238–43.

106. See my discussion in chapter 3, section 3.2.4.

107. This phenomenon is manifested in the vow granting of God, which will be discussed in chapter 5.

108. Cartledge, *Vows*, 169.

109. Wenham, *Genesis 16–50*, 224.

fleeing from home, not sure what his future fate would be. It was in such a distressing context that he received a surprising commitment from God: promise of protection, promise of blessings, and promise of bringing him back to Canaan, the Promised Land. Besides he was there right in the house of God (Bethel), which makes the context exactly appropriate for making a vow, solemnly promising to fulfill it in Bethel, if God grants his plea.

Thus, this votive utterance in Genesis 28:10–22 is absolutely relevant to this narrative unit of the Jacob story as well as to the general framework of the Jacob story.[110] It is connected to the preceding and following story: to the preceding story because of its allusion to and echoing of the preceding stories; to the following story because of the literary nature of the votive narrative and assumed institutional nature of the vow. Cartledge, though he did not explain it in terms of this framework, observes this feature when he says "Gen 28:10–22 serves multiple functions, one of which is to integrate the components of the Jacob/Esau and Jacob/Laban cycle."[111] It raises a strong expectation of relevance in terms of its fulfillment, which we will examine in the following chapter(s). Before we embark on that discussion let us examine the content of Jacob's vow.

Protasis

Usually the conditional expressions (protases) are marked by אִם "if." However, it is worth noting that in Jacob's votive utterances אִם occurs only with the first protasis אִם־יִהְיֶה אֱלֹהִים עִמָּדִי וּשְׁמָרַנִי בַּדֶּרֶךְ הַזֶּה אֲשֶׁר אָנֹכִי הוֹלֵךְ "if God will be with me and protect me in this journey" and the rest of the conditionals are marked by *vav* consecutive in order to indicate that technically each of them are marked by the same אִם. Therefore, in the following discussion I will assume that אִם marks each conditional expression implicitly.

---

110. Wenham, *Genesis 16–50*, 224.
111. Cartledge, *Vows*, 166.

Vow-Making of Jacob as a Metarepresentation

אִם־יִהְיֶה אֱלֹהִים עִמָּדִי וּשְׁמָרַנִי בַּדֶּרֶךְ הַזֶּה אֲשֶׁר אָנֹכִי הוֹלֵךְ
"If God will be with me and will keep/protect me in this way/journey that I go."

The expression "if God will be with me and protect me in this journey" is part of the protases which expresses Jacob's distress and his plea to God for his intervention. This plea is apparently a metarepresentation of God's commissive speech act or utterance to protect him as represented in verse 15.

When God promised his protection to Jacob there was no indication that his protection was limited only to Jacob's journey to Haran. Because God declared: "I am with you and protect you wherever you go and I will bring you back to this land because I shall not forsake/leave you until I have done what I said to you" (v. 15). On the other hand it appears that Jacob's echoic plea for protection was limited to that particular context of his distressing situation—protection in his journey to Haran. However, it can be argued that his plea for protection was not limited only to his journey to Padan-Aram (see the apparent implication in verse 21). Rather it includes the whole time span, beginning from his journey to Padan-Aram to his returning back to the land of his fathers in peace (v. 21). Thus the utterances in the protasis: "if you will be with me and protect me in this journey" (v. 20) and "if I return back to my fathers house in peace" (v. 21) are interrelated utterances and are included in the votive plea for protection.

וְנָתַן־לִי לֶחֶם לֶאֱכֹל וּבֶגֶד לִלְבֹּשׁ
"If he will give me food to eat and clothing to wear"

This condition of Jacob's votive utterance is an interpretive echoic utterance of God's utterance in verses 13b–14. Although it is vague in terms of linguistic expression it is apparent that God's promise to Jacob comprises the prosperity of material wealth and the blessings of many descendants.

One may think that according to this utterance Jacob asks God only for the provision of food and clothing "just enough to subsist on."[112] However, Cartledge remarks that "it could just as likely be understood as a hendiadys for 'all that I need.'"[113] Thus, the context of the vow granting in the subsequent chapters of the votive narrative shows that this expression requires interpretive use of the linguistic representation rather than a

112. Ibid., 170.
113. Ibid.

metalinguistic use. It does not seem natural to understand the utterance of Jacob: "if you give me food to eat and clothes to wear" literally, as if Jacob asked God to give him only something to eat and wear nothing less and nothing more.

The linguistic feature of not making his request explicit about things which this expression includes, something more than food and clothing, could be explained as loose talk, which is common in human communication.[114] Sperber and Wilson explain loose talk as follows:

> An utterance, in its role as an interpretive expression of a speaker's thought, is strictly literal if it has the same propositional form as that thought. To say that an utterance is less than strictly literal is to say that its propositional form shares some, but not all, of its logical properties with the propositional form of the thought it is being used to interpret. From the start point of relevance theory, there is no reason to think that the optimally relevant interpretive expression of a thought is always the most literal one. The speaker is presumed to aim at optimal relevance not at literal truth.[115]

For example, if I say "I do not have shoes for the wedding" that does not necessarily mean I do not have any shoes at all. Rather, it could mean I do not have the appropriate shoes. Assuming that I have shoes and my audience also knows that I have shoes, what I said does not resemble my thought literally, but by logical interpretation. Thus, loose use of language in communication is indeterminate in the propositional sense, but its contextual implications are mutually manifest for both the speaker and hearer. Here there is a logical resemblance between Jacob's representation (if you give me bread to eat and clothes to wear) and what it represents (a plea for the blessing of prosperity), that is they resemble one another interpretively because they share logical and contextual implications in that situation.

The implication of this utterance becomes more apparent in his votive utterance in the apodosis, committing himself to give a tithe to God out of everything God will give him: "I shall give a tenth out of all you will give me" (v. 22). This aspect of the utterance becomes more obvious when we discuss the concept of tithing in the ancient Israelite context below. If Jacob does not request God for the blessing of prosperity then why

---

114. Sperber and Wilson, *Relevance*, 233–37; Carston and Powell, "Relevance Theory," 157–59.

115. Sperber and Wilson, *Relevance*, 233.

does he make a votive promise to give tithe from everything God will give him? If his request for "bread to eat and clothes to wear" was connected to his promise "to give tithe from everything that God will give him" then the expression should be understood as a loose talk rather than literal. Thus, Jacob's request is for more than food and clothing—it is a request for prosperity which also includes wives, children, shelter, water, and all other blessings.

He was in a desperate situation, being empty-handed in his forties (Gen 26:34). Now he runs away from his father's house for his life, not knowing whether there is any possibility that he will come back and share the inheritance of his father so he spoke in this way.

וְשַׁבְתִּי בְשָׁלוֹם אֶל־בֵּית אָבִי וְהָיָה יְהוָה לִי לֵאלֹהִים
"If I return back to my father's house in peace"

This expression is echoic to the utterance of God which says:

> The land on which you are lying I shall give it to you and to your descendants. ... Behold I am with you and protect you wherever you go and I will bring you back to this land because I shall not forsake/leave you until I have done what I said to you. (vv. 13, 15)

When we compare Jacob's utterance "If I return back to my father's house in peace" and God's utterance of promise to Jacob in his dream: "Behold I am with you and will protect you wherever you go and I will bring you back to this land" it shows that they are in apparent interpretive resemblance, which proves that the utterance of Jacob is an echoic metarepresentation of the thought or utterance of God. It is echoic because it implies that Jacob has an endorsing attitude to the utterance of God to protect him and to bring him back to the land of his fathers. We can work out the explicatures and implicatures of both utterances, and compare them so that we can see the interpretive resemblance between them better. The explicatures of God's utterance have the following main points:

1. God will be with Jacob wherever he goes and will protect him—Jacob may go to different places including even going out of the Promised Land; in fact Jacob was on his way out of the Promised Land at that particular time.

2. God will bring him back to the Promised Land—Jacob's coming back to the Promised Land is fully dependant on God's act of bringing him back. It is God who will bring him back but nobody else.

3. God shall not forsake him until he has fulfilled what he has promised to Jacob—it is guaranteed that God will fulfill what he has promised to Jacob.

4. God will give the Promised Land to Jacob and his descendants to inherit—Jacob and his descendants are now chosen by God as the heirs of the Abrahamic covenant. God will do all the above and everything necessary for Jacob so that Jacob and his descendants inherit the Promised Land.

Jacob's utterance: "If I return back to my father's house in peace" is meta-represented echoically to the utterance of God in 2: "I will bring you back to this land." However, Jacob did not include in his echoic utterance the rest of God's utterances listed above which are in fact an integral part of God's commitment to bring him back to the promised land. For example Jacob's utterance did not explicitly include his desire of inheriting the land when he returns back to the Promised Land. However, we can assume that he presumed that his audience can draw this information by inference because that was why God would bring him back to Canaan anyway. Hence, the rest of the above list of God's utterances are implicatures of Jacob's utterance which can be reconstructed inferentially. In this way Jacob's utterance is optimally relevant, avoiding unnecessary processing effort in effect. Therefore, there is no need for Jacob to say "If you will be with me wherever I go and protect me and bring me back to this land in peace so that I inherit this land, and if you shall not forsake me until you fulfill what you have promised me."

In summary, this votive utterance of Jacob is again loose talk. I assume that what Jacob said and what he actually thought is connected logically, by inference, not in the linguistic form. I do not think that Jacob was only interested in coming back to the Promised Land in peace but not interested in inheriting it. In fact, probably inheriting the Promised Land was the ultimate goal of his desire to return to the land of his fathers, to which the narrator intended to allude. Thus apparently this utterance is also echoic to what God promised to him in his dream, except that he chose this expression because it is optimally relevant to express his emotional feeling of distress and his desperate need of divine protection and the placing of his hope in God for help. Hence, there is an apparent interpretive resemblance between the utterance of God and Jacob here too and Jacob's metarepresented utterance is an echoic one because he has an attitude of endorsing God's utterance.

Apodosis

וְהָיָה יְהוָה לִי לֵאלֹהִים "he will be my God."

Noh's analysis of the metarepresentational use of conditionals shows that some conditionals may have both metarepresentational antecedents (protases) and metarepresentational consequents (apodosis).[116] Thus, I argue that Jacob's utterance: "you will be my God," which is an apodosis (consequent), is echoic depending upon God's utterance "I am the LORD God of your father Abraham and God of Isaac." This metarepresentation is relevant in this context on the basis of contextual implication. The expression "I am the LORD God of your father Abraham and God of Isaac" implies that he is their protector, provider, and one who has made a covenantal relationship with them. Reciprocally they committed themselves to worship him faithfully. Thus the votive utterance of Jacob: "you shall be my God" is an echoic expression of God's utterance: "I am the LORD God of your father Abraham and God of Isaac," in verse 13, which has different contextual implications, in terms of what God did and will do for Abraham, Isaac, and their descendants and how they should worship him. Hence, in short, what Jacob says is presumably: "God, you said that you are the God of Abraham and Isaac. If you will be with me and protect me in this journey, give me food to eat and clothes to wear, return me back to my fathers house in peace, then you will also be my God." Thus Jacob achieves the relevance of up-fronting his plea to God by metarepresenting God's utterance of promise to him in his dream.

וְהָאֶבֶן הַזֹּאת אֲשֶׁר־שַׂמְתִּי מַצֵּבָה יִהְיֶה בֵּית אֱלֹהִים
"This stone which I set as a pillar shall be the house of God"

We have already discussed above that Jacob's votive utterance at Bethel denotes that he designated a particular stone he erected and the place where it was erected as a dwelling place of God.[117] Thus Jacob recognizes Bethel

---

116. Noh, *Metarepresentation*, 205–8.

117. Wenham, *Genesis 16–50*, 224. We have already discussed that possibly Jacob's erecting the pillar in Bethel was intended to signal the conviction of Jacob about the presence of Yahweh in Bethel, as his behavior of changing the name of the place from

as a sanctuary of God. The contextual implication of this utterance is that no other place is compatible with Bethel unless Yahweh himself shows that he chose some other place. Hence, as Yahweh himself requires, the tithe should be returned in Bethel and votive promises must be fulfilled only in Bethel.[118] Jacob has therefore ostensively committed himself to fulfilling his vow in Bethel if and when God has granted his plea and brought him safely back to Canaan from Padan Aram.

וְכֹל אֲשֶׁר תִּתֶּן־לִי עַשֵּׂר אֲעַשְּׂרֶנּוּ לָךְ
"I shall give you a tenth out of all you will give me"

One of the apodoses of Jacob's votive utterances was that he commits to give a tenth of everything God will give him. One may argue that there is no clear metarepresentation in the utterance of Jacob to the utterance and thought of God because there is no interpretive resemblance between the utterances of God and Jacob. However, I suggest that the clause "out of all you will give me" shows that Jacob is making an inferential reference to the utterance or thought of God which is apparently God's commitment to bless Jacob with prosperity as the clause "out of all you will give me" shows. If that was not the case, then we might ask "Where did he get the thought of the expression 'out of all you will give me'?" Thus the votive utterance of the tithe shows that the narrator has recovered the implied information of "if you give me bread to eat and cloth to wear" as it was intended to include the blessing of prosperity as well, as we discussed above. This phenomenon is clearer when we understand the institution of tithing (see Appendix 3).

In summary, presumably the connection of Jacob's votive plea for "food to eat and clothes to wear" with his votive utterance "to give a tenth of everything God will give him" implies that Jacob made a votive plea to God to bless him with prosperity as well, thus echoically metarepresenting God's thought to bless him with prosperity.

Conclusion

In this chapter we read Genesis 28:10–22 from the metarepresentational perspective. The degree of metarepresentational dependence of verses

---

"Luz" to "Bethel" signifies (v.19).
118. See our discussion in chapter 3.

Vow-Making of Jacob as a Metarepresentation

16–22 upon verses 10–15 supports the internal unity of Genesis 28:10–22 and beyond, contrary to the views that have sometimes been proposed by some critics.

Our discussion in this chapter shows that Jacob's votive utterance is echoic; it is linked to Yahweh's earlier commissive speech act to which it has apparent interpretive resemblance. Thus, it shows that Jacob's attitude toward God's commissive speech act cannot be a "doubt" because the condition in a votive utterance never marks doubt; rather it marks the petitioner's emotional state or condition caused by distress, his trust in the deity for relief, his plea to the deity for help, and his commitment to respond to the deity in thanksgiving in a specific way, if the deity grants his plea. The use of אם "if" in the votive narrative leaves the response of the deity open, thus allowing for both possibilities of granting the votive plea or not. It does not imply any sense of divine obligation.

Finally, based on the above discussion I would again emphasize that the votive utterance of Jacob has raised a strong expectation of relevance: Will God grant Jacob's votive plea? If God grants it, then will Jacob fulfill his vow to God? These questions will be answered in the following chapter when we investigate the following narrative episodes.

5

Vow Granting and Vow Fulfilling

Introduction

JACOB'S VOTIVE UTTERANCE AT Bethel (Gen 28:10–22) functions as a framework for the interpretation of the following Jacob story (Gen 29:1—35:15). This is because his vow has raised expectations of relevance. The reader of the Jacob story is now entertaining the following thoughts: Will God grant his votive plea? Will Jacob fulfill his vow? The narrator's public representation of the following narrative episodes (29:1—35:15) shows that he aimed to answer these questions.

The story of Jacob in Gen 29:1—35:15 may be read from different points of view depending on the readers' assumptions. Here it is read from the narrator's point of view as it is ostensively signaled in narrator's public representation of the story. As remarked elsewhere, Cartledge, though he failed to read Genesis 29:1—35:15 within the framework of a votive narrative, correctly observes that the vow of Jacob in Bethel was presented within a large narrative unit and it integrates the narrative components of the Jacob/Esau and Jacob/Laban story.[1] Concurring with this, it has already been maintained that according to the narrator's point of view, Genesis 28:10–22 was employed as a staging or abstract of the whole narrative/discourse unit of Genesis 28:10—35:15 in order to influence the interpretation of everything that follows in the story.

Brown and Yule have observed that providing such an abstract of a narrative discourse right at the beginning of the story is a common feature

1. Cartledge, *Vows*, 166.

of most narratives.[2] Accordingly, in the close reading of Genesis 28:10–22 in chapter 4, it has been suggested that the vow of Jacob, which includes the commissive speech act, raised an expectation of relevance of the granting of the vow by God and of the fulfilling of the vow by Jacob in the contemporary audience, gearing them to search for it in the story that follows. Thus, there are two different types of expectations of relevance: firstly, that the votive plea may be granted, if granted then that the votive promise should be fulfilled and that failure to fulfill leads to the risk of further adverse consequences; secondly that, as in all communication, the audience has an expectation of relevance for themselves.

Jacob's votive utterance:

> If you will be with me and protect me in this journey, if you give me bread to eat and clothes to wear, if I return back to my father's house in peace, then, you shall be my God, this stone which I set as a pillar shall be the house of God, I shall give tenth out of all you will give me.

According to the contemporary social and cultural context of Jacob story, this votive utterance automatically raises expectations of relevance in the audience in these two ways. Examining whether each condition of the vow of Jacob is granted and whether Jacob fulfilled his votive commitment will be the organizing theme of this chapter.

The public representation of the narrative is ostensively organized to lead readers to an evaluation of this phenomenon as the narrator reflects his own point of view in the story about whether God granted an answer to Jacob's votive plea and whether Jacob fulfilled his votive promise to God. Further, if Jacob should fail to fulfill his votive promise, then the expectation of relevance about the inevitable adverse consequences for the failed votive promise must have been raised in the audience

Therefore, understanding the evaluative nature of this narrative, as ostensively represented by the narrator, is crucial for the task of its interpretation and translation. All the ostensive signals in the narrative will be pointed out in order to explain this.

However, it is worth noting that they are linguistically underdetermined. This is because it is not relevant to express what is mutually manifest in the cognitive environment of both speaker and audience, and such communicative behavior is explained by relevance theory. Ronald Sim remarks this phenomenon nicely as follows:

---

2. Brown and Yule, *Discourse Analysis*, 133.

Reading and Translating Genesis 28:10—35:15 as a Votive Narrative

Ostensive stimuli draw on parts of the cognitive environment that speaker and hearer mutually share, in order to make the speaker's informative intention(s) manifest to the hearer. The presumption of relevance leads the audience to make sense of what is said, by supplying additional information where necessary, and deriving cognitive benefits that are adequate for the processing effort. This quest for optimal relevance makes it possible to communicate unexpressed as well as expressed information.[3]

For instance, the communicator of the Jacob narrative in Genesis does not state explicitly something like "God granted answers to Jacob's votive plea," or "Jacob fulfilled his votive promise to God," or "Jacob failed to fulfill his votive promise to God so that he suffered adverse consequences." Presumably, on the contrary he assumes that since his audience mutually shares the cognitive environment about the Hebrew concept of נדר "vow" and the nature of the social institution of vowing, he can simply present the votive narrative, assuming that they will imagine these features for themselves inferentially from the story. Though we do not know exactly what he assumed, we can suggest that the narrator mutually shares a cognitive environment with his audience about the votive institution, and that it is not surprising that he leaves fulfillments to be inferred as the cognitive effects, thus fulfilling their expectations of relevance. Therefore, reading this story from the relevance theoretic perspective will significantly help to understand the inferential and evaluative aspects of the story more comprehensively.

Definition of the Evaluative Narrative

William Labove notes that a narrator may have so many ways to tell the same story, or to make different points of the same story significant, or even "to make no point at all."[4] What makes a narrative 'a good narrative' is its being evaluated by the narrator. Such a narrative answers questions like what was this all about (abstract)? Who did it? When? What? Where? Labove describes these as orientation of the narrative. Then what happened (the narrative feature of complicating action)? So what (evaluation)? And what happened finally (coda[5] or result)? The evaluative nature

---

3. Sim, *Handbook for Translators*, 47.
4. Labove, "Transformation," 231.
5. Coda is "one of the many options open to the narrator for signaling that the

of a narrative is one of its most important features. It is a linguistic or public representation of the narrator's cognitive point of view about what he is getting at and why he is telling the story. Thus, the narrator's point of view in a discourse is intended to play a very important role in the real social life of his prospective readers. Gunther Kress and Theo van Leeuwen observe this feature when they claim that texts are produced by the producers in order to play a very real role in social life:

> [L]iterary and artistic texts as much as mass-media texts, are produced in the context of real social institutions, in order to play a very real role in social life—in order to do certain things to or for their readers, and in order to communicate attitudes towards aspects of social life and towards people who participate in them...[6]

Wenham also observes this feature of the biblical narratives when he says "Old Testament narrative books do have didactic purpose, that is, they are trying to instill both theological truth and ethical ideal into the readers."[7] Such feature of a narrative can be reflected as the abstract of the story, right at the beginning of the narrative.

Labove lists some of the characteristics of a fully developed narrative: abstract, orientation, complicating action, evaluation, result or resolution and coda and he explains them as follows.[8] "Abstract" is the narrator's summary of the whole story at the beginning of his narrative. What Labove calls "abstract" is similar to what Brown and Yule describe as "staging." Orientation refers to the narrator's effort to identify time, place, person(s) and their activity or situation and it can occur at any necessary place of the narrative. The complicating actions and the termination or resolution of that action in a particular story may be presented by complex chaining and embedding. Such strategies of narrative representation are employed by a narrator because of the communicative assumption that how a narrative is told affects us. Bader elaborates this feature in her words as follows:

> The sense of the movement of a story from its beginning through its resolution is controlled by the narrator. ...The narrator

---

narrative is finished." For example: Since that time he never comes to disturb me, you know. I do my work quietly and peacefully. No more fight (Labove, "Transformation," 227–34).

6. Kress and van Leeuwen, "Repesentation," 378–79.

7. Wenham, *Genesis 16–50*, 3.

8. Labove, "Transformation," 227.

Reading and Translating Genesis 28:10—35:15 as a Votive Narrative

> or story-teller tells the story in a particular manner, carefully choosing words to guide the reader. Additionally, the narrator makes decisions about what information to include and what to leave out. That person chose whether to show or tell the readers about characters, events, and the various ways in which different characters reacted to or evaluated the events.... How the story was told affects us.[9]

Brown and Yule also note that narrative presentation has a natural order both in terms of the narrator's cognitive organization as well as his linguistic or public presentation of the story, in which the narrator begins from the starting point and proceeds to the narrative progression up until the conclusion. Naturally the process of arranging a discourse may follow a cultural stereotype which is shared by the narrator's audience.[10] However, Brown and Yule remark that such formal arranging is influenced/dictated by the narrator's point of view and consequently he "manipulates the knowledge which the reader needs."[11] Adam Jaworski and Nikolas Coupland also concur with this view when they say:

> [N]arratives are not at all objective or impartial ways of representing events.... [E]ven "factual" narratives are intimately tied to the narrator's point of view, and the events reconstructed in a narrative are his/her (re)constructions rather than some kind of objective mirror-image of reality.... [T]he meaning of the narrative is jointly constructed by the selectively filtering actions of both speaker and listener.[12]

Thus, the narrator's point of view may direct him to choose a particular linguistic form and organization. I have adapted one example here with its accompanying explanation from Brown and Yule in order to illustrate this point:

a. Mary, Queen of Scots, was executed by the English Queen.

b. Mary, Queen of Scots, was assassinated by the English Queen.

c. Mary, Queen of Scott, was murdered by her cousin, Elizabeth.

In each case of the above examples the agent who caused the patient to die and the patient who suffered the death are the same—Queen Elizabeth and Queen Mary respectively. However, the point of view the narrator

---

9. Bader, *Sexual Violation*, 81–82.
10. Brown and Yule, *Discourse Analysis*, 145.
11. Ibid., 144–48.
12. Jaworski and Coupland, *Discourse Reader*, 32.

Vow Granting and Vow Fulfilling

represented by each sentence is distinct as summarized as follows: in 'a' the action is represented as a legal process sanctioned by the constitutional monarch (the English Queen). In 'b' the action is represented as an illegal, politically motivated act of assassination authorized by the constitutional monarch (the English Queen). In 'c' the action is represented as an illegal, criminal act of murder carried out by her cousin Elizabeth.

Thus, Brown and Yule note that in each case "the writer reveals a different assessment of the character and motivation of the act" which lead him to choose different lexical forms which will make his point of view salient for his readers. Thus, it is a fact that the narrators imagine the knowledge of others (metarepresent) as well as their point of view and then strategically organize what will be said in order to influence their readers.[13]

Similarly Daniel Marguerat, Yvan Bourquin and Meir Sternberg describe the story from the narrator's point of view. Both cognitive organization and linguistic or public presentation of "evaluative narrative" reflect his/her point of view about the participants or characters of the biblical stories so that the readers can identify with them and share the narrator's view/feeling about them. The linguistic organization of the narratives is strategically and artistically represented in order to influence and appeal to the readers.[14] In Marguerat and Bourquin's words:

> [T]he narrator tries to influence for his own ends this interaction which will not fail to take place between the reader and the network of characters. To this end the narrator counts on a permanent mechanism of reading which is partly unconscious: the evaluation of the characters.[15]

Thus, every bit of the biblical narrative is fashioned by the narrator's particular point of view employed in linguistic organization in order to influence his prospective readers.[16] Hence, they conclude, that every aspect of the biblical narratives is saturated by the value system and worldview of the narrator.[17] Similarly, the medieval Jewish biblical scholar Rabbi Moses ben Nahman, who wrote a commentary on Genesis observes the literary feature of the Bible as an

13. Brown and Yule, *Discourse Analysis*, 147–48.
14. Marguerat and Bourquin, *Bible Stories*, 66–67; Sternberg, *Poetics of Biblical Narrative*, 129–31.
15. Marguerat and Bourquin, *Bible Stories*, 67–68.
16. Ibid., 68; Sternberg, *Poetics of Biblical Narrative*, 31.
17. Marguerat and Bourquin, *Bible Stories*, 68.

> [I]nter-relationship between the point of view of narrator, character, and reader, artistic use of sound and imagery, tone of dialogue, plot sequence, strategies of characterization, as well as the effects of gaps, repetition, irony, and suspense in biblical narratives.[18]

Therefore, as Bader remarks, the readers of a story should allow the intention of a story to guide them in the direction intended by the narrator.[19] This is because the cognitive point of view of a narrator about the story he intended to represent to his audience and his communicative intention he wanted to achieve through the same is usually strategically manifest by his public representation.[20]

In summary, the term "evaluative" in this discussion depicts the narrator's point of view to the narrative, which he or she is intends to communicate and it denotes his cognitive analysis of the situation of the narrative, characters of the story, and events he has undertaken to narrate and his strategic organization of linguistic representation in order to influence his prospective reader(s) so they share his point of view. Hence, in narrative representations "the narrator's point of view controls the discourse and gives the narrative cohesion and unity."[21] Pagolu says that it is safer to read and interpret a story from the narrator's point of view rather than "to read the text from a hypothetical reconstruction of the story."[22] Therefore, our question regarding Genesis 28:10—35:15 will be: "What is the narrator's point of view of the story?" The aim is to answer this question from the close reading of the text as follows.

God Grants Jacob's Votive Pleas

There is a natural order for seeking the fulfillment of the votive utterance. This is because, according to the institution of vow, the fulfillment of the apodosis is totally dependent on the fulfillment of the protasis. The petitioner is obliged to fulfill his vow only if God grants his votive plea. Therefore, first, our discussion will focus on whether the narrator ostensively showed that God granted Jacob's votive plea. And then we will investigate whether Jacob fulfilled his vow to God.

18. Levine, "Inner World," 306.
19. Bader, *Sexual Violation*, 82.
20. Sperber and Wilson, *Relevance*, 54–64.
21. Bader, *Sexual Violation*, 82.
22. Pagolu, *Religion of the Patriarchs*, 158.

Vow Granting and Vow Fulfilling

This nature of the votive narrative can be observed in other similar narratives in the Hebrew Scriptures. For example, the two clear examples, the votive narrative of Hannah (1 Sam 1:11–28) and the votive narrative of Jephthah (Judges 11:30–39), present both votive utterance and the fulfillment of the vow: vow making, vow granting, and vow fulfilment. If a votive narrative simply stops at the stage of votive utterance (vow making) without reporting whether the deity has granted and whether the petitioner has fulfilled his vow, then the purpose is elusive, and the audience is left in suspense. However, the narrator of Genesis 28:10—35:15 presents vow making, vow granting, and vow fulfillment.

Accordingly, we can describe the narrative elements in 28:10–20 as orientation or background to Jacob's vow-making: orientation about the place, about the major participants (God and Jacob), about the situation (encounter of Jacob with God who established a covenant with him which is full of promises for him and his descendants), and about Jacob's response or reaction to the event. Then the narrator strategically presents the votive utterance of Jacob in verses 20–22 which functions as the thesis or abstract/staging of the whole narrative unit which will continue through 29:1—35:15. Thus the narrative element in verses 20–22 creates a beautiful framework of coherence for the story.

As noted above, the three main votive pleas and the votive commitments of Jacob represented to God in his votive utterance are (Gen 28:20–22):

- אִם־יִהְיֶה אֱלֹהִים עִמָּדִי וּשְׁמָרַנִי בַּדֶּרֶךְ הַזֶּה אֲשֶׁר אָנֹכִי הוֹלֵךְ "If God will be with me and will protect me in this way I go"
- וְנָתַן־לִי לֶחֶם לֶאֱכֹל וּבֶגֶד לִלְבֹּשׁ: "and will gives me bread to eat and cloth to wear"
- וְשַׁבְתִּי בְשָׁלוֹם אֶל־בֵּית אָבִי "and I return back to my father's house in peace"

Then

- וְהָיָה יְהוָה לִי לֵאלֹהִים: "the LORD shall be my God"
- וְהָאֶבֶן הַזֹּאת אֲשֶׁר־שַׂמְתִּי מַצֵּבָה יִהְיֶה בֵּית אֱלֹהִים "and this stone which I set as a pillar shall be the house of God"
- וְכֹל אֲשֶׁר תִּתֶּן־לִי עַשֵּׂר אֲעַשְּׂרֶנּוּ לָךְ: "and of all that you will give me I shall give you tenth."

Reading and Translating Genesis 28:10—35:15 as a Votive Narrative

The rest of the story talks about this theme or abstract. Therefore, I will be looking for verbal correspondence and perhaps overt evidence of metarepresentation about these utterances in 29:1—35:15.

Cartledge argues on the one hand that there is no clear indication for God's granting the votive plea of Jacob immediately following the vow in Genesis 28:10-22. He further adds that the vow "clearly relates back to the dream; but since it is unfulfilled, the story is incomplete and cannot be regarded as a self-contained narrative."[23] On the other hand, he observes that Jacob's safe arrival at Laban's house and direct reference to God's granting the votive plea appears in chapter 31. He notes some of the explicit references refer back to the vow of Bethel in this chapter as follows: God's instruction to Jacob to return to his father's land, the allusion to the vow as denoted by God's utterance: "I will be with you" (31:3); the allusion denoted in Jacob's utterance: "but the God of my fathers has been with me" (31:5); the allusion in the utterance of Jacob: "God has taken away the cattle of your father and given them to me" (31:9); and God's reminder to Jacob about his vow at Bethel saying: "I am the God of Bethel, where you anointed a pillar and made a vow to me. Now arise, go forth from this land, and return to the land of your birth" (31:13). Then he says: "The intended implication is that God has now granted all of Jacob's requests except the safe return to Canaan, and this is now at hand." His final observation is that Genesis 35:1-7 is the final fulfillment of Jacob's vow and it contains some verbal relations to Jacob's vow. He further observes that the passage of chapter 31 is "interconnected to what is past and what is to come" while 35:1-7 is interconnected with 28:10-22 which shows a "conscious formulation of the author."[24]

Similarly other scholars such as Pagulo, Wenham, Gunkel, and Westermann also observe that the narrator has represented the partial fulfillment of the vow of Jacob.[25] However, they all fail to read the subsequent story from the perspective of a votive narrative. Consequently they do not follow through the granting of the votive plea and fulfilling of the votive pledge in all the details in such a way that all the textual data of the story could be explained in that framework. As a result they fail to explain why the Dinah story is presented between Jacob's safe arrival in his father's land

---

23. Cartledge, *Vows*, 173.
24. Ibid., 173-74.
25. Westermann, *Genesis*, 553; Wenham, *Genesis 16-50*, 323; Gunkel, *Genesis*, 335; Pagolu, *Religion of the Patriarchs*, 158.

(Gen 33:17–18) and Jacob's eventual act of fulfilling his votive promise to God in 35:1–15.[26]

Jacob's votive plea was granted to Jacob (section 3:1); whether Jacob fulfilled his votive pledge, as particularly presented in 33:17–20 will be evaluated (section 4). In chapter 4, I argued that Jacob's votive utterance in 28:20–22 was a metarepresentation of God's promise to him in his dream in Genesis 28:13–15 which comprises the following features:

- הָאָרֶץ אֲשֶׁר אַתָּה שֹׁכֵב עָלֶיהָ לְךָ אֶתְּנֶנָּה וּלְזַרְעֶךָ "The land on which you lie, I will give to you and to your descendants."

- וְהָיָה זַרְעֲךָ כַּעֲפַר הָאָרֶץ וּפָרַצְתָּ יָמָּה וָקֵדְמָה וְצָפֹנָה וָנֶגְבָּה "And your offspring shall be like the dust of the earth, and you shall spread abroad to the west and to the east, and to north and to the south."

- וְנִבְרְכוּ בְךָ כָּל־מִשְׁפְּחֹת הָאֲדָמָה וּבְזַרְעֶךָ "All the families of the earth shall be blessed in you and in your offspring."

- כִּי לֹא אֶעֱזָבְךָ עַד אֲשֶׁר אִם־עָשִׂיתִי אֵת אֲשֶׁר־דִּבַּרְתִּי לָךְ . . . וְהִנֵּה אָנֹכִי עִמָּךְ וּשְׁמַרְתִּיךָ בְּכֹל אֲשֶׁר־תֵּלֵךְ "I am with you and will keep you wherever you go and I will bring you back to this land; . . . I will not leave you until I have done what I have promised you."

- וַהֲשִׁבֹתִיךָ אֶל־הָאֲדָמָה הַזֹּאת "I will bring you back to this land."

It is difficult to differentiate between God's answer to Jacob's votive plea and the fulfillment of God's promise to Jacob in his dream. However, since Jacob's vow is a metarepresentation of God's words, there may be no need to distinguish the two. Yet it is worth noting that the vow, though it was a metarepresentation of the promise of God, supersedes it. Jacob takes God up on his promise and adds his own votive commitment should the promise be fulfilled.

An important feature of this story is that the narrator was careful to indicate specifically the connection between the following story (29:1—35:15) and Jacob's votive utterance (28:20–22), rather than between the following story (29:1—35:15) and God's promise in his dream (28:13–15). For example, he refers back to the utterance of vow: "I am the God of Bethel, where you anointed a pillar and made a vow to me" in Genesis 31:13; 35:1. Hence, the narrator has provided sufficient linguistic evidence that his intention was to evaluate both God and Jacob in relation to Jacob's votive utterance. A close reading of the episodes of this story shows that the narrator organized his linguistic representation of the event-line of the

---

26. This phenomenon will be discussed and explained in the following chapter.

story beautifully to show how God granted Jacob's votive plea before he eventually tells us whether Jacob fulfilled his votive pledge to God. In fact, interestingly enough, the event-line of the story was organized according to the chronological order of Jacob's votive plea, except for the protection which manifests in different parts of the story. Accordingly, the representation of the story is organized first showing how God protected Jacob in his journey to Laban, second, how God blessed Jacob with prosperity, and third how God brought Jacob back to his father's house in peace, just as he requested in his vow. In the following discussion we will investigate God's granting Jacob's votive plea in this order by close reading of every relevant part of the story.

God Grants Protection (Gen 29:1–14; 31:1–55; 32:1—33:20)

The root of the Hebrew verb employed to express Jacob's votive plea was שמר "keep, watch, preserve, protect" (28:20). Cartledge notes that the Hebrew verb שמר has the connotation of protection and provision.[27] A close reading of the narrative shows that in fact Jacob enjoyed the protection and provision of God in every situation both in Padan Aram and in Canaan. However, the narrator presents particularly three situations as a clear evidence of God's answer to his votive plea to Yahweh for protection as follows.

God's Protection during Jacob's Journey to Laban (29:1–14)

Chapter 29 is considered as a continuation of the Bethel story. Allen Ross observes that the literary structure and the content of the story in Genesis 29 show that it is a continuation of the Bethel experience of Jacob.[28] Wenham, however, interprets the narrative in Genesis 29–31 as a distinct story of the "accounts of Jacob's relationship with Laban" which is organized palistrophically.[29] Nevertheless, he also remarks that this story is connected to both the preceding and following story. Though both Ross and Wenham observe the continuation of the story, they stop short of reading it in the framework of the votive narrative.

27. Cartledge, *Vows*, 170.
28. Ross, "Genesis," 75.
29. Wenham, *Genesis 16–50*, 228.

Vow Granting and Vow Fulfilling

The expression וישׂא יעקב רגליו "Jacob lifted his feet," in 29:1, significantly marks that the following story is a continuation of the Bethel event. It shows that Jacob left Bethel with refreshed faith in Yahweh and a cheerful expectation about the answer to his plea and the fulfillment of God's promise in his dream. It is most probable that Jacob had a cheerful attitude: relieved from distress, and believing that he will be granted his votive pleas because God has renewed the Abrahamic covenant with him. The Broadman Bible Commentary describes the expression as "a vivid picture of his eagerness after his experience at Bethel."[30] Wenham concurs with this understanding when he explains that the expression "suggests referring back to Jacob's experience at Bethel, so that he now goes on his way cheerfully."[31] The narrator's intention was to represent the following events as granting Jacob's votive plea.

The narrative element of 29:1–14 is here considered to be an episode of the same votive narrative unit begun in Genesis 28:10–22. In Genesis 29:1–14 the narrator tells us that Jacob's journey to Laban was completed quickly and safely through the protection and guidance of God. Jacob reaches Harran (v. 4) and by God's providence he meets with the shepherds who eventually helped him to meet Rachel, his future bride. The story shows that Rachel came to the well at that particular time by God's providence (v. 6) and Jacob meets her and then after introducing himself he kisses her in greeting (v. 11–12). Rachel helps him to meet his uncle Laban whom Jacob desperately needs to meet, which also should be understood to be a divine providence (Gen 29:11–14).[32] The story also implies that the initial situation providentially facilitated for Jacob an opportunity to introduce himself as a strong good desirable workman, particularly as a shepherd, for Laban (Gen 29:9–12),[33] through which he will eventually acquire the blessing of wives, children, and material prosperity. Although the text does not claim these phenomena explicitly, these are the contextual implications which were part of the presumption of the reporter and left for the readers to derive from the text based on the contextual assumption of the votive narrative.

The narrator presents Jacob's external expression of kissing his cousin Rachel, weeping, and telling her who he was as Jacob's relief from his distress after his journey (11–12). When Laban met him and took him to

30. Francisco, "Genesis," 212.
31. Wenham, *Genesis 16–50*, 229.
32. Ibid.; Gunkel, *Genesis*, 317.
33. Gunkel, *Genesis*, 318.

his home Jacob told about himself and what brought him to him so that Laban was convinced that Jacob was his nephew. Laban provided shelter for one month and then Jacob worked for wages. Thus, God brought about that Laban was willing to give him protection and let him to live with him (29:13–14). One of the most important features of this episode, which the audience can infer for themselves, is that God protected Jacob on his way to Laban and that he arrived at Padan Aram safely, which is part of the grant of his votive plea: "If you will be with me and protect me in this journey."

God's Protection from the Threat of Laban (31:1–55)

It is preferable to decide episode boundaries for the organization of episodes. Genesis 31:1–55 seems intended to resolve the threat of Laban when Jacob was on his way to return home peacefully and 32:1 narrates that Jacob resumes his journey to his father's home after the conflict was resolved. However, commentators differ whether the episode about the conflict between Jacob and Laban ends on 31:54 or 32:1.[34] The Masoretic Text inserts the chapter break in 31:54 while Septuagint translates 32:1 as part of the episode of 31:1–54. Other translations like NRSV and NIV make the chapter break at 31:55 rather than 54.[35] Thus, though it is not easy to decide where the preceding episode ends, Wenham's view and that of the writer is that 31:55 or 31:1—32:1 is more appropriate because the return of Laban to his home in 32:1 concludes the episode.[36] We established Jacob as the thematic character or the major participant of the narrative in chapter four. Accordingly, the narrator removes Laban after a satisfactory resolution of the narrative tension in 31:1–55 and closes one episode, and then picks up the thread in a new development by returning to Jacob as a participant in the following episode in Genesis 32:2—33:17.

However, the important point to be noted here is that the Jacob-Laban episode is an integral part of the preceding story of Jacob as well as the following story of Jacob and Esau, and the Dinah story. The narrative elements in the following cross-references (28:10–22; 31:3, 13; 33:18; 35:1, 3, 6–7, 6–15)[37] show this congruency by the anaphoric reference

---

34. Wenham, *Genesis 16–50*, 266.

35. Chapter breaks themselves are not reliable guides to the narrative structure because they are very late additions.

36. Wenham, *Genesis 16–50*, 266.

37. Ibid., 267–68.

(metarepresentation) back to the vow of Bethel in 28:10–22.³⁸ Here the narrator is showing that the story is an answer to the votive plea of Jacob at Bethel for divine protection. The main theme of the episode as the protection of God is presented as follows: אָמֶר יְהוָה אֶל־יַעֲקֹב שׁוּב אֶל־אֶרֶץ אֲבוֹתֶיךָ וּלְמוֹלַדְתֶּךָ וְאֶהְיֶה עִמָּךְ "Then the LORD said to Jacob, 'Return to the land of your ancestors and to your kindred, and I will be with you'" (31:3). We observe that "ואלהי אבי היה עמדי" "God has been with me" is a distinguishing feature of this episode (vv. 3, 5, 24, 29, 42) which is apparently attributed to the promise of God to Jacob in 28:15 and to the metarepresented votive utterance of Jacob in 28:20,³⁹ as the following comparison between them shows:

- Gen 28:15 אָנֹכִי עִמָּךְ וּשְׁמַרְתִּיךָ "I will be with you"
- 28:20 אִם־יִהְיֶה אֱלֹהִים עִמָּדִי וּשְׁמָרַנִי "if God be with me and protect me"
  31:3 וְאֶהְיֶה עִמָּךְ "I will be with you"
- 31:5 וֵאלֹהֵי אָבִי הָיָה עִמָּדִי "God has been with me"

Thus, this story is the continuation of the Bethel event and the story of Genesis in general (see the close reading of 28:10–22).

Accordingly, the narrator indicates in the story "the Yahweh-centered" motive of Jacob's flight back to Canaan (31:3, 5).⁴⁰ Gunkel's suggestion concerning Jacob's flight to Canaan (on the one hand he describes it as a flight of a pious person instructed by God, and on the other hand he describes it as a flight of deceiving/cunning person who tried to avoid Laban's hatred) seems contradictory.⁴¹ The narrator's representation on the contrary shows that Jacob suffered from the hatred of Laban and his children and that he tried to escape the danger (31:1). Laban's attitude toward Jacob had changed into hatred, which Jacob perceived as a threat to his life. But God intervened in this situation and instructed him to go back to Canaan and confirmed his promise at Bethel to protect him (vv. 3, 5). So one can observe that on God's level, YHWH instructs Jacob to return to his father's house; and on a human level, tension occurs between Laban and Jacob so Jacob wants to get away from Laban, and attempts to run away from him in secret.

---

38. Wenham, *Genesis 16–50*, 267–68. This will be discussed in the following section of this chapter and in chapter 6.

39. Ibid., 268.

40. Gunkel, *Genesis*, 331.

41. Ibid., 331.

Reading and Translating Genesis 28:10—35:15 as a Votive Narrative

The narrator explains why. He represents Laban as a trickster, who values wealth more than his children, his grandchildren and his son-in-law; "a man governed by avarice."[42] Wenham comments that Laban even "looked on Jacob more as a slave than as a son-in-law."[43] He sold his children when he told Jacob to work fourteen years to marry his daughters (31:15), he cheated Jacob by refusing to pay his wages which Rachel and Leah describe as "he ate all our money" (30:25–26; 31:7, 15).[44] Jacob's speech to Laban also shows his frustration and disappointment because Laban refused to pay his wage. The expression "Send me away, that I may go to my own home and country; give me my wives and my children for whom I have served you, and let me go; for you know the service which I have given you" (Gen 30:25–26) demonstrates clearly that Jacob was angry with his uncle because he had exploited him. The narrator implies that Jacob knew that Laban would not allow him to take his property, his wives, and his children with him to Canaan, so that he took action to escape with all his belongings (v. 31). Hence, he presents the main reason for his escape and then concludes: therefore, Jacob had to flee in secret (Gen 31:17–21).

Thus, the narrator represents that these circumstances on the human level triggered a life-threatening narrative complication for Jacob, which also created a suitable context for God to grant Jacob's votive plea for protection. He describes how Jacob and Rachel both cheated Laban. Jacob did not tell Laban that he wanted to go back to Canaan (31:20) and Rachel stole her father's household gods (31:19). This behavior provoked Laban to take vengeance on Jacob and he set off in hot pursuit after Jacob (vv. 22–23). Laban's pursuit for revenge threatened Jacob's safety and his successful departure to Canaan as instructed by God. Laban's vengeful intention was very dangerous for Jacob as the narrator retells us by an embedded metarepresentation: "It is in my power to do you harm; but the God of your father spoke to me last night, saying: 'Take heed that you speak to Jacob neither good nor bad'" (Gen 31:29). Consequently, the narrator tells us by metarepresenting the utterance of Jacob, that God now limits Laban's threat as follows:

31:42 לוּלֵי אֱלֹהֵי אָבִי אֱלֹהֵי אַבְרָהָם וּפַחַד יִצְחָק הָיָה לִי כִּי עַתָּה רֵיקָם שִׁלַּחְתַּנִי אֶת־עָנְיִי וְאֶת־יְגִיעַ* כַּפַּי רָאָה אֱלֹהִים וַיּוֹכַח אָמֶשׁ׃

> If the God of my father, the God of Abraham and the Fear of Isaac, had not been on my side, surely now you would have sent

---

42. Wenham, *Genesis 16–50*, 268, 269.
43. Ibid., 254.
44. Ibid., 273.

Vow Granting and Vow Fulfilling

me away empty-handed. God saw my affliction and the labor of my hands, and rebuked you last night (Gen. 31:42).

Thus, the circumstances on the human level worked out to create an appropriate situation to exhibit God's granting of Jacob's votive plea for protection in Bethel.

Once again this textual evidence shows that the narrator organized this episode as a continuation of the patriarchal story in general and of the Bethel experience of Jacob in particular, specifically as an answer to the votive plea of Jacob in Bethel. He employs significant anaphoric expressions to the Bethel experience as exemplified above. He highlights the intervention and protection of God for Jacob and his family, which is inferentially attributed to the answer to his votive plea. Therefore, God's intervention was the termination or resolution of the narrative tension. Accordingly 31:45–55 could be described as a narrative signal employed by the narrator to show that the Jacob-Laban episode has ended.

God's Protection from the Threat of Esau (Gen 32:2—33:17)

The second evidence which the narrator employed to show that God answered Jacob's votive plea for his protection in 28:20–22 concerns the story of God's protection of Jacob from the anger and threat of Esau. Esau determined to kill Jacob in order to take revenge on him for deceiving him and taking his birthright as well as the blessing of his father. Cartledge makes a very important observation regarding this matter when he says that when Jacob pleaded with God to bring him back to Beersheba in peace he meant "without fear of Esau, from whom he is fleeing."[45] The episodes of this story are:

1. Jacob encounters the angels of God as an assurance of his protection from Esau (32:1).
2. Yet Jacob is so gripped with fear of Esau that he prays to God earnestly (Gen 32:9–12). In fact his prayer metarepresents the promise God made to him in Bethel (Gen 28:14) as the following synopsis shows:

God's promise:

---

45. Cartledge, *Vows*, 170.

- וְהָיָה זַרְעֲךָ כַּעֲפַר הָאָרֶץ וּפָרַצְתָּ יָמָּה וָקֵדְמָה וְצָפֹנָה וָנֶגְבָּה "and your offspring shall be like the dust of the earth, and you shall spread abroad to the west and to the east and to the north and to the south" (28:14).

Jacob's prayer:

- וְאַתָּה אָמַרְתָּ הֵיטֵב אֵיטִיב עִמָּךְ וְשַׂמְתִּי אֶת־זַרְעֲךָ כְּחוֹל הַיָּם אֲשֶׁר לֹא־יִסָּפֵר מֵרֹב "you have said, 'I will surely do you good, and make your offspring as the sand of the sea, which cannot be counted because of their number.'" (32:13 MT, 12 NRSV)

3. And he also attempts to pacify the anger of Esau (32:2–21).

4. God gives another assurance of his protection to Jacob through his experience in Penuel (32:22–32).

5. Finally, Jacob meets Esau peacefully (33:1–17).

These episodes are aimed to show that if it were not for God's protection, Jacob could by no means defend himself from the vengeance of his brother Esau. Rather, Esau, who was accompanied by four hundred men, would have easily destroyed the vulnerable Jacob and his family (32:6–7). In this regard it is worthwhile to refresh our memory that the narrative tension which was introduced between Esau and Jacob in 27:1—28:5 when Esau decided to kill Jacob had not been resolved by the flight of Jacob to Padan Aram (28:10–22). Rather, the narrator presents the resolution in Genesis 32:2—33:17 when Esau accepts Jacob without any violence because of God's providence and protection for Jacob. Thus the main coherence between the Jacob-Laban episode and this episode is that both stories narrate how God protected Jacob from Laban and Esau during difficult life-threatening situations. Therefore, the nature of the story significantly shows the point of connection between the preceding and the following episodes.

Assurance of God's Protection in the midst of Fear (32:1–32)

Gunkel suggests that the passage in 32:2 about the appearing of the angels is incoherent.[46] He further claims that "the text does not support the usual explanation that the angelic revelation is supposed to assure Jacob of God's protective presence."[47] However, we must understand that the general mo-

---

46. Gunkel, *Genesis*, 342.
47. Ibid., 343.

tif of the episode is primed or geared to show the fulfillment of the vow in 28:10–22 as it is explicitly stated in 31:3, 13:

וַיֹּאמֶר יְהוָה אֶל־יַעֲקֹב שׁוּב אֶל־אֶרֶץ אֲבוֹתֶיךָ וּלְמוֹלַדְתֶּךָ וְאֶהְיֶה עִמָּךְ:

אָנֹכִי הָאֵל בֵּית־אֵל אֲשֶׁר מָשַׁחְתָּ שָּׁם מַצֵּבָה אֲשֶׁר נָדַרְתָּ לִּי שָׁם נֶדֶר עַתָּה קוּם צֵא מִן־הָאָרֶץ הַזֹּאת וְשׁוּב אֶל־אֶרֶץ מוֹלַדְתֶּךָ:

> Then the LORD said to Jacob, "Return to the land of your ancestors and to your kindred, and I will be with you. . . . I am the God of Bethel, where you anointed a pillar and made a vow to me. Now leave this land at once and return to the land of your birth."

Thus, the appearing of the angels clearly shows the presence of God with Jacob in order to protect him from Laban, as we are told in the preceding story, and reassures him that he will also continue to be with him and protect him from the threat of Esau as the following story shows. Thus the story is not a fragment as it has been thought to be.

The narrative complication or tension of the episode occurs in Mahanaim and Penuel. The narrator makes a significant comment about the events in Mahanaim and Penuel because they intensify the presence of Yahweh with Jacob in order to protect him from Esau as he promised in Genesis 31:3: "Return to the land of your ancestors and to your kindred, and I will be with you."

Now Jacob is on his way back to Canaan as God instructed him. However he was in great fear and distress remembering Esau's threat to kill him about twenty years previously. Probably these places were not too far from where Esau lived because the narrator tells us that he came to meet Jacob (32:6). However, we do not know how far or how close they were. Mahanaim was the place where the angels of the Lord appeared to Jacob while Penu'el was where Jacob wrestled with a strange person throughout the night (22–32).[48]

In Mahanaim

The root of the term "Mahanayim" is מחנה *camp, army* which is suffixed with "-ayim"[49] which is a plural marker and it has been suggested as a

---

48. Ibid., 343–44

49. The suffix to Mahanayim looks like that of the dual plurals which comprises accented patah, plus yod, plus hireq, and plus final mem. However, it is different because it is suffixed by accented qames, plus yod, plus hireq, and plus final mem.

Reading and Translating Genesis 28:10—35:15 as a Votive Narrative

plural of locative rather than number.[50] However, "Mahanaim" may imply more than one camp, probably associated with the camp of the army of the angels of God as well as Jacob's camping at that place dividing his possession into two groups/camps (32:7–8, 21) because of his fear of Esau.[51] Jacob behaves like a woman in a labor pain because of his fear of Esau. He prays to God earnestly and appeals to his promise:

10 וַיֹּאמֶר יַעֲקֹב אֱלֹהֵי אָבִי אַבְרָהָם וֵאלֹהֵי אָבִי יִצְחָק יְהוָה הָאֹמֵר אֵלַי שׁוּב לְאַרְצְךָ וּלְמוֹלַדְתְּךָ וְאֵיטִיבָה עִמָּךְ:

11 קָטֹנְתִּי מִכֹּל הַחֲסָדִים וּמִכָּל־הָאֱמֶת אֲשֶׁר עָשִׂיתָ אֶת־עַבְדֶּךָ כִּי בְמַקְלִי עָבַרְתִּי אֶת־הַיַּרְדֵּן הַזֶּה וְעַתָּה הָיִיתִי לִשְׁנֵי מַחֲנוֹת:

12 הַצִּילֵנִי נָא מִיַּד אָחִי מִיַּד עֵשָׂו כִּי־יָרֵא אָנֹכִי אֹתוֹ פֶּן־יָבוֹא וְהִכַּנִי אֵם עַל־בָּנִים:

> O God of my father Abraham and God of my father Isaac, O LORD who said to me, "Return to your country and to your kindred, and I will do you good." ... Deliver me, pleas, from the hand of my brother, from the hand of Esau, for I am afraid of him; he may come and kill us all, the mothers with the children. (32:9, 11)

However, his fear seems more intensified even after he prayed to Yahweh. He prepares a huge gift to Esau in order to calm down or appease his anger. But he was so uncertain about what would happen that he was in deep anxiety and depression and he could not even sleep. He even does things which do not make sense. Why did he cross the river at night? Why did he take his wives and children to the other side of the river during the night.[52] Thus Jacob felt so helpless that night. He was in a life or death struggle.[53] In that difficult night Jacob remained alone, probably to pray, and he encountered an attacker (from his point of view) with whom he fought for his life.[54]

The main focus of this episode is to show that God actively worked to protect Jacob and bring a resolution to the contention of Jacob and his brother Esau, which was started 20 years previosly, in favor of Jacob. Thus the narrator labors to represent this phenomenon in a vivid and dramatic manner. The representation of the events show that God was with Jacob

50. Edelman, "Mahanaim."
51. Ibid.
52. Wenham, *Genesis 16–50*, 292.
53. Ibid., 294.
54. Ibid., 295.

and he was actively working for him, not only to protect him but also to make a turning point in his life as well as in his descendants' life by making them the blessed descendants of Abraham, as the changing of his name shows: וַיֹּאמֶר לֹא יַעֲקֹב יֵאָמֵר עוֹד שִׁמְךָ כִּי אִם־יִשְׂרָאֵל כִּי־שָׂרִיתָ עִם־אֱלֹהִים וְעִם־אֲנָשִׁים וַתּוּכָל: "You shall no longer be called Jacob, but Israel, for you have striven with God and with humans, and have prevailed."[55]

In Penu'el

As I have mentioned above, the narrator tells us that in Penu'el Jacob struggled for his life with a stranger who was disguised as a man[56] but who actually was God who was working to make a turning point in Jacob's life.[57] The new naming of Jacob by the stranger (God) captures this feature beautifully. The previous name "Yacob" and his act of struggling for his life with God are structured in a beautiful form of rhyming assonance, which is clearly a word play on Yabbok and Yacob.[58] The expression ויאבק יעקב "Jacob was struggling," triggers the inferential and referential connection with Genesis 25:26. According to the story in Genesis 25:26 there is a rhyming assonance between בעקב "his hand was in the heel of his brother" and יעקב which was a proper name of the child associated with his act of holding his brother's heel. The name יעקב is taken from the root עקב and it has the following nuances: as a noun it could mean heel, hoof, rear of a troop, footstep; it could also mean over-reacher, deceitful, deceitfulness as a denominative adjective.[59] It could also be used as a denominative verb which could mean "take by the heel, supplant, to cause one to fall, to cause a downfall, to supersede, substitute or replace someone else."[60] The narrator shows that in this narrative עקב is used as a denominative verb יעקב. Esau affirms this use when he says: "Is he not rightly named Jacob? For, he has supplanted me these two times. He took away my birthright; and behold, now he has taken away my blessing" (Gen 27:36).

Thus the narrator in this episode indicates that when God changed the name of Jacob to Israel he actually affirmed that Jacob has succeeded

---

55. Gunkel, *Genesis*, 350; Wenham, *Genesis 16–50*, 294.

56. The book of Hosea describes the unknown person who struggled with Jacob as God; Hos 12:4.

57. Pagolu, *Religion of the Patriarchs*, 168; Wenham, *Genesis 16–50*, 295.

58. Wenham, *Genesis 16–50*, 295.

59. Payne, "Jacob."

60. Ibid.

in his supplanting behavior: "Your name shall no more be called Jacob, but Israel, for you have striven with God and with men, and have prevailed" (Gen 32:28). Thus, this story recapitulates the early stage of the narrative tension between Esau and Jacob in order to show that this story is a coherent part of the larger narrative unit (25:19—37:1).

The story also tells us that God changed the name יעקב *Yacob* to ישראל *Israel*[61] (Gen MT 32:29; RSV 32:28). It seems that the narrator employed a word play here as well. The new name "Israel," now given to Jacob, is taken from the root שָׂרָה *sarah*.[62] The term *sarah* has three nuances: when it is construed as a nominative form it could mean 'princess, noble lady; when שָׂרָה is construed as a verb it could mean "to persist, exert oneself, contend, persevere, and have a power." It could also mean the proper name of Sarah the wife of Abraham the patriarch, which yields or leads to the sense of "mother of the nations and kings" (Gen 17:15). When שָׂרָה is juxtaposed or combined with אל "god" and when the relation between the two words is copulative then it could mean "God is prince or God rules." But when it is construed as a genitive construction it could mean "prince of God."[63] However, when it is construed as a verb (which seems the case in this context because it is prefixed by the imperfect marker י which shows that it is a normal perfect of the verb שָׂרָה) juxtaposed with אל then it could mean "God struggles, persists, perseveres, contends, or one who struggles with God."[64] However, the sense of the root *sarah* does not imply a physical confrontation and strength of Jacob in his struggle with his contenders because there is no such evidence in the story. Rather, it signifies Jacob's trust in Yahweh and the promise of Yahweh for Jacob to protect him in his struggle with his contenders. Thus Israel, the new name of Jacob, denotes the interwoven nature of the relationship between Jacob and God in his success and victory against his contenders and adversaries.

---

61. It is also worth noting that the process of changing Jacob's name to "Israel" is apparently connected to the process of changing the name of Abraham's wife from שרי *Sarai* which is "princess, noble lady" into שָׂרָה *Sarah* which mean "the mother of the nations and kings" (Gen 17:15). However, in the case of ישראל *Israel* שָׂרָה is taken as a denominative verb and combined with אל *God* as a coinage signifying new meaning of contention of Jacob and his descendants with their opponents including Esau. Thus, שָׂרָה *sarah* was the very word employed in Genesis 25:23-26 in order to depict the contention between Jacob and Esau which is now going to be resolved by the victory of ישראל (the new name of Jacob) which will be achieved by the help of Yahweh as the following story narrates.

62. Payne, "Israel."

63. Slayton, "Penuel," 223.

64. Wenham, *Genesis 16–50*, 296–97.

Accordingly the name "Israel" depicts that Jacob has succeeded and also will succeed in his struggle with Esau and other contenders and adversaries and eventually will rule over them by the help of God to whom he pleaded. God himself promised to be with him on his way back to Canaan in order to protect him and give him relief from his distress.

Accordingly, the new name "Penuel," given to that particular place where Jacob struggled with God, shows that Jacob succeeded by the protection and providence of God, not by his own strength. The term 'Penuel' was the combination of *pen* "face" and *el* "God" which could mean "the face of God" implying that Jacob the "supplanter" has found favor before God. It is in Penuel that he received the blessing from God which his father Isaac bestowed on him (Gen 32:29). Thus, the events which occurred in Mahanaim and Penuel are clearly coherent with the promise God made to be with Jacob and protect him when he commanded him to go back to Canaan (Gen 31:3, 13). Similarly they are also coherent with the promise which God made to Jacob in Bethel when Jacob made the votive plea (28:10–22).

Once again, there is no indication in the story that Jacob was strong and clever enough to defeat Laban and Esau. If it were not because of God's intervention and protection he would have lost everything to Laban's revenge. Now if the same God had not intervened and rescued him and his family from the hands of Esau his future would have been hopeless.[65] Thus the author shows that Jacob's wisdom in such a difficult time was that he clung to God and he pleaded with him so that he won his favor. Hence, God's protection to Jacob was the main focus of this episode.

The narrator of the story has provided sufficient ostensive linguistic signals to support the inferential process of interpreting each element of the episode within the framework of the votive utterance of Jacob in Bethel. There are seven main ostensive signals employed in this narrative in order to guide the interpretation of the story, specifically pressing the votive conditions of the narrative:

1. The strategic representation of the promise of God to Jacob in his dream in Bethel and Jacob's metarepresented vow of pleading to Yahweh in Bethel to relieve him from his distress (28:10–22). Representing these narrative elements, right at the beginning of the story, functions as a frame work for the interpretation of the subsequent episodes of the story.

---

65. Parry, *Old Testament Story*, 134.

Reading and Translating Genesis 28:10—35:15 as a Votive Narrative

2. The narrator tells us about the trip of Jacob to Paddan Aram after making the vow (29:1) which shows that the trip was made in the context of the Bethel experience in the votive conditions with a refreshed faith and expectation of Yahweh's granting of the votive plea.

3. The narrator's representation of the story is in a very strictly Yahweh-focused context, apparently highlighting him, to whom Jacob made his vow in Bethel, as a main hero of the story in every aspect of Jacob's life (Gen 31:13). For example, even Laban was blessed because of Jacob's relation with Yahweh (Gen 30:30). This shows that the narrator intended to show that Yahweh has really granted Jacob's votive plea.

4. The narrator explicitly and emphatically tells us that the God of his fathers, to whom he made the vow, was with him throughout his life in Paddan Aram and it is the same God who instructed him to go back to the land of his fathers, promising to be with him in order to protect and provide (Gen 31:3–5). Thus, granting his votive plea is represented by implicature.

5. There is explicit anaphoric expression to the votive conditions of the Bethel incident in the story which clearly states that it is the God of Bethel, to whom he made a vow, who blessed him with the wealth,[66] and instructed him to go back to Canaan (31:11–13).

6. The narrator also evidently tells us that it is the same God of Jacob's fathers who protected Jacob from the attack of Laban,[67] apparently as a grant of his votive plea "If you will be with me and protect me" (31:3, 24, 29, 42).

7. Jacob was presented as a weak and vulnerable person before both Laban and Esau and that he was in serious fear, distress, and depression 32:7. Thus, there is no way that Jacob could confront Esau by his own strength. So he pleads with God earnestly to help him and to rescue him from the revenge of Esau, which clearly implies that Jacob was appealing to the commissive speech act of God in Bethel which was also metarepresented in his votive plea:

---

66. We will discuss this in section 3.2.

67. Laban's god(s) vanish(es) from the narrative while Jacob's God is presented as one who controls every aspect of life, even including Laban's. It was not Laban's gods who warned him not to harm Jacob; Laban made the covenant in the name of Yahweh, not in the name of his gods (31:48–53).

> And Jacob said, "O God of my father Abraham and God of my father Isaac, O LORD who said to me, 'Return to your country and to your kindred, and I will do you good,' I am not worthy of the least of all the steadfast love and all the faithfulness that you have shown to your servant, for with only my staff I crossed this Jordan; and now I have become two companies. Deliver me, please, from the hand of my brother, from the hand of Esau, for I am afraid of him; he may come and kill us all, the mothers with the children. Yet you have said, 'I will surely do you good, and make your offspring as the sand of the sea, which cannot be counted because of their number.'" (32:9–12)

This prayer of Jacob can be described as a metarepresentation of his vow in Bethel for the following reasons.

1. There is an appeal to the God of his ancestors Abraham and Isaac (v. 9 NRV, v. 10 MT) which is a metarepresentation of God's words in Genesis 31:13 which further reflects 28:13, 22.
2. There is an appeal to God's instruction to Jacob to return to Canaan (31:3) which further reflects God's promise in Bethel (28:15) to bring him back, which is also metarepresented in Jacob's vow in 28:21.
3. There is an appeal to God's blessing of prosperity which is a metarepresentaion of God's promise in 28:15 to bless him and to multiply his descendants which also farther reflects Jacob's votive plea for prosperity in 28:22.

It is in this context that the narrator tells us that Jacob struggled with God and refused to let him go unless he blesses him. It is in the same context that God changed his name saying: "Your name shall no longer be called Jacob, but Israel, for you have struggled with God and with men, and have prevailed" (32:28). This utterance of God must have given Jacob new hope and encouragement so that he could also overcome the threat of Esau.

Jacob Meets Esau Safely

When Jacob was preparing to meet Esau he was gripped by the fear. He was very apprehensive about what would happen when Esau met him. This was because he knew that he would not be able to defend himself and his family if Esau wanted to attack him. No doubt that he must have told his family what he did to Esau twenty years ago and that he had run away from his brother for fear of his life. Now he was coming to meet him, but he was not sure whether Esau still wanted to take revenge. Therefore he warned all his family members to be nice and humble when they met Esau in order to pacify his anger and in order to avoid anything which might trigger it. He told them to bow down humbly to Esau when they meet him. He divided his children among three groups: the maidservants and their children, Leah and her children, and Rachel and Joseph, thinking that if Esau attacked the front group the next group would escape; if he attacked both the front and the next groups, Rachel and Joseph might escape. He put the children of the maidservants in the front, Leah and her children next, and Rachel and Joseph at the rear because he loved Rachel so much. And then he himself went ahead of them bowing to the ground seven times even before he approached Esau in order to appease his anger. The rest of his family also bowed to him. However, he saw that Esau's reaction to him was something which he never expected. Esau runs to Jacob and embraces him and kisses him rather than attacking him (Gen 33:4). Thus Jacob meets Esau peacefully, in spite of his fear.

In summary, the narrator's public representation of the story depicts that the conflict between Jacob and Esau was resolved smoothly in an amazing way, which must have brought great relief to Jacob. The narrator does not tell us explicitly what made Esau behave so nicely with Jacob. However, he leaves it for the readers to imagine for themselves. The narrator represents the events of the story as the work of God in favor of Jacob. The intended implicature is that God influenced Esau to accept Jacob in love rather than attacking him. Thus, in a miraculous way, Esau greets him and welcomes him with warm love, contrary to Jacob's expectation. Hence, once again the narrator of this episode shows that God answered Jacob's votive plea for protection (Gen 31:3).

God Grants Prosperity (29:14b—32:10)

In our exegetical discussion on 28:20 I argued that the expression ונתן־לי לחמ לאכל ובגד ללבש "and will give me bread to eat and clothing to wear" should be understood comprehensively. Thus, Jacob actually appealed to God to grant him the blessing of wealth (כבד Gen 31:1; 30:43) as this was implied and perceived from his votive promise: "and of all that you give me I will surely give one tenth to you" (Gen 28:22). In this episode we observe that the narrator shows that God has granted this request. The blessing has two themes or aspects: the blessing of wives and children and the blessing of wealth.

The Blessing of Wives and Children

In 29:14b—30:24, the story tells us how God's providence worked out for Jacob to bless him by the gift of two wives and many children, who will eventually become the twelve patriarchs. Though Laban gave Leah his daughter to Jacob as a wife by tricking him (29:23-25), though there was strife between Rachel and Leah, and though Jacob did not love Leah (29:31) God had still blessed him with two wives, and with many children through them. The story tells us that most of the patriarchs were born of Leah. He explicitly tells that it is God who blessed him with eight children from Leah: six from Leah herself (29:31-35; 30:16-20) and the other two through her maid Zilpah as a surrogate mother (30:9-13). The other four children were born of Rachel: two from Rachel herself (30:20-24; 35:16-19) and the other two through her maid Bilhah as a surrogate mother (29:31—30:22; 35:16-19). The only daughter mentioned in this episode as born of Leah to Jacob is Dinah (30:21). The narrator's intention of mentioning Dinah in this context is strategically aimed to anticipating the events of chapter 34.

As I noted above the narrator's representation of the story about the blessing of God to Jacob by giving him the wives and the children shows the providential work of Yahweh. This blessing is part of the fulfillment of the promise of God (to multiply his descendants like the dust of the earth and spread to the east and to the west and to the south and to the north, Gen 28:14) in general and grant to his votive plea in particular. Thus the representation of the story about Jacob's receiving of the blessing of children through Rachel and Leah was employed in order to show that it was the fulfillment of God's promise and grant to his votive plea not simply to narrate a mere coincidence.[68] For example, the narrator ostensively signals this phenomenon when he tells us that the mother's joy at giving birth of each child is expressed to God (29:32, 33, 35; 30:6, 11, 18, 20, 23, 26). Also Leah's and Rachel's initial pregnancies are ascribed to God (29:31; 30:22-24). Besides, 29:31—30:24 is full of overt mentions of God's blessings of wives and children including the naming of the children. In fact, this view was correctly perceived by the later generations of Israel, so that they say "Like Rachel and Leah who built up the house of Israel" (Ruth 4:11-12). Thus this blessing of the patriarchs to Jacob was directly connected to the Bethel experience. It is also a partial fulfillment of God's promise to Jacob in particular and to the promise of God to Abraham in general:

---

68. Wenham, *Genesis 16-50*, 239.

Reading and Translating Genesis 28:10—35:15 as a Votive Narrative

> [A]nd your descendants shall be like the dust of the earth, and you shall spread abroad to the west and to the east and to the north and to the south; and by you and your descendants shall all the families of the earth bless themselves (Gen 13:14–16; 28:14).[69]

I argue that this episode is part of God's grant of the votive plea of Jacob for two reasons. First, in my close reading of 28:10–22, I have argued that Jacob's votive plea was a metarepresentation of God's utterance of promise in his dream. Thus, it is very difficult to choose between the fulfillment of God's promise to Jacob in his dream and God's grant of Jacob's votive plea, except that the grant of the votive plea has a short term time span while God's promise to bless Jacob does not have a specific time limit. Hence, there is no need to distinguish the two, since the latter is an echoic use of the former.

Secondly, it seems that according to the ancient Israelites' worldview the blessing of children (mainly sons), and wealth are essentially perceived as a blessing from Yahweh. This worldview implies that one is incomplete without the other because the "strength" and "honor" of the house is measured by the number of its sons.[70] Thus Jacob's votive plea for the blessing of the wealth was intrinsically inclusive of the blessing of the children. Thus, this episode could be perceived as part of the grant of Jacob's votive plea and is clearly a coherent part of the narrative unit. In fact when Jacob crossed the river Jordan with his big family and wealth on his way back to Canaan he remembered his journey to Padan Aram and his Bethel experience and acknowledged this fact (Gen 32:10 NRSV/32:11 MT).

The Blessing of Material Prosperity

The story in the next episode, Genesis 30:25–43, represents in a significant way that God blessed Jacob with wealth as a grant of his votive plea in Bethel. Scholars differ as to where the episode ends: 30:43 or 31:1–2.[71] However, the story clearly continues from the preceding episode, except that 31:1–2 introduces a complication or conflict into the narrative which functions as a staging or background for the following episode. This will continue intensifying the narrative tension which eventually will lead to

---

69. Wenham, *Genesis 16–50*, 238, 250.
70. De Vaux, *Life and Institution*, 41.
71. Wenham, *Genesis 16–50*, 252.

Vow Granting and Vow Fulfilling

the conflict's resolution by God as the main agent. So it does not matter where the preceding story ends.

The narrator emphatically states that Jacob did not become rich because he was a clever or hard working man; rather he remarks that it was because Yahweh blessed him. However, as the following reading shows, the narrator does not comment upon divine blessing to Jacob, rather, he puts the claim of God's blessing of prosperity into Jacob's mouth, by an echoic metarepresentation:

קָטֹנְתִּי מִכֹּל הַחֲסָדִים וּמִכָּל־הָאֱמֶת אֲשֶׁר עָשִׂיתָ אֶת־עַבְדֶּךָ כִּי בְמַקְלִי
עָבַרְתִּי אֶת־הַיַּרְדֵּן הַזֶּה וְעַתָּה הָיִיתִי לִשְׁנֵי מַחֲנוֹת

> I am not worthy of the least of all the steadfast love and all the faithfulness that you have shown to your servant, for with only my staff I crossed this Jordan; and now I have become two companies. (Gen 32:10)

Thus, the narrator claims that it is God who made Jacob prosper as Jacob himself has acknowledged that it is God who made him prosper exceedingly. This metarepresentation is possibly echoic because the narrator has an endorsing attitude claiming that truly God has granted Jacob's votive plea for prosperity as Jacob himself made clear. This feature also makes the metarepresentation emphatic.

Accordingly, the story tells us that Jacob stayed with Laban for twenty years (31:38): he served Laban for fourteen years as a dowry for Leah and Rachel; and then he worked only for six years for the spotted flocks as his wage (v. 41). He became exceedingly rich (30:43) within those six years despite the fact that Laban was so hard on him and cheated him (31:7). How did he get such a huge wealth within the six years? The narrator has an answer:

> ... yet your father has cheated me and changed my wages ten times, but God did not permit him to harm me. If he said, "he speckled shall be your wages," then all the flock bore speckled; and if he said, "The striped shall be your wages," then all the flock bore striped. Thus God has taken away the livestock of your father, and given them to me. (31:7–9)

More specifically, the narrator also tells us in a particular way that Jacob acquired this wealth because God granted his votive plea as it was revealed in his dream:

> During the mating of the flock I once had a dream in which I looked up and saw that the male goats that leaped upon the

flock were striped, speckled, and mottled. Then the angel of God said to me in the dream, "Jacob," and I said, "Here I am!" And he said, "Look up and see that all the goats that leap on the flock are striped, speckled, and mottled; for I have seen all that Laban is doing to you. *I am the God of Bethel, where you anointed a pillar and made a vow to me.*" (Gen 31:10–13; emphasis mine)

Led by this dream Jacob proposes a very modest or humble suggestion to Laban to have only multicolored goats and sheep as his wage (30:31–36).[72] This suggestion was very attractive to Laban.[73] What is more striking is that Jacob invites Laban to separate all the multicolored animals from the flock as his own so that he may have the newborn multicolored animals from that time onward in order to prove that he was an honest man (30:34). Thus, from Laban's point of view Jacob was asking something very insignificant or he is asking for nothing.[74] So Laban removes all the colored animals and takes them away about three days walking distance from where Jacob tends the flock in order to make sure that the spotted animals will never breed with the flock under Jacob's care.

However, prompted by the dream, Jacob applies a device which he thought will influence the flock to bear only colored young goats and sheep. Probably this practice was based on the belief that if a pregnant animal or woman regularly sees a particular beautiful or ugly thing attentively it can have an influence on the physical appearance of the young or baby they will bear.[75] Thus, Jacob peels the tree branches to make strips and puts them in the watering troughs so that the animals may see them when they mate in order to influence the physical appearance of the young which the animals will bear. He does this only when the strong female animals were in heat, not the weak ones. Consequently all the strong animals bear colored young which belong to Jacob while the few remaining weak single colored animals are left for Laban. Thus Jacob accumulated a lot of wealth and he became "exceedingly prosperous." But the narrator tells us that his wealth was not based on only on the flocks, but that he owns maid servants, men servants, camels, and donkeys (Gen 30:41).

However, the narrator does not imply that his wealth was acquired by the magic of striped branches. Rather, he connects both the choice of

72. Wenham, *Genesis 16–50*, 255.
73. Ibid.; Gunkel, *Genesis*, 330.
74. Wenham, *Genesis 16–50*, 255.

75. For example, such belief is common in my community, such that the pregnant women are usually encouraged to look at a beautiful color and beautiful or handsome people rather than some ugly looking things or people.

having colored animals as his wage and employing the device of striped branches to what God has told Jacob in his dream (31:10–12). The story clearly shows that Jacob himself acknowledged that his "impressive flocks are the result of divine blessing" (Gen 31:7–13).[76] Thus, from the narrator's point of view Jacob's acquiring such wealth is Yahweh's grant of his votive plea in Bethel: "Lift up your eyes and see, all the goats that leap upon the flock are striped, spotted, and mottled; for I have seen all that Laban is doing to you. *I am the God of Bethel, where you anointed a pillar and made a vow to me*" (Gen 31:10–13a).

As I already mentioned above even Laban learned by *divination* נחשתי and acknowledged that his wealth came from Yahweh because of Jacob's presence in his house (30:27). Thus his wealth was attributed to the blessing of the patriarch by Yahweh: "the nations of the world will be blessed by you." Hence, even those who associate with the patriarchs will be blessed (Gen 12:3; 14:1920; 21:22–23; 22:18; 26:12–16, 28–29; 28:14; 39:5; 23).[77] Hence, it is no wonder that Jacob buries the Teraphim, which was the Aramean god believed to "help the votary in his house and home, blessing his family and his flock," under the tree in Shechem,[78] when God confirmed with him that he was the one who had blessed him, protected him, and brought him back to Canaan, granting his votive plea. Therefore Jacob did not want to associate with any other gods except with Yahweh. The narrator even dissociates Jacob from Laban and his religious practices when he says "Laban the Aramean" (Gen 31:24) probably for the same reason, in order to distance himself from any religious association of Aramean culture from that time onward. This story has a definite moral implication regarding the expected behavior of descendants of Jacob.

In summary the public representation of the narrator's point of view of the story clearly depicts that the blessing of wives, children, and wealth to Jacob was Yahweh's grant of answer to Jacob's votive plea in Bethel.

God Grants Return to Canaan Safely (Gen 31:3; 33:17–18)

In Genesis 31:3 the narrator tells us that God commanded Jacob to return to Canaan, the land of his fathers and he promised to protect him as already discussed above. In 31:17–18 he tells us that Jacob obeyed God in that he set out on his way to Canaan. As he promised, God protected

---

76. Cartledge, *Vows*, 172.
77. Wenham, *Genesis 16–50*, 255; Gunkel, *Genesis*, 329.
78. Gunkel, *Genesis*, 334.

Jacob so that he arrived in Canaan safely. Thus, the narrator's main focus in 33:18 is on Jacob's return to Canaan safely which is a conclusion of the episode began in 31:3 in particular and the fulfillment of the long awaited promise of Yahweh and his grant answer to Jacob's votive plea in 28:10–22 in general: "And Jacob came safely to the city of Shechem, which is in the land of Canaan, on his way from Padan Aram; and he camped before the city" (33:18). This expression is loaded with information, and it is very emphatic and vivid. The narrator says that Jacob made it to Canaan at last as God promised him twenty-six years ago! Indeed, God had answered his votive plea in Bethel and had brought him to Canaan so that he will possess it. Jacob built a house there, as a sign of claiming it as his permanent home (33:17). Thus it alludes to the promise of God in 28:15: "I am the LORD, the God of Abraham your father and the God of Isaac; the land on which you are lying I will give to you and to your descendants." Wenham, Pagolu and other scholars correctly observe that Jacob's coming back to Canaan in peace was God's answer to Jacob's votive plea in Bethel.[79]

In summary, the close reading of the story in the context of the votive institution shows that the narrator publicly represents his mental representation about the fulfillment of Jacob's vow, in a remarkable way. He briefly but vividly narrates in this passage that God granted Jacob's votive plea to return home so that he arrives in Canaan safely because God brought him safely, and he builds a house for himself as a partial fulfillment of God's promise to Abraham, Isaac and to Jacob himself in Bethel (Gen 13:14–17; 26:3–4; 28:10–22). The granting is recognized in the way various tensions are resolved by God, which also significantly highlights God's granting of Jacob's plea for his protection. This feature of the narrative is overlooked by scholars.

Thus, the narrator assumes that he has achieved the communicative and informative intention of the story in terms of providing ostensive signals about Jacob's vow in Bethel and God's granting of the same, constraining his audience who must have been geared to the expectation of relevance about whether God granted Jacob's votive plea. He is affirming that God did grant an answer to Jacob's votive plea.

Jacob Fails to Fulfill his Votive Pledge

In the above discussion I argued that the narrative representation of the story shows that the expectation of relevance regarding God's grant of

79. Pagolu, *Religion of the Patriarchs*, 168; Wenham, *Genesis 16–50*, 287.

Vow Granting and Vow Fulfilling

Jacob's votive plea was achieved, because God granted all his requests. The next expectation of relevance which the reader is geared to search for in the following narrative must be "since God has granted his votive plea, then Jacob will go straight to Bethel in order to fulfill his votive pledge." Similarly, in normal circumstances, any one who reads this narrative unit within the framework of a votive narrative and in the context of the institution of the vow expects Jacob to fulfill his vow to Yahweh in Bethel right away. The optimal expectation of relevance at this point requires that Jacob should fulfill his votive promise to Yahweh at Bethel promptly, as expected in the votive institution (see chapter 3 section 3.2.7).[80]

Though it seems improbable, the Testament of Levi suggests that it was about ten years since Jacob returned to Canaan safely up until this incident of the Dinah story.[81] Under normal circumstances, this is an undesirable delay for fulfilling one's votive pledge and the narrative shows that Jacob failed to fulfill his votive pledge to God in Bethel as follows:

19 וַיִּקֶן אֶת־חֶלְקַת הַשָּׂדֶה אֲשֶׁר נָטָה־שָׁם אָהֳלוֹ מִיַּד בְּנֵי־חֲמוֹר אֲבִי שְׁכֶם בְּמֵאָה קְשִׂיטָה:

20 וַיַּצֶּב־שָׁם מִזְבֵּחַ וַיִּקְרָא־לוֹ אֵל אֱלֹהֵי יִשְׂרָאֵל:

> And from the sons of Hamor, Shechem's father, he bought for one hundred pieces of money the plot of land on which he had pitched his tent. There he erected an altar and called it El-Elohe-Israel. (Gen 33:19–20)

אֵל אֱלֹהֵי יִשְׂרָאֵל "El-elohe-Israel" means El, the Supreme God is the God of Israel (his new name). The way in which Jacob lays claim to God in this utterance is apparently connected to his votive pledge to God in Bethel: וְהָיָה יְהוָה לִי לֵאלֹהִים "The LORD shall be my God" (28:21).[82] Thus, the strongest implicature of the expression "There he erected an altar and called it El-elohe-Israel" seems that the action of Jacob is intended to fulfill his votive pledge made at Bethel in Shechem.[83] And so the narrator implies that

---

80. But the sacred donations that are due from you, and your votive gifts, you shall bring to the place that the LORD will choose (Deut 12:26).

81. Baarda, "Shechem episode," 13–14.

82. Wenham, *Genesis 16–50*, 301.

83. The place Jacob settled when he returned from Padan Aram is referred as Succoth in verse 17 and Shechem in verse 18. Gunkel argues that both Shechem and Succuth refer the same place (Gunkel, *Genesis*, 356). However, some scholars argue that the place Jacob returned was called 'Salem' (Pink, *Gleanings*, 300; Wenham, *Genesis 16–50*, 300). Their argument was based on the sentence וַיָּבֹא יַעֲקֹב שָׁלֵם עִיר שְׁכֶם אֲשֶׁר בְּאֶרֶץ כְּנַעַן (Gen 33:18). Thus they perceive שָׁלֵם as a reference to a place while many scholars perceive it as a denominative adverb which is used to qualify the verb וַיָּבֹא "he

Reading and Translating Genesis 28:10—35:15 as a Votive Narrative

Jacob failed to fulfill his votive pledge to Yahweh in Bethel. Unfortunately, this point of view of the narrator is overlooked by all the scholars again as far as I know.

There are two possible ways in which Jacob failed to fulfill his vow to Yahweh. First, the significant element in 33:17-20 is that Jacob makes a transaction to purchase a piece of land from the sons of Hamor. The narrator attempts to represent his cognitive point of view, in his linguistic representation regarding Jacob's action of setting an altar to Yahweh on that piece of land in Shechem: "There he erected an altar and called it El-elohe-Israel" (33:20). Thus the narrative represents details that convey the implicature that Jacob actually attempted to fulfill his vow of Bethel by erecting the altar in Shechem.[84] The expression "There he erected an altar..." connotes that Jacob was expected to erect it in Bethel, not in Shechem (28:22; 35:1), because all the votive promises must be fulfilled in a place chosen by God as we observed in chapter 3.[85]

Parry observes that the mention of Bethel and Shechem in the story is intentional, has literary significance and shows a specific attitude to these places.[86] Parry's observation concurs with Walter Brueggemann's observation. Brueggemann notes that according to the archaeological remains "Shechem was a major shrine before the appearance of Israel." Thus Jacob's building an altar at Shechem (30:20) was probably intended to claim that older cult place for the Israelite use of worshiping Yahweh.[87] Noth also observes that Jacob stayed in Shechem and Bethel because they were associated with the sanctuaries built in these places.[88] The Hebrew Bible and

came" thus "he came in peace" (Pelikan, *Luther's Works*, 182–83; Speiser, *Genesis*, 259; Gunkel, *Genesis*, 356; Hartley, *Genesis*, 292; Mathews, *Genesis*, 573). I concur with the second interpretation and interpret it as "safe and sound," "happy to have escaped the danger" from Esau and Laban, because this interpretation fits the context of granting Jacob's votive plea by God to return to his father's house in peace. Hence, according to the votive narrative framework this interpretation strengthened a reflection of 28:21 "to my father's house in peace." Based on the commissive speech act of God to him in Bethel and his votive plea to Yahweh, Jacob, after fleeing from family conflict, hoped to return in peace. The narrator also tells us that Jacob declined to follow Esau in Seir as he promised to and he went to Succoth instead. The probable but possible implication would be that Jacob did not want to go out of Canaan any more. Besides, although now at peace with Esau, he prefers not to depend on him too closely.

84. Wenham, *Genesis 16–50*, 301.

85. "But the sacred donations that are due from you, and your votive gifts, you shall bring to the place that the LORD will choose" (Deut 12:26).

86. Parry, *Old Testament Story*, 134.

87. Brueggemann, *Genesis*, 275.

88. Pagolu, *Religion of the Patriarchs*, 158.

Vow Granting and Vow Fulfilling

Talmud also imply this phenomenon, but indicate that God chose Bethel than Shechem, when they say that Shechem was the place where Abraham passed through in his first arrival to Canaan up to Bethel where there was a great tree of Moreh, and where God appeared to him (Gen 12:6).[89]

Adam Zertal observes that even before the Israelites came to Canaan, Shechem was a cultic place. There was a stronghold or tower known as "beth-el-berith," which is probably a cultic place outside of the city of Shechem. There were about four fortified temples unearthed by the archaeologists during the 1913–27 excavations.[90] There were also statues of gods, and there was a particular temple with altars put in the courtyard in front of the temple. This temple was used for four hundred years.[91] Thus probably Jacob went to Shechem to worship the Lord by building an altar there in order to fulfill his vow, thinking that Shechem was compatible with Bethel. Hence he made a grave mistake and incurred guilt by breaking his votive promise to worship the Lord in Bethel. A Jewish Rabbi Tanna shows his negative attitude toward Shechem by the following words: "[It was] a place predestined for evil; in Shechem Dinah was ravished; in Shechem his brethren sold Joseph; and in Shechem the kingdom of the House of David was divided."[92]

Secondly, another possible way would be that Jacob ignored or forgot to fulfill his vow in Bethel. However, the second reason is unlikely because the votive institution of ancient Israel was so strong. Besides, all the stressful experiences which Jacob went through because of Laban and Esau, must have prompted him to remember his vow and his obligation to fulfill it at Bethel. In both cases Jacob incurred guilt before God which resulted in breaching God's protection for him and his family as we observe in chapter 34.

Finally, the narrator employs the representation of 33:18–20 as a summary of the narrative:

> And Jacob came safely to the city of Shechem, which is in the land of Canaan, on his way from Paddan-aram; and he camped before the city. And from the sons of Hamor, Shechem's father, he bought for a hundred pieces of money the piece of land on which he had pitched his tent. There he erected an altar and called it Elelohe-Israel.

---

89. Epstein, *Nashim*, 158, 165.
90. Pagolu, *Religion of the Patriarchs*, 72.
91. Zertal, "Shechem."
92. Epstein, *Nezikin*, 692.

Reading and Translating Genesis 28:10—35:15 as a Votive Narrative

This functions as a conclusion of the evaluative narrative and as a connector of the whole story back to 28:10-22 and simultaneously connecting it to the following story (chapter 34). By the same expression, he triggers the expectation of the shared contextual assumptions of the adverse consequence of the unfulfilled votive promise.

Hence, this passage raises the expectation of relevance in the readers' mind so that the reader can perceive the story of chapter 34 as an adverse consequence of the unfulfilled or failed votive promise.[93] Thus, the story of this passage was aimed to highlight or remark the cause of the tragedy in chapter 34 to the reader showing that it happened because Jacob failed to fulfill his vow in Bethel. Wenham observes this phenomenon when he notes that the usual style of the Genesis narratives of closing an episode or a narrative unit by providing a preview for the next chapter was exhibited in 33:18-20, which functions as a trailer for chapter 34. In his words:

> [I]t is customary in Genesis for the end of one episode to include a trailer for the next one. This is exactly what is found here. 33:18-19 records Jacob's arrival at Salem, the city of Shechem, and his purchase of land from the sons of Hamor. This sets the scene for the events of chap. 34.[94]

Conclusion

It is generally accepted that the longer and more complex a narrative is the more difficult it is to claim one or another suggestion as the narrator's point of view. However, it has been shown that Jacob's vow at Bethel has very strong and specific implications as a social institution which comprises vow making, vow granting, and vow fulfilling. And this has implications, in particular whether the expectations raised by the conditional pleas may be granted, and the expectation in such case that the commitments made will place the vow maker under an inescapable obligation to make good his commitment. Furthermore, there is also further expectation, if the fulfillment is ignored or unnecessarily delayed, that the vow maker risks adverse consequences.

The linguistic or public representation of the cognitive organization of the narrative of Genesis 29:1—33:20 is clearly an evaluative one in

---

93. Wenham notes that the nature of this passage seems aetiological in that presumably the narrator was attempting to explain "the origin of the name Succoth and to note its connection with the patriarch" (Wenham, *Genesis 1–15*, 300).

94. Ibid., 309.

Vow Granting and Vow Fulfilling

which the narrator linguistically represents his point of view about God and Jacob regarding the fulfillment of the votive utterance of Jacob in Bethel (Gen 28:10–22).

It seems to be correct that granting the vow is never explicitly referred to, but is repeatedly a contextual implication, which is derived by inference. Thus, the story shows that:

1. God grants Jacob's appeal for protection
2. God grants Jacob's appeal for prosperity and provision
3. God grants Jacob's appeal to return to his homeland in peace
4. Jacob failed to fulfill his votive pledge to God

On the one hand, the narrator presents God as a divine power who faithfully granted Jacob's votive plea, as his caring and loving patron. On the other hand, he represents Jacob as God's chosen patriarch but as one who failed or delayed to fulfill his votive promise to his patron God. At different points in the narrative each of these is a strong inference, within the institution of vow, throughout chapters 29–35. Often the granting of the vow is not straightforward, but is recognized in the way that various tensions are resolved, which also dismisses Jacob's role in resolving them and highlights God's granting. Clearly a number of scholars have also observed God's granting of Jacob's vow, but they failed to read the whole narrative within the framework of a votive narrative. Consequently, no scholar has read 33:17–20 as indicating that Jacob failed to fulfill his votive commitment.

Thus, since the story is presented within the framework of the social institution of vow and in the context of the votive narrative a narrator would be entitled to presume that his audience can imagine for themselves the imminent adverse consequence of the failed votive promise of Jacob. This would be so if the narrator and readers of the story have the same mutually shared knowledge or cognitive environment about the unfulfilled נדר "vow" so that he is able to move straight to represent the subsequent story in chapter 34. The narrator manifestly intends that the readers of the story will draw the conclusion from what he has said, but constrained by his optimally relevant ostensive stimulus of the narrative as well as mutually shared knowledge about the utterance of נדר in Genesis 28:10–22 and the institution of vow.

Genesis 28:10–22 clearly gives the actual votive utterance in context and 29:1—35:15 details Yahweh's granting of Jacob's votive pleas, and Jacob's failed fulfillment of his votive pledge to Yahweh. The expectation of fulfilling the votive promise also comprises an imminent adverse consequence if Jacob fails to fulfill his votive promise, which we are going to discuss in chapter 6.

6

Dinah Story as an Adverse Consequence of the Unfulfilled Vow

Introduction

ALTHOUGH GOD HAD GRANTED all of Jacob's votive pleas Jacob had failed to fulfill his vow in Bethel. Certainly, Jacob had attempted to fulfill it in Shechem, probably thinking that Shechem was compatible with Bethel. However, this is the same as not fulfilling his vow because Shechem was not a place chosen by God. This will immediately trigger another expectation in the mind of any vow-oriented society: namely that he must suffer an adverse consequence for the unfulfilled vow. The crisis of Genesis 34 was this adverse consequence.

The votive narrative of Jacob has been read in the light of the Hadiyya institution of the vow; and the Dinah story will be read in the light of the Hadiyya marriage institution. It is an integral/congruent part of the Jacob narrative and presented as an adverse consequence of the unfulfilled vow. There are three points to investigate from the narrator's point of view before the discourse analysis:

Almost all biblical scholars read the Dinah story as if it were an independent story. Consequently, they treat verses 30–31 of the chapter as if it were the resolution of the narrative tension which was created in verses 1–4. On the contrary, Dinah's story is an integral part of the preceding story, strategically put there by the narrator to show that the crisis of Genesis 34 happened to Jacob because he failed to fulfill his votive promise to Yahweh. This episode continues up to 35:15, verses 30–31 is a further intensification of the narrative tension, not a resolution, and 35:1–7 is the resolution. This claim can be substantiated by ostensive textual evidence.

Almost all the biblical scholars approach this episode from the perspective of character evaluation. However, a close reading of this episode shows that the narrator intends to explain why such a terrible crisis, which threatened the very existence of the chosen people of God, happened to Jacob and his family. This argument can also be substantiated by elucidating the narrator's ostensive linguistic signals.

Whether Shechem raped Dinah or he attempted an abductive marriage is briefly considered. Most scholars describe the sexual violence which Shechem committed to Dinah as "rape." However, my reading of the story, which is informed by my own social community's practice of abductive marriage, is that Shechem attempted abductive marriage rather than rape.[1] This can be substantiated if ostensive linguistic signals can be found.

Review of Previous Work on the Dinah Story

Dinah's story has had readings from three different perspectives: ethical and moral, source criticism, and social scientific; each based on the evaluation of the character of the participants.

The Perspective of Character Evaluation

Robin Parry has done an excellent review of the previous works on Genesis 34; the following is a summary of the main points he makes about Jewish readings.

Talmud and Other Jewish Literatures

The Talmudic reading of Genesis 34 proceeds from assumptions about the status of the women in Israelite society and their relationship with the Gentiles. The episode was perceived as a punishment by God for Dinah's undesirable behavior and the undesirable relationship of Jacob with

---

1. Fleshman, "Simeon and Levi," 112. These terms are culturally defined. In English abductive marriage may constitute rape and honourable intentions of marriage do not override this. But in Hadiyya (and Hebrew?) culture, an abductive marriage is not categorised that same way as a rape without any honourable intentions. Hence to impose Western categories on an Eastern text is inappropriate.

the Gentiles. The Talmud blames Dinah's whorish behavior (which she may have imitated from her mother Leah, Gen 30:16) and makes Dinah responsible for going out for the terrible consequence in her life. Rabbi Huniah describes that by having sexual relations with a Gentile, Dinah became a Canaanite, and then claims that later her brother married her as a Canaanite woman and had a child from her (Gen 46:10).[2]

The Talmud also interprets the episode as a punishment to Jacob because he failed to give Dinah in marriage to a circumcised man, so that God allowed her to have a sexual relation with an uncircumcised Gentile; thus "Jacob's pride was punished by his daughter's rape."[3] However, Rabbi Berekhiah holds Dinah responsible for the result, because she exposed herself to the danger; he justifies Jacob's silence as prudent and defends the action of Levi and Simeon as right because the Hivites were planning evil against the Israelites (Gen 34:23).[4] Thus the Talmud describes the circumcision of Shechem as "circumcised from an unworthy motive."[5]

The Book of Jubilees treats the Dinah story as relevant to the Genesis story in general and to the Jacob story in particular because it sets a model of prohibition of marriage relations between Israel and Gentiles. According to the Book of Jubilees the crime in the Dinah story is not rape, "but sex and marriage with a Gentile."[6]

Another non-canonical text, the Testament of Levi, presents a different perspective. In this testament the author retells the story of Genesis 34. The intention of the narrator or the aim of the author seems to be to clear Levi from any blame for massacring Shechemites. One can imagine why he is doing that. The narrator was aware that one of the mutually shared relevant accessible contextual assumptions of his readers about Levi is that he was the father of all the priests of the Israelites who were chosen by God. Logically, if God chose Levites for his service then their father Levi must be guiltless and right in his action and behavior. Therefore, he should be cleared from the blame of unjustified killing of the Shechemites. Thus the Testament of Levi claims that it was Levi who initiated the idea of revenging Dinah and he received the command to revenge from God in a vision. By doing this, in fact, God aimed to appoint and inaugurate

---

2. Parry, *Old Testament Story*, 99.
3. Ibid., 97.
4. Ibid., 98.
5. Epstein, *Nashim*, 112.
6. Charles, *Jubilees*, 153–54; Parry, *Old Testament Story*, 88.

Levi and his descendants as priests.[7] The Testament of Levi implies that the "execution of vengeance upon Israel's enemies is likewise connected with the priesthood of Levi and his descendants."[8] Thus God was directly involved in the vengeance, and therefore Levi is not to blame because he obeyed God.

The Testament of Levi also interprets the relevance of the Dinah story in terms of God's punishment against the Shechemites for their long-standing, recorded abuse of strangers, which also shows that God will eventually dispossess the Canaanites and will give the Land to Israelites.[9]

Similarly Theodotus, a Hellenistic Jewish[10] author also attempts to clear Levi from the blame of massacre. He believes that it was Simeon who decided to kill Hamor and Shechem because Shechem refused to accept the crime of rape he committed against his sister, and then later he involved Levi. Thus it was Simeon who took the initiative of killing, and then he convinced Levi to be involved in the action.[11]

The book of Judith interprets the deceit and revenge of Levi and Simeon as justified action by God for the defense of Israel.[12] Josephus interprets the tragedy to the Shechemites as an action inspired by God to prohibit the marriage relationship between the Israelites and Gentiles (*Ant.* 1.21.1–2).[13] Josephus also observes that the initiative taken by God to remind Jacob to fulfill his votive plea which he made in Bethel was connected to the tragedy of Dinah, but he failed to explain how the story was relevant to Jacob's narrative in general and to the votive narrative of Bethel in particular because he failed to read the Dinah story from the votive narrative point of view.[14]

Parry remarks that Philo the Jewish philosopher interprets the Dinah story allegorically as an individual's inner person: the virgin Dinah represents the soul of a person which in turn is incorruptible judgment and justice on its journey to God; Shechem, the son of Hamor, represents folly and irrationality; defiling the virgin Dinah represents those passion-loving fools who do not give rational attention to soul (virgin) because

---

7. Baarda, "Shechem Episode," 20–73.
8. Ibid., 25.
9. Parry, *Old Testament Story*, 89.
10. Whether he was a Jew or Samaritan is debated (Holladay, *Epic Poets*, 57ff.).
11. Baarda, "Shechem episode," 18.
12. Parry, *Old Testament Story*, 90.
13. Ibid., 91.
14. Ibid.; Whiston, *Josephus*, 60.

soul never intends doing wrong. Levi and Simon represent the vindicators of the suffering soul who will eradicate the folly and irrationality of persons from the world so that the soul may be her true virgin self.[15] Thus he claims that Dinah (soul) was never defiled, the suffering was that of the soul unwilling to be influenced to do wrong.[16] Philo's interpretation was based on ethnocentrism in that he stereotypes, by implication, the Hivites as bad people while stereotyping the Israelites as good people. Apart from this allegorical interpretation Philo does not give an explanation about the relevance of the Dinah story to the Jacob Narrative.

Early Church Fathers

According to Parry the early church fathers (100 CE–1000 CE) did not make extensive use of this story except for drawing some specific ethical lessons from it. For example, Tertullian interprets the zealous Levi and Simeon, who massacred the innocent Shechemites, as the prefiguring representatives of zealous Jews who killed Jesus.[17] Ambrose condemns the massacre by Simeon and Levi and admires Jacob's prudence, temperance, and sound reasoning.[18] Jerome warns parents to keep their daughters at home or keep them from bad friends and company in order to avoid similar consequences.[19] St. Gregory allegorically interprets Dinah as representing a person who is trapped by sin. Shechem represents the devil who, "after uniting himself with the sinning soul, deceives it so that it loses its sorrow and penitence," because a sinner who has lost the sense of sorrow for the committed sin cannot repent.[20]

Medieval and Reformation Readings

Medieval interpreters (1000 CE–1300 CE) and Reformers (1500 CE–1600 CE) approach Genesis 34 from the objective of unveiling the "inner life of the biblical characters."[21] Thus, in the artistic literary device of the Genesis

---

15. Parry, *Old Testament Story*, 92–93.
16. Ibid., 93.
17. Ibid., 95.
18. Ibid., 95–96.
19. Ibid., 96.
20. Ibid., 96.
21. Levine, "Inner World," 334.

34, they search for the meaning of keeping one's self away from anything which may cause an evil desire and pride which will lead one into temptation and sin. Thus mediaeval and reformation interpreters focus on the evaluation of the behavior of the characters of the story rather than explaining the relevance of the Dinah story to the Jacob narrative. Medieval writers blame Dinah for leading Shechem into sin and the eventual consequence of the Shechem crisis. Accordingly they used her as an example and warning for women who knowingly or unknowingly tempt men sexually as Dinah did, which resulted in trouble for herself, her family and even her enemies the Shechemites.[22]

Martin Luther and Calvin blame Dinah for being a cause of the tragedy. Luther notes that Dinah's sin is her curiosity which led her to go around without her parents' permission eventually leading Shechem into temptation. Shechem's sin was that he was a spoiled son of a rich man who thought that everything is permitted and who behaved dishonorably. Thus he defiled the daughter of a noble man, Jacob. According to Luther, the worst thing about Shechem was that he did not repent of his sin, so he deserved punishment. Shechem's father Hamor, too, deserved the punishment because he had not brought up his son in a godly manner; he did not correct and rebuke his son for his sin; he did not apologize to the Israelites, mainly because he was proud; and finally he lied to his people in order to convince them to condone the crime so that they eventually agreed and they too were punished with him and his son.[23]

Luther evaluates Jacob as a model for faithful saints because of his patience, godliness, and trust in the Lord despite the heartbreaking circumstances he experienced. Reformers, including Luther, observe that Jacob's silence when he heard the bad news of Dina's tragedy was because he was obsessed with deep sorrow; or wondering what happened to the promise of God to protect him.[24]

Luther comments that Levi and Simeon are justified for taking revenge against the Shechemites because they did what God wanted them to do with the Shechemites as a punishment for their sin. However, he makes them responsible for committing such a cruel execution of vengeance.[25]

---

22. Ibid., 99–102.

23. Ibid., 104–5.

24. Pelikan, *Luther's Works*, 187–220; Calvin, *Genesis*, 218–29; Parry, *Old Testament Story*, 104.

25. Pelikan, *Luther's Works*, 210.

Dinah Story as an Adverse Consequence of the Unfulfilled Vow

He notes that Jacob was angry that Simeon and Levi went beyond what they should have done; thus they acted unjustly.[26]

Luther believes that this tragedy was allowed to happen by God, because nothing would happen to Jacob without God's permission. God did not want to protect Jacob from this tragedy. He wanted to use it as a means to punish the Shechemites because they refused to repent.[27]

Calvin has a similar understanding. He gives more focus to evaluating the behavior of Simeon and Levi than to the other characters of the story. Except for Jacob, he evaluates all of them as accountable for the tragedy. He makes Dinah responsible for moving around without her parents' permission, which led Shechem into temptation.[28] On the other hand, he perceives Shechem as one who had a sincere love and attraction to Dinah but he holds him responsible for his lack of self control.[29] However, he commends Shechem for coming to his senses and making an effort to redeem the situation; yet he condemns the evil motive behind the decision to accept the circumcision rite of the Israelites.[30] He also condemns the cruelty and massacre of their hospitable friends by Simeon and Levi in a peaceful time. In their anger, they lost all awareness of the imminent danger of revenge by the Canaanites against their family.[31]

He observes that the narrative representation was organized in such a way as to influence the readers to have sympathy for the Shechemites and to dislike the behavior of Simeon and Levi.[32]

Just like their predecessors, post-reformation commentators (1600–1800 and beyond) also focus on evaluating the characters of the narrative rather than explaining the relevance of the Dinah story to the Jacob narrative. On the one hand, Bishop Babington holds Dinah and Shechem responsible for the tragedy. He concludes that both Dinah and Shechem rightly suffered the consequence of their sins, because no one will go without being punished for the sins they commit. However, he disapproves of the irrational cruelty of the children of Jacob. On the other hand, Mathew Henry strongly condemns the cruel massacre by Simeon and Levi, and

---

26. Pelikan, *Luther's Works*, 211.
27. Ibid., 211–14.
28. Parry, *Old Testament Story*, 106–7.
29. Ibid., 107.
30. Ibid., 107–8.
31. Ibid., 108.
32. Ibid., 107–8.

Reading and Translating Genesis 28:10—35:15 as a Votive Narrative

holds Dinah responsible for being a cause for the temptation of Shechem and for exposing herself to the tragedy.[33]

Wider Literary Readings

The above discussion shows that there are different possible interpretations depending on the assumptions one may bring to a character evaluation of the story. However, some biblical scholars did attempt to explain the relevance of the Dinah story to Jacob narrative, but they have different views of which the following are only a few examples.

Walter Brueggemann argues that Genesis 33:18—34:31 has "no relationship with anything before or after."[34] On the contrary, Brisman perceives the Dinah story as connected to the Jacob story because it turns "from the story of Jacob in his own generation to those of Dinah and Joseph, Jacob's children."[35] Consequently, he describes the Dinah story as a strong nationalistic reaction of Jacob's children to their father's dangerously compromising behavior in response to the Shechemites' strategy of making ethnic relationship by marriage. This would have resulted in the assimilation of the chosen people of God, which would eventually lead to their possible extinction.[36] In Brisman's words "To a nationalistic ear, this cry of 'peace!' is no peace but the threat of assimilation."[37]

Wenham remarks that it is difficult to describe the relevance of the Dinah story to Jacob story, nor is it easy to pinpoint the point of view of the narrator about the event.[38] However, Wenham argues that the Dinah story is relevant to Jacob narrative and attempts to substantiate this view by supplying some textual evidence from the Jacob narrative. For example, he notes that Jacob, after he enjoyed "God's protection in Mesopotamia, gained descendants, and bought land in Canaan, but has not quite reached his destination in Bethel," where he will fulfill his vow as mentioned in 35:1–15. Jacob was still on the move to his prospective destination, Bethel, when he was interrupted and threatened to be destroyed because of the Dinah tragedy.[39] Thus he observes that the rape of Dinah and the revenge

---

33. Ibid., 109–10.
34. Brueggemann, *Genesis*, 274.
35. Brisman, *Voice of Jacob*, 92.
36. Ibid., 92–98.
37. Brisman, *Voice of Jacob*, 94.
38. Wenham, *Genesis 16–50*, 308.
39. Ibid., 300.

Dinah Story as an Adverse Consequence of the Unfulfilled Vow

of her brothers was not the end of the story; rather they are the cause of a dangerous situation for Jacob and his family which eventually forced him to proceed to Bethel though he admits that it is difficult to pin down the specific relation of the Dinah story to the theme of Genesis in general and to the Jacob story in particular. He lists some of the intratextual evidences in Genesis which show its relevance:

1. The story occurred in Canaan which shows Jacob's return to Canaan.
2. It is connected to the story of the marriage relationship of Jacob and Leah who bore him six sons and one daughter.
3. It shows that Jacob was not fond of Leah and her children and that he was not concerned about their humiliation. Probably this caused the emotional reaction of Simeon and Levi against the Shechemites.
4. Dinah's mention in 30:21 anticipates the story of Genesis 34.
5. The necessity of circumcision of Shechemites was connected to the command to circumcise in Genesis 17.
6. The usual style of the Genesis narrative of closing an episode or a narrative unit by providing a preview for the next chapter was exhibited in 33:18–20 which is a functional trailer for chapter 34.
7. Genesis 35:1–5 presupposes the preceding story presented in chapter 34 about the possible revenge of the enraged Canaanites for the murder of the Shechemites.[40]

Then he draws the moral teaching of the story as one intended to ban the intermarriage relationship between the people of Yahweh and pagans.[41]

Meir Sternberg in his literary analysis proposes that the author of the Dinah episode evaluated the action and the actors of the episode by the standards of legislation about the Israelites' social relation to others which strictly prohibits any exogamous marriage relation. He believes that the biblical narrators in their representation interact with inter-textual contexts and other social and institutional contexts of their audience in order to influence/persuade them to their point of view.[42] For example, he suggests that presumably the narrator of the Dinah story represented this episode in the context of Deuteronomy 7:1–4 which commands the Israelites not to make any covenant with Canaanites, not to show any mercy

---

40. Parry, *Old Testament Story*, 130; Wenham, *Genesis 16–50*, 308–9.
41. Wenham, *Genesis 16–50*, 319.
42. Sternberg, *Poetics of Biblical Narrative*, 444–45; Sternberg, "Biblical Poetics," 483.

Reading and Translating Genesis 28:10—35:15 as a Votive Narrative

to them, and not to marry with them when they enter into Canaan.[43] How did Simeon and Levi know about the doctrine of Deuteronomy? Sternberg suggests that probably such tradition was going on about such prohibition prior to legislating it in Deuteronomy.[44] So Sternberg proposes that the narrator was sympathetic with Simeon and Levi and he considers them as heroes for defending this religious legislation, at every cost no matter what.[45] He further remarks that Simeon and Levi received the divine protection (which is represented in chapter 35:5) for "doing right in keeping the prohibition" of exogamous marriage.[46] But he fails to explain the relevance of God's utterance: "God said to Jacob, 'Arise, go up to Bethel, and settle there. Make an altar there to the God who appeared to you when you fled from your brother Esau'" which in fact the narrator strategically represented in 35:1 between the crisis and the resuming of God's protection.

Sternberg argues that the narrator denounced Jacob as an "indifferent parent" and a coward who failed to fight against the exogamous marriage attempt,[47] Shechem as "rapist criminal," and again Shechem and his father Hamor as suitors who approached Dinah's marriage affair as a business and commercial transaction (but it was ruled out by Dinah's family).[48] However, he admits that the narrator never make such judgment explicitly in his own words: "The dilemma raised by the story is so complex and each choice so problematic that he cannot fully identify with any of the positions taken."[49]

A recent thorough and inspiring work on the Dinah story is Parry's monograph. Parry summarizes different interpretations of the Dinah story, which are based on character evaluation, before he gives his own view. He observes that, on the one hand, some read it in the favor of Simeon and Levi. They suspect the genuineness of Shechem and his father Hamor when they approached Jacob and his children to negotiate for the marriage of Dinah. They blame Shechem for the action of rape before the negotiation. They also suspect the dubious intention of Hamor and Shechem in their speech to the Hivites (Gen 34:20–24) which would encourage them to claim the possession of the Israelites if they were not destroyed by them

43. Sternberg, "Biblical Poetics," 483.
44. Ibid., 483ff.
45. Sternberg, *Poetics of Biblical Narrative*, 455, 472, 474–75.
46. Sternberg, "Biblical Poetics," 483.
47. Sternberg, *Poetics of Biblical Narrative*, 474.
48. Ibid., 456.
49. Ibid., 475.

first.⁵⁰ Thus they justify the crime of Levi and Simeon as if they were forced by the Shechemites to commit such a horrendous crime which was even condemned by their own father Jacob (Gen 49:6–7). Many scholars also condemn Jacob for not being sympathetic to his daughter.⁵¹ They perceive him as an unsympathetic father who does not care for his humiliated daughter.⁵²

Others observe that the narrator is positive toward Shechem. He shows that Dinah's father Jacob showed favor to Shechem out of a sense of responsibility for his family and their safety.⁵³ The narrator also portrays Dinah as wronged by Shechem but as persuaded and eventually convinced by him, and as seeing marriage as the only way forward.⁵⁴ Generally, Shechem, Hamor, and the people of Shechem were portrayed as innocent people who were sincere in their marriage negotiation but who were deceived by the children of Jacob. The narrator presents the sons of Jacob as angry savage figures who killed the innocent Hivites and plundered their property and who took Dinah from Shechem's house against her will.⁵⁵ He does not present them as acting wisely rather he portrays them as complicating matters for Jacob and his family, which might have led to the complete destruction of the promised seed by the imminent revenge of Canaanites. They made Jacob miserable.

After summarizing other literary readings of the Dinah story Parry gives his own view about the relevance of the Dinah story to Jacob narrative. He comments that as Abraham moved from Shechem to Bethel, Jacob was also to move from Shechem to Bethel as presented in chapter 35, but this was interrupted by the Dinah tragedy. In his words, "Chapter 34 is a rude and dramatic interruption in this predictable ending. The divine promise is suddenly thrown into jeopardy yet again."⁵⁶ Though he falls short of reading the Dinah story from the votive narrative perspective, he believes that Dinah story is an integral and congruent part of the Jacob story, but he holds that it is incorporated in Jacob narrative to show the issue of "exogamy and its implications for the divine promise of descendants

---

50. Parry, *Old Testament Story*, 117.
51. Ibid., 118.
52. Ibid.
53. Ibid.
54. Ibid.
55. Ibid.
56. Ibid., 135.

and land inheritance."⁵⁷ The tragic confrontation between the Shechemites and Israelites is the result of rejecting assimilation with pagans.⁵⁸

However, some biblical scholars such as Candlish, Strahan, and Pink observe a literary connection between Genesis chapters 33 and 34. Accordingly they perceive the event of chapter 34 as a tragedy which happened to Jacob because God's protection for Jacob was breached at that time as a punishment of God. Consequently Jacob suffered divine retribution, which ruined his only daughter Dinah and which also further escalated to a threat of revenge by the Canaanites. They believe that Jacob incurred this adverse consequence because of three possible reasons:

1. Because of Jacob's unbelief and disobedience (because he did not believe God's promise to give him the land, he bought piece of it from the children of Hamor in Shechem).⁵⁹ In addition Pink observes that probably God was not pleased with Jacob when he built the altar in Shechem, as his utterance in 35:1: "Go to Bethel and build an altar for me . . ." indicates. Thus, Pink, though he does not explain why the crisis of Genesis 34 happened, correctly observes that this utterance of God has a very significant contextual implication: God was not happy with the altar Jacob built in Shechem rather than building it in Bethel.⁶⁰

2. Robert S. Candlish presumes that the adverse consequence of the Dinah story of Genesis 34 to Jacob resulted from his heart not being quite right with God. This behavior of Jacob manifested when he stopped in Shechem at the border of Canaan (Gen 33:17–20) rather than proceeding to Bethel to fulfill his vow according to the preface of God's word in 31:13. Thus he neglected or delayed to pay his vow in Bethel and he built the altar in Shechem rather than building it in Bethel. It was in Bethel where the "hallowed stone of which he had vowed that it was to be God's house" was, not in Shechem.⁶¹ He further notes that Jacob's naming God as "God of Israel" rather than "God of Bethel" also shows that Jacob's personal religious faithfulness to God was not right at that particular time.⁶² Hence, since his

---

57. Ibid., 136.

58. Brisman, *Voice of Jacob*, 94; Wenham, *Genesis 16–50*, 319; Parry, *Old Testament Story*, 136.

59. Pink, *Gleanings*, 300.

60. Ibid., 301.

61. Candlish, *Studies in Genesis*, 563–65.

62. Ibid., 565–66.

faith to God was falling away he was not able to discipline his family well, so that Dinah went out to see the daughters of the land rather than staying at home as a "discrete and chaste" girl, consequently exposing herself to temptation.[63]

3. The tragedy of the Dinah story happened to Jacob because he was associated with pagans.[64]

We will investigate the content of these three claims further from the votive narrative perspective and from the institution of vow in my close reading of the Dinah story in section 3 of this chapter.

Source Criticism Readings

Most of the nineteenth- and twentieth-century scholars approached the reading of the Dinah story mainly from the perspective of identifying different sources and interpreting it accordingly. Consequently they propose source A (Shechem variant) which was ascribed to J; source B (Hamor variant) which is ascribed to E; and the final redaction to combine them.[65] According to source A, which is held to be much older than source B, Shechem abducted Dinah then fell in love with her. He reassures Dinah that he loves her and then he takes the initiative of negotiation with her family. But according to source B, Shechem raped her but did not abduct her and take her to his house. Otherwise why did the brothers say "we will take our daughter and move away" (v.17)? Then he loved her and he pleaded with his father to negotiate for him to marry Dinah.

The Hamor variant approves the punishment for the crime of rape.[66] On the contrary, the Shechem variant opposes the crime of massacre and predicts the imminent future punishment of the two tribes of Simeon and Levi (Gen 49:5–7).[67] The redactor combined these two variants in order to fit his ideological agenda and produced the final story.[68] Unlike other Patriarchal and Israelite stories, the Shechemites' innocence was positively

---

63. Candlish, *Studies in Genesis*, 566–67.
64. Strahan, *Hebrew Ideals*, 263.
65. Alders, *Genesis II*, 153–54; Gunkel, *Genesis*, 362.
66. Parry, *Old Testament Story*, 114.
67. Gunkel, *Genesis*, 361; Parry, *Old Testament Story*, 114.
68. Skinner, *Genesis*, 417–22; Westermann, *Genesis*, 544; Gunkel, *Genesis*, 358–62; Parry, *Old Testament Story*, 110–15.

evaluated in this story while the deceitful and treacherous behavior of Dinah's brothers was criticized.[69]

There is limited interest in pursuing the source criticism approach further because, as Parry remarks, it contradicts the assumption that the text is a coherent narrative unit and so makes the text unstable data.[70] Besides, source criticism does not prove the existence of its hypothetical source documents.[71] The synchronic approach has been used in analyzing the final form of the text as it is presented in the Hebrew Scripture.

Social Scientific Readings

Feminist readings

Feminist interpretations approach the Dinah story from a particular ideological perspective. Feminist hermeneutics can be described as cultural hermeneutics which evaluates and describes life-affirming (not harmful) and life-denying (harmful) cultural practices involving women in order to absorb what is life-affirming and challenge what is life-denying. Feminists read the biblical stories with suspicion and examine them to detect and expose whether they are oppressive and damaging to women in terms of depriving them of their human rights.[72] This feminist hermeneutic of suspicion challenges the view of the normative value of every scriptural text, associating some with patriarchal culture.[73] It depicts the biblical culture as a male dominant androcentric culture and it reads the Bible as a book condoning male dominance.[74] In Parry's words the feminists "consider the text of the Bible to be both patriarchal and androcentric and thus potentially harmful to women."[75] Therefore, the Bible needs to be liberated both from the patriarchal prejudice of reflecting male dominance and from the existing biblical interpretation regarding women.[76]

---

69. Gunkel, *Genesis*, 361.

70. Parry, *Old Testament Story*, 115–16.

71 For an extended critique of source critical analyses of Genesis 34 on their own terms see Parry, "Source Criticism."

72. Blyth, "Terrible Silence," 26.

73. Leeb, "Translating," 115; Blyth, "Terrible Silence," 8.

74. Blyth, "Terrible Silence," 3ff.

75. Parry, *Old Testament Story*, 218.

76. Ibid., 220.

Dinah Story as an Adverse Consequence of the Unfulfilled Vow

Feminist interpretation of the Dinah story shows that ideology plays a critical role in biblical interpretation. Feminist theology argues that the marriage negotiation of the Dinah story shows that the ancient Israelite culture was patriarchal and androcentric because Dinah was treated as an object. She was the voiceless victim because the discussion took place between the males to transfer the object-female (Dinah) in an economic transaction to the subject-male (Shechem). Her consent was never considered. That was a disgrace for women.[77]

Danna Nolan Fewell and David Gunn reject the argument of Meir Sternberg (see section 2.1) from the feminist point of view.[78] Sternberg, based on the narrative analysis, suggests that the narrator of the Dinah episode evaluates both the action of Shechem and the action of Simeon and Levi in the light of the later books of law. He believes that the narrator is sympathetic with Simeon and Levi and so he attempts to justify their action and considers them as heroes while denouncing Shechem and Hamor as criminals, and criticizing Jacob as an indifferent parent and a coward.[79]

Fewell and Gunn, however, blame both Shechem and Dinah's brothers, Simeon and Levi. They are more sympathetic with Shechem arguing that though he was a criminal for raping Dinah, he took steps to marry her as restitution, and Dinah agreed. Sternberg describes the character of Dinah as a helpless victim who needed to be rescued by her brothers. However, Fewell and Gunn argue that "she could have made her own choice" but her voice was denied by the dominant males.[80] Unlike Sternberg, they are also sympathetic with Jacob and Hamor because they tried to make "the best of the flawed world" in order to resolve the matter peacefully. They note that it is dangerous to advocate that a woman marry her rapist, but that was the best choice for her in that particular cultural context; Shechem's house is the best place for her to stay.[81] However, they argue that the brothers never express the interest of their sister, but only their own interest. When Shechem took her it was against her will, and now when her brothers took her, again it was against her will. She has no voice in both cases because the dominant men did not allow her to have a voice in her own case.[82] Her brothers were so much more concerned about their honor

---

77. Ibid., 227.
78. Fewell and Gunn, "Tipping the Balance."
79. Sternberg, *Poetics of Biblical Narrative*, 446, 472.
80. Fewell and Gunn, "Tipping the Balance," 211.
81. Ibid., 210, 221.
82. Ibid., 211.

than they were about Dinah that they killed her reformed fiancée and took her away against her will. They did not value her preferences; because of male superiority; they considered her as helpless and powerless, a weak person who needed to be rescued.[83]

Sternberg responds vigorously to Fewell and Gunn's criticism of his interpretation in his 1992 article.[84] He reaffirms his previous interpretation by elaborating the deuteronomic doctrinal context of the narrator's point of view. He asserts that the biblical narrators' presentations reflect their view of the moral values held by their audience. He argues that there is no androcentric ideological interest manifested in the narrative representation of Dinah episode. The reason why the narrator did not include Dinah's voice in his representation is because "it would disturb the tale's focus of interest."[85] Dinah's voicelessness in the episode from the perspective of the narrator's mental and linguistic representation of the discourse reflects the socio-cultural code of antiquity, and the strict doctrinal objection of the Scriptural legislation to exogamous marriage.[86] He remarks that the Scripture "pushes to the limit of absolute veto regarding" any marriage relationship with the Canaanites. Thus Dinah's voice or voicelessness in the episode does not affect the uncompromising doctrinal judgment against the proposed marriage relation between Hivites and Israelites. Therefore, including Dinah's voice in the episode is irrelevant for the narrator.[87]

Some feminists reject any sympathy Fewel and Gunn have for Shechem arguing the story should be read from the perspective of the victim (Dinah), not from the perspective of the powerful (Shechem).[88] They do not recognize the view that the narrator had a neutral position in that though he makes Shechem responsible for the rape he presents him as one working for restitution. They allege that this view supports the sentiment that "love can make rape" and it is "not so bad."[89] They interpret the narrator's presentation in verse 3: "And his soul was drawn to Dinah daughter of Jacob; he loved the girl, and spoke tenderly to her" (Gen 34:3) as an attempt to calm Dinah because she refused to consent, not a genuine love.[90]

---

83. Parry, *Old Testament Story*, 225.
84. Sternberg, "Biblical Poetics."
85. Ibid., 480.
86. Ibid., 481.
87. Ibid.
88. Parry, *Old Testament Story*, 226.
89. Ibid., 225.
90. Ibid., 226.

Dinah Story as an Adverse Consequence of the Unfulfilled Vow

In conclusion, the feminist interpretation of the Dinah story reads the narrative from the feminist ideological perspective and challenges interpretations which make Dinah responsible for the massacre or tragedy by attributing to her the cause of the problem because she took the liberty of moving around in such a dangerous place. The purpose of the feminist hermeneutical approach to Genesis 34 is to make the lost voice of Dinah heard in order to restore her honor, thus making the story gynocentric.[91] But surely all readings, including feminist readings of the Bible, should be submissive to the narrator's point of view and listen to it carefully.

Social Anthropological Readings

Social anthropology reads the Dinah story from the perspective of endogamy and exogamy as well as shame and honor in social groups. It assumes that originally Israelites were exogamous people. When they were Bedouins/nomads the Israelite women were given to foreigners. Even in some cases when the Israelites seek refuge with a sedentary people who are usually politically more powerful, they used to give their women to their host as well as to more powerful neighboring people as part of sexual hospitality.[92] Social anthropology perceives the crisis of the Dinah story as part of the shift of the Israelites' marriage custom from exogamous practice to endogamous marriage practice when they started becoming sedentary from nomadic life. The Dinah story happened in the endogamous context. Israelites considered Dinah's marriage to Shechem as one which will destroy "lineage solidarity and deprive a member of the Terahite line of a potential wife."[93] Steinberg remarks that since Jacob consented to exogamous marriage during the negotiation he is responsible for bringing strife to the family.[94] However, she observes that Jacob's children objected to the matter for "reasons relating to family honor; family honor appears linked to control of the sexuality of women."[95] Thus when Shechem dishonored Dinah, he actually dishonored the entire family. Hence, particularly the honor of the men, whose honor and power is related to the control of the sexuality of their community's women, was threatened.[96] She notes that

---

91. Blyth, "Terrible Silence," 9, 14.
92. Parry, *Old Testament Story*, 119–20.
93. Steinberg, *Kinship and Marriage*, 110.
94. Ibid., 110.
95. Ibid., 110.
96. Ibid., 111; Bechtel, "Dinah," 33.

anthropological study shows that men who cannot control and defend the sexuality of their community's women "are also thought to be unable to defend themselves against attacks from outsiders."[97] Thus Shechem's sexual violation of Dinah was a shameful act against the children of Jacob. Levi and Simeon took the action of revenge in order to restore their honor by proving that they have power to defend themselves and to protect the sexuality of their women.[98] Bechtel puts it nicely:

> The reaction people had to being shamed was to take revenge or save face. This need for revenge suggests that their pride had been violated by their shaming. Revenge would restore pride by reversing the position of those of involved.[99]

Thus, Bechtel in her anthropological reading of Genesis 34 argues that the Dinah story must be read from a group-oriented society[100] perspective. Based on this assumption she claims that "Dinah was not actually raped but consented to Shechem's sexual advance."[101] She objects that most interpretations of this narrative are based on grid/individual-orientation. Bechtel suggests that Dinah should be understood as a member of a group-oriented society, who behaved like an individual-oriented person when she transgressed the community's boundary by going against the community's custom/norm of sanction about shame when she had sex with Shechem who was outside of her group. Dinah lost her sexual power, which keeps the existence of her community, to an uncircumcised outsider. Thus she brought shame on her community.[102]

Bechtel evaluates Jacob, Shechem, Dinah, and Hamor as good models who were open and willing to negotiate and compromise their group values in order to create a bonding and peace between the two ethnic groups. She argues that the story presents Jacob and Hamor as the heros

97. Steinberg, *Kinship and Marriage*, 111.
98. Ibid.
99. Bechtel, "Shame," 76.
100. Grid-orientation claims that the main source of identity of the people "comes from within the individual's self." Thus individuality is greatly valued. Such society internalizes the grid in the conscience of the people in order to control the behavior of the people. On the contrary, in the group-oriented society, the main source of identity of the people comes from the consciousness of belonging to the strongly bonded group. In such a society the use of sanction of shame to control the behavior of the people is common. However, Bechtel suggests that there is no society that is purely grid-oriented or purely group-oriented (Bechtel, "Shame," 51–52).
101. Bechtel, "Dinah," 19–31.
102. Ibid., 32.

of the story because they are models for tolerance and flexibility in order to create peace between the two groups. She argues that, on the contrary, the story presents Simeon and Levi as those who negatively stereotype the outsiders. They have a militant attitude toward the outside groups, so that they were threatened by the outsiders through what happened to Dinah. Thus they decided to take revenge on all the Shechemites, because they perceived it as a group crime, in order to restore their own group's honor. But they acted foolishly because they did it independently without involving their father and they failed to see the danger which their action would bring to the whole community. Based on this argument Bechtel argues that this story was intended to challenge their militant attitude, which is the moral lesson of the story.[103]

Similarly Pieter M. Venter employs a triadic construct method, using inter-related concepts: progeny or heirship, marriage, and ownership of land in Genesis 34; and law, identity, and marriage in Jubilee 30 in order to explain the ethical message of the Dinah story.[104] He compares the narrative presentation of the story of both Genesis and Jubilee and then he draws a conclusion that the intended moral impact which was propagated by the Jubilee was maintaining the purified ethnic identity of the contemporary Jews. Hence, he uses the triads in negative term such as avoiding intermarriage with any outsiders.[105] Thus he argues that the identity of Israel was expressed by a triad of interrelated concepts and therefore the Dinah story deals with the identity of Israel.[106]

Summary

The review above shows that the different readings of the Dinah story are usually aimed at drawing out a moral lesson from the story by evaluating its characters and their behavior. The conclusion of this evaluation differs depending on the starting assumptions one may have. Some scholars hold a character responsible for the crisis while other scholars view the same character as innocent. For example, some scholars perceive Dinah as a cause of the crisis while some scholars perceive her as an innocent victim. Some scholars perceive Shechem as an innocent young man who wanted to redeem his mistake by paying Dinah's family abundant dowry and by

103. Parry, *Old Testament Story*, 121.
104. Venter, "Triadic Construct."
105. Ibid., 6.
106. Ibid., 20.

marrying Dinah while others perceive him as undisciplined wild young man. Some evaluate Jacob as a wise character who gave priority to peace, while others evaluate him as unsympathetic father who failed to care for his own daughter and for the family honor. Some evaluate Hamor, the father of Shechem, as an innocent man who negotiated for peace and for the bonding of two groups while others evaluate him as a selfish deceiver who wanted to manipulate negotiation for material gain. Some evaluate Simeon and Levi as the foolish, brutal, militant persons of the family while others evaluate them as heroes who fought for innocent Dinah, to protect the blood of the chosen line of Israel from contamination and possible assimilation and to restore the honor of the family.[107]

On the other hand, many scholars have observed that the story of Dinah does not intend to blame Shechem, or Dinah, or Jacob, or Simeon and Levi, or Hamor. In Bechtel's words the "story contains contradictions, ironies, paradoxes and ambiguities that they raise a question: Does the story really intend to indicate that Dinah is raped?"[108] Parry correctly observes that reading the Dinah story from the perspective of character evaluation in order to draw a moral lesson has an apparent problem because every reading varies depending on the assumptions one may have.[109] Therefore, we should question whether the narrator intended to evaluate the characters of the narrative of Genesis 34 at all. Since such a claim has not been established by strong ostensive textual evidence so far this will be used to explain and establish the narrator's point of view by substantiating it with the ostensive textual evidence provided within the story.

Close Reading of the Dinah Story (Gen 34:1—35:15)

Examining the Hadiyya Marriage Institution for the Reading of the Dinah Story

The issue of whether Dinah was raped or not will be dealt with very briefly in the light of the Hadiyya culture before explaining the relevance of her story to the Jacob narrative. From this perspective what happened to Dinah was an abductive marriage, not rape, as many scholars have thought, and suggest a new approach. Before the actual analysis of the Dinah story, I gathered some empirical data on Hadiyya marriage customs. I read the

107. Parry, *Old Testament Story*, 122.
108. Bechtel, "Dinah," 20.
109. Parry, *Old Testament Story*, 122.

Dinah Story as an Adverse Consequence of the Unfulfilled Vow

Dinah story to some of the community members in order to find out whether they would think that Shechem raped Dinah or attempted to marry her by abduction. The results will throw some light on the reading of Genesis 34 (without influencing it) because of the Hadiyya people's diverse ways of fulfilling the marriage institution and will later be seen to be relevant.

It will then be shown how Shechem's attempted abductive marriage became a threat to the very existence of the chosen line of God's people as an adverse consequence of Jacob's unfulfilled vow at Bethel, evidently showing that Dinah story is a congruent part of Jacob's votive narrative.

Marriage and Rape among the Hadiyya People

There are six ways of fulfilling the marriage institution among the Hadiyya people and most of these types of marriage practice are widespread among African cultures.

Marriage by Wedding "ladiisimma"[110]

Among Hadiyya marriage institutions, a wedding is considered the most desirable and honorable way for both the couple and the family. According to Hadiyya tradition, a young man used to decide to marry a girl whom he had never met. In such a case the young man and one of his best friends would go to the girl's house in order to see her appearance and her manners. However today, if he already knows the girl this procedure is not needed. If the boy is happy with the girl then he will ask his father to go and negotiate his marriage to the girl. The consent of both families before the marriage is essential. Once all the concerned parties are agreed, the boy's family will give gifts to the girl and her family and then the boy's family will usually propose a date for the wedding. Since all the traditional formal marriage procedures can be performed on the wedding day, this is considered the most desirable, and honorable procedure by both the nuclear and extended families.

---

110. The term *ladiisimma*, literally "putting a skirt on a lady," denotes the action of giving a girl away for marriage. When they talk about a man marrying a woman they say *meento eebaako* which means "he has brought women." This is because in Hadiyya marriage tradition women leave their family and join their husband's family.

Reading and Translating Genesis 28:10—35:15 as a Votive Narrative

Levirate Marriage "lago gassimma"

This type of marriage usually occurs between brother-in-law and sister-in-law. This happens when a woman's husband dies and the family of the deceased wants to keep the widow within the family. Thus the family will force the brother-in-law to marry her. It also depends on whether the woman is willing to accept her brother-in-law as a husband or not.

Sororate Marriage (not lexicalized)

Sororate marriage concerns the provision of a dead wife's sister or very close relative as a new wife for a surviving husband. Sororate marriage in the Hadiyya community is not a required norm, but it is commonly practiced marriage if it is consented by both the family of the deceased women and the family of the widower, by the sororate woman, and by the widower. The substitute woman must be a sister of the deceased women or her close relative. The main reason of providing a substitute is to take care of the children of the deceased woman. But sometimes a substitute woman is given even to a widower who did not have a child from his deceased wife, in order to maintain the family relationship.

Cohabitation[111]

Such marriage occurs between a widow and a man, usually one who has another wife. In the Hadiyya marriage tradition, usually, the woman leaves her family or her home and goes to the home or family of her husband in marriage. But in this particular case the man comes to the home of the widowed women when she consents to welcome him and starts living with her. Usually this kind of marriage is done without any formal family or community approval, thus it is not binding. Therefore, if the woman is not happy with the man she may send him out of her house without any formal family or community approval or if the man is not happy with the woman he may leave her house and go without any formal family or community approval.

---

111. Not lexicalized, rather it is described by a pragmatic clause . . . *aagaako* "he has entered in to . . .," which manifests a man's coming to live with a widow for a marriage relationship.

Dinah Story as an Adverse Consequence of the Unfulfilled Vow

Marriage by Eloping "heerancha"

According to this tradition a boy and a girl who love one another make arrangement secretly and the girl will disappear with her lover. Thus, elopement is strictly consensual, and even an engaged girl can elope. Once the girl has eloped a messenger will then be sent to the girl's family to inform them that the girl is with them (with the family of the man) that they should not look for her (in some Hadiyya dialects, they say metaphorically "the heifer is with us; so do not look for it!"). Formal negotiation will follow then in order to give gifts to the parents of the girl so that they will endorse the marriage. The process may take a shorter or longer time depending on different reasons. Though this type of marriage is not considered as honorable, it is a well-accepted way of marriage among the Hadiyya people.

Marriage by Abduction "gosimma"

Abductive marriage is widely practiced among the Hadiyya people. The particular nature of this practice is that it is violent, so that some girls may even lose their lives in an attempt to refuse, and it may spark a fight between different groups because the Hadiyya people are a shame/honor conscious community. Thus, since the Hadiyya people are an exogamous community, shaming and restoring the threatened group honor is very serious matter, because abductive marriage is very humiliating for the girl and her family.

According to this tradition the man who intends to marry a girl by abduction first spies out the scene and then kidnaps and abducts the girl with the help of his friends for the purpose of marriage. He then takes her to a hiding place (usually with another family), and has a sexual intercourse with her by force right away, and makes sure that her family will not find the place where he hides her at least for one week to a month, depending on the seriousness of the reaction of the girl's family. In the meantime the man does his best to convince the girl to consent to marry him. And then the family of the man will plead with the family of the girl so that they will let their son marry their daughter.

Abductive marriage can sometimes be aborted in several cases. However, it will be endorsed in most cases, depending on different reasons. Sometimes it may provoke a serious fight between the two families, especially if the girl's family is very proud of their status in the community;

such a family is likely to be very aggressive in order to restore their threatened honor. They will feel humiliated and dishonored so that they will do whatever they can in order to abort the marriage and bring the girl back home (see appendix 6 for some real-life examples of abductive marriage among the Hadiyya people).

RAPE

Though rape apparently occurs among the Hadiyya people this behavior is not lexicalized so far, and it is always concealed. A rapist always attempts to maintain anonymity. Rape is perceived as a sexual attack on women by men, only to satisfy their sexual appetite. Usually rape is committed by individuals—group rape is not known among the Hadiyya people. The attacker never keeps the woman with him in his house or in any other place. If he does and if the victim is a girl then it is perceived as an abductive marriage—*gosimma*; never as a rape.

Interview with the Hadiyya Community Members

The research method I employed in order to explore this matter was simple: first I summarized the Dinah story (see appendix 4) and then I read the summary to the Hadiyya audience and ask them what has happened to Dinah according to the story: whether she was raped or it was an abductive marriage.

All participants unanimously said "*ooki gosimma*," which mean "that is an abductive marriage." I asked them why. They responded by saying it is evident that he took the girl and kept her with him and he is negotiating with the girl's family for marriage. Probably the boy abducted the girl because he knew that they will not let him marry her or she refused to marry him. So first he had to marry the girl by abduction and then negotiate.

Regarding my question why it is not a rape, all participants unanimously responded that it is not a rape, because if it were a rape then he wouldn't keep the girl with him or initiate the negotiation for marriage. Instead he would do it in secret and then disappear. He wouldn't behave like this. This answer was not a surprise to me because I already expected that the Hadiyya people, with their practical knowledge about different ways of fulfilling the marriage institution of the community, would think that what Shechem did with Dinah was an abductive marriage and not a rape.

Dinah Story as an Adverse Consequence of the Unfulfilled Vow

This response clearly shows that it might be better to interpret the story as an abductive marriage rather than as rape which is the usual interpretation. Now it is left to prove that Shechem attempted an abductive marriage to Dinah and that the episode is represented as the adverse consequence of the unfulfilled vow of Jacob.

Reading the Dinah story in the Light of the Hadiyya culture

Reading the Dinah story with the Hadiyya contextual assumptions about the diverse ways of fulfilling the marriage institution in mind will give a better understanding of the story.

Narrative Structure and Interpretation of Gen 34:1—35:15

Setting (34:1–2a)

וַתֵּצֵא דִינָה בַּת־לֵאָה אֲשֶׁר יָלְדָה לְיַעֲקֹב לִרְאוֹת בִּבְנוֹת הָאָרֶץ: וַיַּרְא אֹתָהּ שְׁכֶם בֶּן־חֲמוֹר הַחִוִּי נְשִׂיא הָאָרֶץ

Now Dinah the daughter of Leah, whom she had borne to Jacob, went out to visit the women of the region. And Shechem son of Hamor the Hivite, prince of the region, saw her. (Gen 34:1–2a)

This section of the text could be understood as the setting of the narrative. The narrator introduces the situation, the participants—daughters of the land, Dinah and Shechem, and the geographical location where the narrative event-line takes place. Both Dinah and Shechem are formally introduced to the narrative. At this juncture it is worth noting that Jacob who is the thematic participant of the votive narrative (28:10—35:15) is included in the participant introduction as Dinah's father in both mentions of Dinah and Shechem (1–3a).

Parry suggests that the expression about Dinah's going out to see the daughters of the land (וַתֵּצֵא דִינָה בַּת־לֵאָה אֲשֶׁר יָלְדָה לְיַעֲקֹב לִרְאוֹת בִּבְנוֹת הָאָרֶץ: Gen 34:1) has the implication of drawing our attention "to the issue of exogamy."[112] However, it could also be seen simply as part of the setting which introduces the situation of the event because it need have no

---

112. Parry, *Old Testament Story*, 136.

implicatures beyond Dinah's friendship among the local girls.[113] This situation is relevant to what the narrator is going to tell us in 2b–3: Shechem taking her by force violently. Dinah's going out to see the daughters of the land, away from her family, created a suitable situation for Shechem to abduct her.

The introduction of the two major participants: Dinah and Shechem need a brief comment. Wenham's and Parry's comments indicate that introducing Dinah as a "daughter of Leah" has a communicative significance for the later interpretation of the narrative because it implies that Dinah is a daughter of Jacob's unloved wife. According to them the expression denotes that this was why Jacob did not respond as a responsible father to defend his daughter Dinah (v. 5).[114] However, I consider that this expression is anaphoric to Genesis 30:21. Dinah is introduced in 30.21 וְאַחַר יָלְדָה בַת וַתִּקְרָא אֶת־שְׁמָהּ דִּינָה: "afterwards she bore a daughter, and named her Dinah" cataphorically with chapter 34 in view. Consequently, the referring expression in chapter 34:1 דִּינָה בַת־לֵאָה אֲשֶׁר יָלְדָה לְיַעֲקֹב "Dinah, the daughter whom Leah had born to Jacob" should be read as anaphoric participant introduction of the episode employed in order to recapture the same Dinah of 30:21. Thus it explains why she was introduced previously.

The referential introduction of Shechem as "son of Hamor the Hivite, chief of the country/land" provides a relevant contextual assumption for the interpretation of attempted abductive marriage. This referring expression suggests (as an implicature) that Shechem has the upper hand in terms of social and political power to abduct Dinah compared to the social status of the Jacob and his family, who were recent incomers to the land. Abductive marriage requires physical power to resist possible confrontation by the girl's family and clan, and political and social superiority in order to influence the girl's family to accept the marriage negotiation. A person attempting abductive marriage always tries to exploit any weak side of the girl's family. This is because when a girl is abducted for marriage the girl's family feels that their honor is violated. Consequently they may react to abort the abductive marriage in order to restore their honor. If the girl's family and clan manage to abort the abductive marriage of their daughter and bring the girl back home it is also terribly humiliating for the man, his family, and his whole clan. Thus, besides aborting the abductive marriage the girl's family can be revenged.

---

113. Blyth, "Terrible Silence," 189.
114. Parry, *Old Testament Story*, 136; Wenham, *Genesis 16–50*, 310.

Dinah Story as an Adverse Consequence of the Unfulfilled Vow

Narrative Tension: The Abduction and the Failed Marriage Negotiation (34:2b–12)

וַיִּקַּח אֹתָהּ וַיִּשְׁכַּב אֹתָהּ וַיְעַנֶּהָ[115]

"He seized her and lay with her and humbled/humiliated her." (34:2b)[116]

I have already noted above that almost all scholars claim that Dinah was raped.[117] However, very few scholars believe that Shechem married Dinah by abduction.[118] Although they do not see the sexual relation between Dinah and Shechem as abductive marriage, Bechtel and Wolde also take the position that the story does not denote rape.[119]

Was Dinah really raped? The narrator tells us that וַיִּקַּח אֹתָהּ "Shechem took her" (34:2); וַיִּשְׁכַּב אֹתָהּ "he had sexual intercourse with her," וַיְעַנֶּהָ "and he humiliated her." Gunkel translates the phrase וַיִּקַּח אֹתָהּ "he took her" as he kidnapped her, abducted her."[120] This expression in this particular context of sexual violence (which will be discussed below) denotes that Shechem seized or snatched Dinah by force and took her before he actually had violent sexual intercourse with her.[121] Jubilee says that "they carried off Dinah" which denotes that probably a group of people took or carried her for Shechem which is a common characteristic of abductive marriage.[122] If this is the case, then presumably the expression "Shechem took her" is synecdoche because probably others took Dinah by force and Shechem asked them to do it. Thus, Shechem's action of taking Dinah in this context implies that Dinah was taken aggressively and violently to a particular location which is convenient for Shechem. Probably he took her to his house, because this accords with the above-mentioned participant introduction (son of the ruler).[123] There, he would not have been afraid of

---

115. The vayiqtol and polysydeton construction in this sentence signify the emphasis on each element of the list.

116. My translation.

117. Sternberg, *Poetics of Biblical Narrative*, 446; Wenham, *Genesis 16–50*, 311; Gunkel, *Genesis*, 358; Fields, *Sodom and Gomorrah*; Miller, "Sexual Offences," 50; Parry, *Old Testament Story*, 137; Yamada, "Configurations"; Blyth, "Terrible Silence," 36.

118. Fleshman, "Simeon and Levi," 112.

119. Bechtel, "Dinah," 27ff.; van Wolde, "Inna," 542–43.

120. Gunkel, *Genesis*, 358.

121. Blyth, "Terrible Silence," 48ff.

122. Charles, *Jubilees*, 153.

123. Parry, *Old Testament Story*, 137.

Reading and Translating Genesis 28:10—35:15 as a Votive Narrative

Dinah's family attempting to confront him in order to take her back. Such behavior in abductive marriage is very shaming to the family of the girl if the society is a shame/honor oriented society, which may provoke them to a potential revenge in order to restore their honor.[124]

Second, the narrator tells us that Shechem וישכב אתה "laid her" (literally) ויענה "and he humiliated/humbled her" (Gen. 34:2) which (the combination of both וישכב אתה and ויענה) implies that he had sexual intercourse by force without her consent and before any appropriate marriage approval of Dinah's family (Gen 34:2).[125] Parry also observes that שכב with direct object אתה marks the narrator's negative evaluation of the Shechem's coercive sexual behavior.[126] However, the Hebrew phrase וישכב אתה does not help us in terms of describing Shechem's sexual behavior with Dinah as rape because it seems that "rape" is not lexicalized in Hebrew. For example, a clear sexual activity which should be translated into English as "rape" was mentioned as וישכב עמה "lay or have a sexual intercourse with her" in Deuteronomy 22:25.

Van Wolde attempts to make a distinction between physical sexual violence against Dinah and her social debasement effected by the same in that she interprets ויענה, in this context, "as a debasement of Dinah from a social-juridical point of view" opposed to physical sexual violence.[127] Nevertheless, I argue that pragmatically the two cannot be separated both from the point of view of Dinah's experience as well as from the mental representation of the event by the narrator and his public representation of the same in that particular social context.[128]

וַתִּדְבַּק נַפְשׁוֹ בְּדִינָה בַּת־יַעֲקֹב וַיֶּאֱהַב אֶת־הַנַּעֲרָ וַיְדַבֵּר עַל־לֵב הַנַּעֲרָ

And his soul was drawn to Dinah daughter of Jacob; he loved the girl, and spoke tenderly to her. (34:3)

In verses 3–4, the narrator tells us that Shechem loved Dinah so much that he moved swiftly to settle the matter by marriage negotiation. The expression ותדבק נפש בדינה בת־יעקב ויאהב את־הנער וידבר על־לב הנער "His

---

124. Israelites are described as "heavily group-oriented, and shame relied predominantly on external group pressure, while being reinforced by the internal pressure of fear of shaming . . . [that they] take revenge" (Bechtel, "Shame," 76).

125. Bechtel, "Dinah," 23–26; Blyth "Terrible Silence," 44ff., 54ff.

126. Parry, *Old Testament Story*, 138–39.

127. Van Wolde, "Inna," 543–44.

128. In this context ויענה could mean loss of soundness, purity, and integrity of her virginity and consequently making her defective or deteriorating her moral value of virginity in the society.

Dinah Story as an Adverse Consequence of the Unfulfilled Vow

soul was bonded with Dinah the daughter of Jacob and he loved the girl and he spoke to her heart" denotes Shechem's deep emotional expression of love, which can be explained better in the context of abductive marriage than in the context of rape (despite the arguments of Blyth and others).[129] In terms of the abductive marriage, first of all, the abductor abducts a girl because he loves her. He does this because he believes that he does not have any other way of making her his own. Then the abductor does his best to win the consent of the abducted girl. This is because it is also common that in the course of marriage negotiation, the girl's family may ask whether the girl consents to marry the abductor before they proceed with any further formal negotiations. If that is not the case there is no need for the negotiation because there is no guarantee that she will stay with him in the marriage relationship. The girl may run away any time when she finds an opportunity to escape, no matter what. Thus the expression "he spoke to the heart of the girl" implies that Shechem was keen in this regard, and his affectionate behavior and his verbal expression of love was aimed to attracted Dinah's heart so that she should consent to marry him if her family also consents to let him marry her. It is interesting that the narrator included even this feature of the event in his narration. Whether the expression "he spoke to her heart" implies that Dinah eventually consented to marry Shechem is controversial as the discussions of Sternberg and Leeb, among others, show and I do not intend to address it here.[130] But we know that at least he tried to engage her heart though we do not know whether he was successful.

Did Shechem suddenly fall in love with Dinah after having sexual intercourse with her by raping or did he love her even before having sexual intercourse with her? Bechtel remarks that "sociological studies reveal that rapists feel hostility and hatred toward their victims, not love."[131] On the contrary, the story tells us that Shechem loves Dinah, his heart was bonded to her, and he immediately sought to engage her heart and then proceeds to marriage negotiation. This feature of the episode will make better sense if it is interpreted in the context of abductive marriage. Shechem must have fallen in love with Dinah, not after sexual intercourse with her, but before, and that is why he abducted her for marriage. Thus the relationship between Shechem's love for Dinah and his violent sexual intercourse with Dinah will make sense when it is interpreted in the context of the abduc-

---

129. Blyth, "Terrible Silence," 138ff.
130. Sternberg, "Biblical Poetics," 475–79; Leeb, "Translating," 116.
131. Bechtel, "Dinah," 29.

tive marriage. Otherwise it is less plausible to hold that he raped her only to satisfy his selfish sexual desire, after which he unexpectedly fell in love with her.[132] Hence, although I sympathize with Dinah's point of view about what happened to her, according to my reading of the story Shechem's violent sexual behavior with Dinah and his excited move to settle the matter by marriage negotiation is better understood as an abductive marriage attempt rather than as rape.

This is exactly what happens with the abductive marriage practice as the Hadiyya practice of abductive marriage shows: first, the man who intends to marry a girl by abduction spies the scene, when he finds an opportunity he comes with a few other strong men, snatches the girl while she is trying to scream and call for help, he has sexual intercourse with her by force, and then he takes her to a place which he and his friends believe is a convenient place to hide her from her relatives in order to avoid any possible confrontation with the girl's family to abort the abductive marriage in order to restore their honor (34:7).

As I mentioned above, the next essential action of the abductor is having sexual intercourse with the girl as immediately as possible. The act of sexual intercourse is violent or forceful because the abducted girl never consents to such sexual intercourse.[133] Full intercourse is necessary for the following reasons. First, usually it is assumed that the abducted girl is a virgin. Therefore, the abductors believe that once an abductor has a sexual intercourse with the virgin girl she will eventually consent to marry him. My own experience also shows that most girls prefer to marry their abductor rather than being taken back home because it is doubtful in the society that they will get another husband. Abductors too assume that the girl's parents and relatives might also be willing to consent for the same reason.

Thus, though the physical behavior of the sexual intercourse of both rape and abductive marriage is evidently violent and humiliating to the girl, there is a clear difference between rape and abductive marriage in terms of the intention and motivation behind them. The sexual action of a rape is motivated to satisfy one's sexual appetite and then abandon

---

132. Sternberg, "Biblical Poetics," 474.

133. I can still recall, once when I was very small boy, I observed personally such violent sexual intercourse of abductive marriage. On one occasion a group of strong young men abducted a girl for the purpose of marriage to their friend. First they spied to locate the girl. Then they snatched her by force and took her to a far off village to someone's house. When they got to the house they put the girl in a quiet corner and let the man have sexual intercourse with the girl immediately. But the girl refused to consent until two young men helped him by holding the girl's legs and arms so that he could have successful sexual intercourse.

the victim. In addition a rapist attempts to keep his rape a secret. Consequently he does not take steps to make himself known to the public in association with the rape. On the contrary, the motivation of sexual act of abductive marriage is intended as a means of securing the consent of the victim and her family to marriage. That is why the abductor keeps the victim with him and takes steps to make himself known to the public as an abductor, sincerely interested to marry the girl, just as Shechem did. Thus there is an apparent difference between the sexual violence of rape and abductive marriage.

Thus Dinah's case is better explained as an abductive marriage, because Shechem's behavior of abducting the girl, having sex with her in a violent manner, keeping her with him, and then initiating marriage negotiation with her parents and family seeking their consent, evidently exhibits the nature of abductive marriage. Therefore, reading this story as an abductive marriage is more plausible than reading as a rape.[134]

As I mentioned above, another essential step of the abductive marriage is initiating marriage negotiation by sending messengers to the family of the girl after abducting her. The messengers will inform to the family that the girl is with them and they are ready to do anything they demand of them, as a restitution and as a marriage dowry. The negotiation may take some time because in some cases the parents may not be willing to accept the deal easily. This is what Shechem and Hamor did. In verse 4 the narrator tells us that Shechem asked his father Hamor to go and initiate negotiation with the family of Dinah:

וַיֹּאמֶר שְׁכֶם אֶל־חֲמוֹר אָבִיו לֵאמֹר קַח־לִי אֶת־הַיַּלְדָּה הַזֹּאת לְאִשָּׁה׃

So Shechem spoke to his father Hamor, saying, "Get me this girl to be my wife." (34:4)

In verse 6 we are told that Shechem went to Jacob for the negotiation. In verse 7 the story tells us that Jacob's children came from the field probably called by their father about this matter. In verses 8–12 the narrator tells us that Hamor spoke to the family of Dinah politely and persuasively. He pleaded with them saying: "Let me find favor with you, and whatever you say to me I will give. Put the marriage present and gift as high as you like, and I will give whatever you ask me; only give me the girl to be my son's wife" (vv. 11b–12).

---

134. Even the story of the Israelites in Judges which allowed the Benjaminite men to marry other Israelite women by abduction, (Judg 21:19–24) shows that probably the behavior of abductive marriage is not totally foreign to the ancient Near Eastern culture after all.

Reading and Translating Genesis 28:10—35:15 as a Votive Narrative

It is natural for the family of a girl to consult one another and make a decision before they respond to the negotiators just as Jacob and his children did (vv. 5, 7). It is also reasonable for Jacob, as the head of the family, to seek to resolve this matter by consenting to the marriage because in his situation that seems the best option for Dinah, for Jacob and his family, and for Shechem and Hamor as the whole narrative representation of vv. 4–12 shows. Hence, at this stage Jacob's silence of verse 5 was likely from a prudence thinking that it is good to discuss with his children what to do.

Narrative Tension Intensifies (34:13–31)

However, the narrator tells us that things got out of Jacob's hand for the worse when his children במרמה "tricked" Shechem and Hamor (34:13–17) and eventually massacred them (34:25–29). The revenge was not directed only against Shechem and Hamor but against the whole Shechemite group because a conflict of abductive marriage in a group oriented society is an issue of honoring and shaming the whole clan, not only the abductor and his immediate family. They killed all the Shechemites presumably in order to avoid any possible retaliation if they revenge against Shechem and Hamor only. Unfortunately Jacob's children were ignorant about the Shechemites' connection to the Canaanites and Perezzites about which Jacob was very well aware of (34:30).

The most important feature in this episode is that the narrator develops his point of view that Jacob was in a difficult situation in both cases. Even if Jacob and his family agree to resolve this crisis by consenting with the marriage of Dinah and Shechem, the Shechemites' motive was opportunistic, because ultimately they may suppress Israel and grab all their property for themselves (34:23). This proposal was treacherous because the Israelites, the minority ethnic group (only one family at that time), would eventually be absorbed by the Shechemites, which would lead to a subsequent extinction of the chosen people of God from existing as a distinct social and ethnic group for Yahweh. Social scientists have observed that any powerful dominant social group who works to build a homogeneous cultural nation creates a strategy to assimilate a minority group.[135]

However, the revenge of Levi and Simeon which resulted in killing all the Shechemites and plundering their property, their wives, and their children risked the worst and most dangerous revenge of the Canaanites

---

135. Hutchinson and Smith, *Ethnicity*, 12–13.

Dinah Story as an Adverse Consequence of the Unfulfilled Vow

and Perezzites against the Israelites.[136] Thus, the Israelites' very existence was in danger of extermination by the imminent revenge of Canaanites and Perizzites. Consequently, the narrator tells us that the revenge of Levi and Simeon did not resolve the crisis; rather it triggered another danger for Jacob; thus complicating the situation further (34:30–31). Hence, the narrator shows that in both cases Jacob was in a very difficult situation because the very existence of the chosen people of God was threatened with extermination.

The narrator also shows that Levi and Simeon behaved strangely to their father (v. 31) that Jacob was angry with them and he never affirmed the action of Levi and Simeon even until his death (Gen 34:30; 49:5–7). Jacob was angry at what Simeon and Levi did because they had killed all the Shechemites unjustly when there was no declared war between them (49:5–7). He also foresaw that the aftermath of their killing may trigger revenge against his family which will put the whole family in danger (Gen 34:30; 49:5–7).[137]

However, Simeon and Levi are still exaggerating the problem ignoring the aftermath. Their response to Jacob is quite interesting and it could be interpreted in the context of abductive marriage: הַכְזוֹנָה יַעֲשֶׂה אֶת־אֲחוֹתֵנוּ: "Should our sister be treated like a whore?" (Gen 34:31). This kind of exaggerated response, from the family of the abducted girl, who were already boiling with anger because their honor had been threatened by abducting their daughter, is expected and it is meant to show that they hold the abductor responsible for his action. Thus, what Simeon and Levi are saying to Jacob is that if Shechem was sincerely interested in marrying Dinah and has a sense of respect and honor for her family he would have come and asked their permission to marry her rather than taking her by force and having sexual intercourse with her and then ask for their permission for marriage. For a shame-and-honor oriented society this is a grave matter.[138] The narrator's public representation remarks this point when he says: "When they heard of it, the men were indignant and very angry, because he had committed an outrage in Israel[139] by lying with Jacob's daughter, for such a thing ought not to be done" (34:7). One can imagine how they must have felt, which eventually led them to revenge her.

---

136. Bechtel, "Dinah," 34. On Israel see also appendix 1.
137. Parry, *Old Testament Story*, 104.
138. Blyth, "Terrible Silence," 115.
139. See appendix 1

It is worth noting that according to the narrator the crisis of the Dinah story was not ended by the massacre of the Shechemites which only made the situation worse for Jacob and his family. Therefore, the response of Simeon and Levi to their father is not the end of the story, rather it remarks a further narrative tension. As the narrative shows the complication was intensified by the fear of revenge (34:30–31). It is the aftermath of the killing which is in focus now. The narrator did not intend to conclude the story in 34:30–31, rather he presents a further intensified narrative tension which will be resolved only by Jacob's fulfilling his vow as Genesis 35:1–15 shows. The mistake that most readers of the Dinah story make is that they stop reading the story at 34:31, yet the narrative is continuing. From this reading Dinah is quite incidental to the story—she drops out and is not mentioned again, probably not because of the androcentric intention of the narrator but because of the narrative motif of the story.[140]

Therefore, I argue that this crisis is congruent to the votive narrative of Jacob and it happened to him as a consequence of his unfulfilled vow and serves to remind him to fulfill it. In order to show this point of view the narrator tells us that Jacob was in difficult situation in both options; and the situation was going from bad to worse until he finally fulfills his vow and restores his breached relationship with Yahweh, his protector and provider.

One may ask why Dinah and the Shechemites suffer for the wrong Jacob did. Our reading of the Dinah episode shows that the narrator was not approving what Shechem did to Dinah. Nor is he approving what Simeon and Levi did to the Shechemites. What he is telling us is that Jacob's failure to fulfill his vow in Bethel breached his relationship with God, his protector and provider. Consequently, God withdrew his protection which resulted in bad relations within his family and with his good neighbors. The story in 34:30–31 implies that Jacob must have been wondering why God allowed such a terrible thing to happen, which really became a threat for the existence of the promised seed; he must have been asking himself, why did Yahweh allow these things happen to him?

Narrative Resolution

We can observe once again that Jacob manifests as a main character/participant of the Dinah story—no mention of Dinah after 34:5; no mention of Shechem, Hamor, and Shechemites after 34:29; and no mention

140. Blyth, "Terrible Silence," 3, 76ff.

of Jacob's children either after 34:31. Thus, all of them vanish from the episode and there is no mention of them again after 34:31. When the minor participants of the story vanish after a satisfactory resolution of the episode which closes with them in 34:31, the narrator picks of Jacob again in 35:1 and proceeds with the narrative-resolution. The resolution comes at the climax of the crisis: a dangerous threat of revenge of Canaanites and Perezites against Jacob and his family. The threat was resolved only by God's intervention when Jacob responded to God's reminder to fulfill his vow in Bethel (35:1–15).

35:1 וַיֹּאמֶר אֱלֹהִים אֶל־יַעֲקֹב קוּם עֲלֵה בֵית־אֵל וְשֶׁב־שָׁם וַעֲשֵׂה־שָׁם מִזְבֵּחַ לָאֵל הַנִּרְאֶה אֵלֶיךָ בְּבָרְחֲךָ מִפְּנֵי עֵשָׂו אָחִיךָ:

> God said to Jacob, "Arise, go up to Bethel, and settle there. Make an altar there to the God who appeared to you when you fled from your brother Esau." (Gen 35:1)

One can observe that this utterance of God is echoic of the event of Bethel. It is directly connected to the Bethel-event in general and to the votive utterance of Jacob in particular. This was exactly what Jacob promised to God in Bethel if God would grant his votive plea (28:18–22).

God spoke to Jacob when he was confused and perplexed by the imminent threat of the Canaanites' and Perezzites' revenge, presumably wondering why God let this terrible crisis happen to the chosen line. What happened to the promise of God made in Bethel to protect him (28:13–15)? Thus the narrator shows that Jacob was not prompted by the adverse consequence of the unfulfilled vow probably because he thought that he has fulfilled his vow in Shechem, the place he considered as compatible with Bethel. Therefore, the narrator tells us that, God had to remind him verbally to go to Bethel and fulfill his vow there. This implies that God was reminding Jacob that if he still refuses to fulfill his vow in Bethel, then he is responsible for the worse consequences yet to come; and he can't blame God for that. At that moment Jacob's memory was prompted because of the contextual assumptions of vow and about the adverse consequence of the unfulfilled votive promise which he remembered he immediately sets off on his way to Bethel:

35:2 וַיֹּאמֶר יַעֲקֹב אֶל־בֵּיתוֹ וְאֶל כָּל־אֲשֶׁר עִמּוֹ הָסִרוּ אֶת־אֱלֹהֵי הַנֵּכָר אֲשֶׁר בְּתֹכְכֶם וְהִטַּהֲרוּ וְהַחֲלִיפוּ שִׂמְלֹתֵיכֶם:

35:3 וְנָקוּמָה וְנַעֲלֶה בֵּית־אֵל וְאֶעֱשֶׂה־שָּׁם מִזְבֵּחַ לָאֵל הָעֹנֶה אֹתִי בְּיוֹם צָרָתִי וַיְהִי עִמָּדִי בַּדֶּרֶךְ אֲשֶׁר הָלָכְתִּי:

Reading and Translating Genesis 28:10—35:15 as a Votive Narrative

> So Jacob said to his household and to all who were with him, "Put away the foreign gods that are among you, and purify yourselves, and change your clothes; and let us rise and let us go up to Bethel, that I may make an altar there to the God who answered me in the day of my distress and has been with me wherever I have gone." (35:2–3)

This textual evidence shows that Jacob responded promptly. Hence, when Jacob responded positively to fulfill his vow in Bethel God's protection resumed: "As they journeyed, a terror from God fell upon the cities all around them, so that no one pursued them." This surely shows clearly that the crises of the Dinah story occurred as an adverse consequence of Jacob's failure to fulfill his vow. Therefore, Genesis 35:1–7 can be seen as a resolution of the narrative tension of the Dinah story of Genesis 34.

Unless Jacob promptly takes action to fulfill his vow in Bethel in order to restore his breached relationship with Yahweh worse was about to happen, not only losing their possessions, even their own very existence will be threatened. The narrative organization and representation of the Dinah story shows that this is the narrator's point of view.

The expression וְנָקוּמָה וְנַעֲלֶה בֵּית־אֵל וְאֶעֱשֶׂה־שָּׁם מִזְבֵּחַ "Arise, ... go to Bethel and build an altar there" in Genesis 35:1 is contrasted to the altar Jacob built in Shechem (Gen 33:20). Some scholars confuse the narrative connection between the reference of Shechem and Bethel in Genesis 33 and in Genesis 35, and perceive it as intended to show a progression of the sanctuary from Shechem to Gilgal, from Gilgal to Bethel, from Bethel to Shiloh, and from Shiloh to Jerusalem.[141] However, though he failed to read the Dinah story in the framework of the votive narrative and within the context of the social institution of vow, Dumbrell rightly observes that the immediate context of Genesis 35 is Genesis 34, which "provides the rationale for the move from Shechem to Bethel."[142] He observes that Jacob's movement from Shechem to Bethel is occasioned by the incident of Genesis 34 in that "Genesis 35 presents us with the account of the movement from Shechem to Bethel, occasioned, we are to understand, by the incident of Genesis 34."[143]

What is the narrative connection between these two places? Apparently it is something to do with the building of an altar. Jacob pledged to build an altar in Bethel in his return to Canaan as a fulfillment of his vow

---

141. Dumbrell, "Role of Bethel," 69.
142. Ibid., 68.
143. Ibid., 68.

Dinah Story as an Adverse Consequence of the Unfulfilled Vow

to God. But he built it in Shechem which was unacceptable to God because Shechem is not the chosen place of God. So the tragedy happens to him and God reminds him to go to Bethel and fulfill his vow. Accordingly, at last, Jacob fulfils his vow in Bethel:

וַיָּבֹא יַעֲקֹב לוּזָה אֲשֶׁר בְּאֶרֶץ כְּנַעַן הִוא בֵּית־אֵל הוּא וְכָל־הָעָם אֲשֶׁר־עִמּוֹ:
וַיִּבֶן שָׁם מִזְבֵּחַ וַיִּקְרָא לַמָּקוֹם אֵל בֵּית־אֵל כִּי שָׁם נִגְלוּ אֵלָיו הָאֱלֹהִים
בְּבָרְחוֹ מִפְּנֵי אָחִיו:

Jacob came to Luz (that is, Bethel), which is in the land of Canaan, he and all the people who were with him, and there he built an altar and called the place El-bethel, because it was there that God had revealed himself to him when he fled from his brother. (35:6–7)

This text shows an apparent narrative connection between Shechem (33:18–20) and Bethel (35:1–15). Dumbrell observes that "there is no other Biblical context which links Bethel and Shechem" except this story.[144]

Finally we observe that the narrator artistically provides a key narrative component in Genesis 35:1–7 in order to accomplish three things regarding the coherence of Jacob's votive narrative:

1. It connects the entire votive narrative unite back to Genesis 28:10–22; we see that 35:1, 7 brings us back to 28:10–22.
2. It connects the episode of Genesis 34 to the immediate preceding story of Genesis 33.
3. It provides a clearly stated resolution (final cognitive effects) of the narrative tension or complication of Genesis 34 because it is when Jacob sets out to Bethel to fulfill his vow that God's protection for Jacob resumed as the narrator says: "As they journeyed, a terror from God fell upon the cities all around them, so that no one pursued them" (Gen 35:5).

Hence, in the light of this close reading of the Dinah story, the episodes of the story could be set out as follows:

- 34:1–2a: setting.
- 34:2b–3: Narrative tension or incitement: abduction for marriage.
- 34:4–10: Negotiation for abductive marriage.
- 34:11–17: The negotiation fails: The sons of Jacob plan to trick Shechem and Hamor.

144. Ibid., 69.

- 34:18–24: Shechem and Hamor naively/innocently accept the deceptive offer of abductive marriage negotiation and get circumcised.
- 34:25–29: Massacre of Shechemites, by Simeon and Levi.
- 34:30–31: Narrative tension intensifies further, threatening the very existence of Israelites.
- 35:1–7: Resolution of the narrative tension: Jacob's going to Bethel and building an altar in Bethel in order to fulfill his vow.
- 35:8–15: Post peak or post resolution: the narrator tells us what happened after the resolution.

Conclusion

It has been shown that the narrative scope of the Dinah story covers 34:1—35:15; the Dinah story is misread because it has not been read in the framework of the votive narrative; Shechem did not rape Dinah, rather he attempted to marry her by abduction; his attempt to abduct triggered a terrible catastrophe because God's protection for Jacob was breached as an adverse consequence of Jacob's unfulfilled vow; the structure of the narrative representation and the resolution of the narrative tension (35:1–7) is a textual evidence for reading the Dinah story as an integral part of Jacob's votive narrative. Finally, further textual evidence in the post-peak of the narrative tension of the Dinah story shows that the tragedy of the Dinah story is intended to represent the adverse consequence of Jacob's unfulfilled vow.

The narrator's strategic design of the linguistic organization of the public representation of the Dinah story does not "allow his readers to give unqualified approval or disapproval to any of the characters in the story."[145] This suggests that his intention rested on something else other than the characters of the story. The artistic tactic of his narrative representation aims to influence his readers to his point of view: the crisis of Genesis 34 happened to Jacob because he failed to fulfill his vow in Bethel. The peaceful relation between Jacob and the Shechemites was destroyed because God's protection to Jacob was breached because of this offence. For Jacob, going to Bethel in order to fulfill his vow to God was part of worshiping Yahweh as his patron deity. To fail to do so implies that he had become unfaithful to him.

---

145. Parry, *Old Testament Story*, xix.

Dinah Story as an Adverse Consequence of the Unfulfilled Vow

Therefore, it can be seen that Genesis 28:10—35:15 is a coherent and cogent votive narrative unit which deals with Jacob's vow making, vow granting, unfulfilled vow, and the adverse consequence of the unfulfilled vow. Thus the narrator used the scheme of the vow of Bethel as a structural framework for the narrative unit. By the adverse consequences of the unfulfilled vow (crisis of Gen 34) Jacob was reminded to fulfill his vow. Jacob, who was shocked by the consequences, fulfills his vow swiftly and then God's protection and patron relationship resumes immediately. To miss this narrator's point of view in reading the Dinah story would destroy the entire discourse structure of this narrative unit as Bar-Efrat says:

> An isolated incident receives its significance from its position and role in the system as a whole. The incidents are like building blocks, each one contributing its part to the entire edifice, and hence their importance. In the building which is the plot there are no excess or meaningless blocks. The removal of any one may cause the entire structure to collapse or at least damage its functional and aesthetic perfection.[146]

Hence, in order to avoid such a tragic effect to this narrative unit, the Dinah story must be read within the context of the social institution of the vow of ancient Israel and within the framework of the vow of Bethel which comprise Genesis 28:10—35:15 as a votive narrative.

---

146. Bar-Efrat, *Narrative Art*, 93.

7

Conclusion with Remarks on Implications for Translation

Overview

THIS RESEARCH HAS DEMONSTRATED that understanding a communicative intention of the utterance or a text within its primary contextual framework is a crucial step for Bible translation and interpretation task. Hence, since an utterance or discourse is totally dependent on the context, access to the contextual assumptions of an utterance of the biblical texts is a key factor in understanding the communicative intention of the narrator before we translate them. In this dissertation we have seen that the context of the biblical discourses comprises both textual and para-textual context which were in the cognitive environment of the primary audience. I have also shown that Genesis 25:19—37:1 is a coherent narrative unit within which the votive narrative of Jacob (Gen 28:10—35:15) is embedded.

Inaccessibility to the original contextual assumptions of the vow and the votive narrative of Jacob story has created such a serious problem for the interpreters and translators that they misunderstood the coherence of the narrative and treated the episodes of the narrative as isolated. This is because the interpreters and translators, who are the secondary communicators of the biblical texts, are not privileged to have access to the full contextual assumptions of the primary communication. We have seen that, as a result, the votive narrative of Jacob in general and the Dinah story in particular have been mistranslated over the centuries. Therefore,

Conclusion with Remarks on Implications for Translation

in my discussion, throughout this dissertation, I have attempted to bring out the correct interpretation of the narrative unit so that it can be translated correctly.

My primary empirical research on Hadiyya cultural conceptions about their vow and their marriage institutions involved a significant number of the Hadiyya community members in order to receive some insight about these issues. Although I myself am a Hadiyya, doing the research was necessary so that I should not rely only on my own views but have evidence of the community's collective opinions. Then I examined the ancient Near Eastern cultural context and other related areas' cultural context about the vow from secondary sources and I have shown that the Hadiyya concept of vow and the ANE concept of vow force us to reconsider our understanding about the Old Testament concept of a vow.

I have explored and defined the ancient Hebrew concept נדר "vow" as it was perceived and used in the ancient Near Eastern cultural context, in that of other related areas, and in the literature of ancient Israel and noted similarities with Hadiyya culture. My research has shown that in all these cases their perception of the vow and practices in relation to vowing are similar to those of their Hebrew counterpart. In all these cultures vow making is conditional, taken in the context of prayer because of distress, and motivated by seeking relief from it. In all cases the content of votive prayers is the promise of public praises in a particular manner, the vow is binding—it must be fulfilled, and the fulfillment of the vow should be in the place where the deity resides. Finally, all unfulfilled vows have adverse consequence.

A description of the essence of the biblical vow has brought out the striking similarities with the concept and practices of vowing in all these other cultures. The biblical vow is a human commissive speech act of solemn commitment directed only to God in the context of distress seeking to get relief from God to be fulfilled only if God honors the petitioner by granting his votive plea. It is a conditional solemn promise to God by humans in which a commitment is made to respond to the deity in a specified way. The Hebrew vow is a conventionalized utterance, operating within a social institution and gives rise to conventional contextual assumptions: the expectation of the grant of a desirable outcome from God and an obligation to fulfill the votive commitment made to God. A further expectation of adverse consequences is raised if the votive commitment remains unfulfilled by the petitioner. These features of the biblical vow are in contrast with the oath, the covenant, and other similar concepts and commissive speech acts. And thus we have established that נדר is a strictly binding social institution which involves a conditional commissive speech act that adverse consequences are to be expected for all unfulfilled vows.

I also showed that the concept נדר comprises distinct encyclopedic information in the cognitive environment of the contemporary audience of the communicator with which the audience interacted in the course of their inferential processing of the votive utterance. The contextual assumptions and implications of the votive utterance of Jacob have been clarified in this way using the cognitive principle of relevance theory.

The metarepresentational reading of Genesis 28:10–22 shows that Jacob made an echoic votive utterance to the commissive speech act of God in his dream (28:13b–15) with an endorsing attitude. Thus, Jacob's votive utterance has apparent interpretive resemblance with the utterance of God. Jacob made a votive commitment to respond to God in thanksgiving if God grants his plea. Consequently, he puts himself under inescapable obligation. Thus, his votive utterance raises an expectation of relevance and, hence, Jacob's vow at Bethel functions as a cohesive theme of Genesis 28:10—35:15. I have shown that the vow-granting, vow-fulfilling, and adverse consequence of the unfulfilled vow of this utterance was represented in Genesis 29:1—35:15:

- God grants Jacob's votive plea for protection (31:1–55; 32:2—33:17).
- God grants Jacob's plea for prosperity and provision (29:14b—32:10).
- God grants Jacob's plea to return to his father's house in peace (31:3; 33:17–18).
- Jacob's laxity in fulfilling his votive commitment to God in Bethel (33:18–20) and the adverse consequence of his laxity (Gen 34:1—35:15).

Therefore, I have described Genesis 28:10—35:15 as a votive-narrative of Jacob. I have also argued that the linguistic or public representation of the cognitive organization of the narrative of Genesis 29:1—33:15 is an evaluative one: the narrator represents his point of view about God and Jacob regarding the fulfillment of the votive utterance of Jacob in Bethel clearly (Gen 28:10–22). On the one hand, the narrator represents God as a divine power who faithfully granted Jacob's votive plea, as his caring and loving patron. On the other hand, he represents Jacob as a God's chosen patriarch but as one who neglected to fulfill his votive promise to his patron God. I have shown that from time to time each of these is a strong inference within the institution of vow, throughout chapters 29:1—35:15.

Conclusion with Remarks on Implications for Translation

Often God's granting of the vow is left to inference, and recognized in the way that various tensions are resolved. Jacob's role in resolving them is not emphasized. This was the narrator's point of view and an intended contextual implication of the story.

I have also noted that the narrator would be entitled to presume that his audience could envisage for themselves the imminent adverse consequences of Jacob's failed votive promise because the story is presented within the framework of the social institution of vow and in the context of the votive narrative. This would be so, since the narrator and readers of the primary communication have the same mutually shared knowledge about the unfulfilled נדר "vow" so that the narrator moves straight to chapter 34 to represent the adverse consequence without any further explanation about Jacob's laxity in fulfilling his vow. The narrator manifestly intends that the readers of the story draw the intended contextual implication from what he has already said, stimulated by the optimally relevant ostensive indications in the narrative as well as mutually shared knowledge about the utterance of נדר in Genesis 28:10–22.

Thus, I challenge interpreters and translators of the story to read the whole narrative unit within the context of the institution of the ancient Israelites' vow and within the framework of the votive narrative which comprises vow making, vow granting and vow fulfilling. Such reading of this narrative unit is crucially important for the task of translating the same.

When I show that Genesis 34 represents the adverse consequences of Jacob's unfulfilled vow I have also argued that Shechem meant to achieve an abductive marriage and did not rape Dinah when he took her by force and had sexual intercourse with her. I attempted to support this view by finding out the opinions of Hadiyya people whose customs include diverse marriage institutions, including abductive marriage. I concluded that describing the narrated sexual relationship between Dinah and Shechem as abductive marriage is more plausible than describing it as a rape.

I have also suggested that the attempted abductive marriage of Shechem could have been a threat for the very existence of the chosen line of God's people because of Jacob's laxity in fulfilling his vow in Bethel. But when Jacob fulfilled his vow in Bethel, reminded by this adverse consequence, his relationship with God was re-established so that God's protection for him and his family was resumed.

Furthermore, I have shown that from the narrator's point of view, the Dinah episode was not intended for character evaluation of the

Reading and Translating Genesis 28:10—35:15 as a Votive Narrative

participants. So if we attempt to read it from the perspective of character evaluation we would be puzzled. Therefore, I argued that the narrative representation of the story shows that the narrator intended to explain that the catastrophe happened to Jacob because of his laxity in fulfilling his vow. This was my major hypothesis and I have maintained it throughout. I have also demonstrated that the structure of the narrative representation in general and the Dinah story in particular (34:1—35:15), as specifically manifested in its resolution of the tension (35:1–7), is the evidence for this claim. This structural evidence clearly shows that the Dinah story is an integral part of the votive narrative.

To sum up my conclusion, the evidences deduced from the votive narrative informed by relevance theory and the Hadiyya culture shows that Dinah story was clearly relevant to the Jacob story in the context of the Bethel story. The expectations of relevance raised by the vow made by Jacob in Bethel (Gen 28:10-22) and the anaphoric expressions employed by the narrator to 28:10-22 in Genesis 31:3, 13; 33:18; 35:1-15, which also includes Jacob's vow fulfilling as a narrative resolution, evidently show that the crisis of Genesis 34 was included in the Jacob story, deliberately putting it in that particular location, in order to explain that this crisis happened to Jacob because he failed to fulfill his vow to God in Bethel. So, I firmly maintain that the communicative intention toward this cognitive effect (conclusion), which will be drawn by inference, is sufficiently provided in the text as a whole by the ostensive communicative signals. Hence, although other readings are possible from the readers' point of view, this is clearly the main communicative intention and translators must aim to communicate this interpretation clearly.

However, the unavoidable challenge the translators face in this regard will be how to provide the needed adequate contextual assumptions of the primary communication of this story for the target readers of the translated text so that they may reconstruct them in order to interpret the story correctly. Though it is a difficult task, it is possible and must be done. Access to this phenomenon is necessary for the target readers so that they would be able to raise similar expectations of relevance of the votive narrative as the original readers did and make appropriate premises and conclusion(s) before they draw the intended cognitive effects as exactly intended by the original narrator. In this regard I wish to make the following brief remarks about how to translate this story at the risk of being simplistic.

Conclusion with Remarks on Implications for Translation

Remarks on Implications for Translation

The task of translation concerns mainly conveying the communicative intention of an utterance or text by making the interpretive resemblance as close as possible to the primary communication.[1] This could be achieved either by direct translation or by retelling it as a story.

A translator of Jacob's votive narrative will face many problems in the course of translating—linguistic, contextual, and others; and the scope of this work will not allow me to discuss them all. However, I want to make a few remarks regarding providing access to the necessary contextual assumptions which the primary audience had about the concept נדר "vow" and the votive narrative of Jacob for the target audience.

As I noted above, we have thoroughly discussed in this work the institutional nature of the Hebrew concept נדר and its encyclopedic information in the cognitive environment of the primary audience, which also comprises vow making, vow granting, and vow fulfilling. This institutional character is pertinent both in the actual practice of vowing and in the mental representation of the Hebrew concept נדר "vow" and votive narratives. It is a mutually shared contextual assumption (cognitive environment) which was manifest to the communicator and his primary audience. The question is then how we can make the cognitive environment of the secondary audience resemble the cognitive environment of the primary audience regarding the institution of the vow. This task is very crucial if they are to understand the relevant and intended cognitive effects from the translation.

Unless the reading of the translation of the Jacob-narrative is inferentially combined with the presumed contextual assumptions of the ancient Israelites' institution of the vow, the intended communication of this votive narrative will not reach the secondary readers. Therefore, it is

---

1. While I was attempting to suggest how to translate both the concept of נדר and the votive narrative of Jacob I made a brief review on other up-to-date Bible translations of the votive narrative of Jacob in order to see if there is any translation which translated the story from the votive narrative perspective. The overview of the sample versions shows that none of them treated the story as a votive narrative; rather they treated the coherent episodes of the votive narrative as isolated episodes. To my surprise, even the Amharic translation of the same story shows that, though the target audience is a vow conscious society, the translation was treated just like the English versions (See appendix 4). Thus, the translators failed to reconstruct this votive narrative, interpret it, and translate it within the context of the institution of vow and within the framework of the votive narrative of Jacob in Bethel. This calls for a suggestion of the better way of representing of this story into the target audiences in the translation task.

necessary to make a contextual adjustment in the translation task of the Hebrew concept נדר and Jacob's votive narrative.

If I were engaged in the real life of translating this narrative, the interpretation of this dissertation (which is my mental representation of the story) must have been naturally followed by the translation (public representation) of the same immediately because, as I noted above, translation and interpretation cannot be separated in the task of translation. Thus my mental representation of the story would be manifested by the linguistic organization of the translation into the target language. Hence, resolving all the relevant translation problems in order to construct an appropriate mental representation of the story and then making this manifest by the public representation of the target language is done at the same time by translators.

However, since I am not intending to do the actual translation of this narrative unit, I wish to remark strongly that all the necessary contextual assumptions which were left to be imagined by the primary audience of this narrative must be made accessible to any secondary audience, which does not have the same institution of the vow. For them, the votive nature of this discourse must be brought out in the translation process. In this regard, the secondary communicators (translators) have a responsibility to help their target audience by facilitating the accessibility of the relevant contextual assumptions.

But, as I mentioned above, how to make them available can be a challenge for Bible translators because of different practical reasons. Therefore, I wish to suggest two possible ways of translating the votive narrative of Jacob into the target languages: firstly, I will propose how to translate the Hebrew concept נדר and then, secondly I will propose how to translate the whole votive narrative of Jacob.

Translating the Hebrew Concept "נדר"

We have discussed the Hebrew concept נדר in chapter three where we listed the possible encyclopedic information of נדר. We need to access certain key contextual assumptions of this encyclopedic information in order to interpret and translate the votive narrative of Jacob. Now I would like to remark that it is equally essential to closely investigate the encyclopedic information of the concept of "vow," if there is any, in the receptor language before we attempt to do a contextual adjustment between them. Therefore, translators should explore the existing social institution and

Conclusion with Remarks on Implications for Translation

other similar comissive speech acts of the target community and compare it with the נדר in order to identify any closest concept in the target language. This will help translators to compare and evaluate whether the contextual assumptions of the concept vow is shared between the source and target languages.[2] If it is believed to be shared it is still better to check what areas of the Hebrew concept נדר are captured and what areas are not captured. For example, as my close investigation in chapter three shows the contextual assumptions of נדר is shared in both Hebrew and Hadiyya. But still I compared and contrasted the Hebrew concept נדר and the Hadiyya concept of vow which is lexicalized as *silet* in the current Hadiyya community. The comparison helped me to see that the two communities have similar concept of "vow" and they have a similar institutional value of the concept, but the Hebrew concept of vow is legislated while the Hadiyya concept of vow is not. For example, in ancient Hebrew a husband can make his wife's vow void while Hadiyya does not have such legislation. Hence, I believe that the translators of the Bible into the Hadiyya language can make a correct decision, where it is needed, in terms of contextual adjustment based on the comparison.

In addition, note that in my comparison of the Hadiyya concept of vow *silet* and the Hebrew concept of נדר "vow," in chapter three, the list of the encyclopedic information of the Hebrew concept of נדר "vow" was longer than the Hadiyya concept of vow *silet*. This is because the concept was legislated in Hebrew; which also shows that the practice of the vow and its institutional value in ancient Israel was accompanied by the legislation in order to prevent misuse or abuse of this institution and clarify some unclear cases of the vow institution which would result in adverse consequence otherwise. This is not the case in Hadiyya. Thus, it is probable that the Hadiyya concept of vow *silet* needs to be complemented in order to capture every feature of the ancient Hebrew concept of נדר "vow" in translation.

Therefore, it is imperative to help the target readers access the comprehensive contextual assumption of נדר by supplying the presupposed encyclopedic information or contextual assumptions, possibly by "spelling out the contextual implications" somewhere in the translation.[3] This access will prompt the new readers to broaden or narrow down the chosen

---

2. Harriet Hill, *Communicating Context*, categorizes the nature of shared contextual assumption between source and target languages into four: shared and believed to be shared, shared but not believed to be shared, not shared but believed to be shared, and not shared but believed to be shared, (see appendix 4).

3. Gutt, *Translation*, 79.

target concept of vow in each context according to the ad hoc principle of relevance-driven processing of lexicalized concepts in communication (see my note on ad hoc in chapter 1, section 1.5).[4] Thus, this will help the reader to understand and interpret the discourse in which the concept נדר occurs in a significant way.

In this regard, particular effort should be made if the target language does not have similar encyclopedic information and institutional value at all like the Hebrew נדר. In such circumstances the translators must help the target audience to access and grasp the ancient Hebrew worldview about the vow and votive narrative. Otherwise the translation of נדר will not be faithful to the original. The translators need to ask, "What is the best possible strategy of making the key encyclopedic information of the concept נדר accessible to the cross-cultural translation readers?" One may choose different strategies. But I propose that if there is no similar institution in the target language, then the translators should flesh out the original concept by employing weak comissive expressions and see how to make them into a strong comissive speech act like the Hebrew נדר. I suggest that this should be done both in the text and outside of the text.[5]

By "in the text and outside the text" we mean the use of a very strong comissive speech act expression in the text and then providing contextual adjustment outside of the text: in the footnote or glossary or introduction page or background-booklet. We may use more than one or all of them. Thus, "outside of the text" refers to providing the encyclopedic information outside of the text. When these two strategies are combined with the teaching, the target audience will be able to grasp the concept of the source language, and then eventually will interpret the discourse in which it occurs correctly.

Translating Jacob's Votive Narrative

When translators are engaged in translating this votive narrative they have to ask the following questions: To what extent are the readers able to see that God granted Jacob's votive plea? Do they understand that Jacob made inadequate fulfillment of his vow in Shechem? To what extend can they understand that Genesis 34 is an adverse consequence of the unfulfilled vow? To what extent has Jacob's dilemma of being trapped in the crisis been brought out? If these features of Jacob's votive narrative are brought

---

4. Carston, *Thoughts and Utterances*, 349–59.
5. Hill, *Cultural Crossroads*, 72–90.

Conclusion with Remarks on Implications for Translation

out clearly in the translation then the secondary communication is successful. I have shown that adequate access to the institutions of vow and abductive marriage will help the interpreters and translators to reconstruct the intended contextual implications of the story. Therefore, translators need to be aware of them and find a way of providing them for the target readers.

However, the Bible translators may have very limited freedom to incorporate all the contextual assumptions of the votive institution and the abductive marriage custom within the main text of the translation. Nevertheless, translators can employ some other techniques in order to guide the readers of their translation to the correct framework of the votive narrative so that they can process every episode of the narrative within that framework. One of the ways could be to provide relevant section headings referring to vow making, vow granting, vow fulfillment, the adverse consequences of the unfulfilled vow, and Shechem's attempted abductive marriage of Dinah. For example, one can provide the general section heading in Genesis 28:10 as "The votive narrative of Jacob" which is followed by different sub-section headings:

1. 28:10–22—Jacob makes a vow to God: The contextual assumptions of the Hebrew concept vow and its votive institution must be made accessible here in order to help the reader reconstruct appropriate contextual assumptions about the following chapters and draw correct contextual implication.

2. 29:1–33:17—God grants Jacob's votive plea: The implications of Jacob's vow in 28:10–22, as discussed in chapter five of this dissertation, must be brought out here.

3. 33:18–20—Jacob fails to fulfill his vow at the chosen place of God (Bethel): The implication of Jacob's laxity in fulfilling his vow in Bethel must be represented clearly in the translation.

4. 34:1–31—Jacob suffers the adverse consequence of the unfulfilled vow: Marriage and marriage institutions (marriage by wedding, levirate marriage, abductive marriage and concubine) of ancient Israel and the attempted abductive marriage of Shechem must be made accessible here. Further subsections may be added here such as 'Shechem's attempted abductive marriage of Dinah' if it is needed.

5. 35:1–15—Jacob goes to Bethel to fulfill his vow and God's protection resumes.

Reading and Translating Genesis 28:10—35:15 as a Votive Narrative

It is worth noting that what I have suggested about how to translate Jacob's votive narrative is just a sketch. I wish to remark again that the main goal of the translators in this regard should be to help the target readers of their translations access the contextual assumptions about the institution of ancient Hebrew vow and the votive narrative framework of the same. In this way the readers of the secondary communication will be able to interpret Jacob's votive narrative from the narrator's point of view.

In addition, the translation also should be organized in such a way that the contextual implications (ethical and moral implications) of this narrative can be drawn by the target readers. One can observe that this story has a theological implication: one should faithfully fulfill his/her votive promises and all other binding utterances to God as well as to others. Besides, we can deduce from the discourse that God is represented as always faithful to his promises. However, when humans fail to keep their vows and other binding commitments to God then they breach their relationship with God, which will result in terrible adverse consequences like suffering and shame in different ways.

The translation also may show that the narrator presumably intended to foster the institution of the God-chosen place of worship, whatever that God-chosen place might be. Therefore, the contextual assumptions about the importance of the institution of the place chosen by God as it is communicated by the narrative should be brought out in the contextual adjustment of the translation. As the story shows, the crisis of Genesis 34 resulted because Jacob failed to fulfill his vow in Bethel, which was the place chosen by God; and this was intended to strengthen the already existing contextual assumptions about the vow and the chosen place. Probably, this was one of the main cognitive effects of the narrative.

Finally I also suggest that this work will provide an opportunity for the OT readers and translators so that they can re-evaluate their reading and their translation of the votive narrative of Jacob in the light of this discussion. Hence, they can see for themselves whether the concept of the Hebrew vow and the votive narrative of Jacob have been perceived and read from the narrator's point of view and accordingly conveyed adequately into target languages in translation.

Appendix 1

Hebrew, Israel, and Jew

ONE OF THE CHALLENGES in biblical interpretation and translation is making distinction among the referring expressions in the Bible so that a right referent should be denoted. Such problem can be observed when the referent is referred by two or more referring expressions. One of such problems occurring in Genesis is the use of Hebrew, Israelite, and Jew, to refer the same nation or individuals associated to this nation. What do their semantic senses mean in the original context? I will attempt to answer this question in brief by explaining the semantic relationship and distinction among them. I acknowledge that my discussion on this issue is heavily based on Harvey's discussion on the same.[1]

Hebrew

The following semantic nuances could be deduced from the biblical use of the referring expression "Hebrew":[2]

A. Patronymic of Abraham and his offspring:

1. Signifies one's belonging to a particular ethnic group. Examples: i. Abraham the Hebrew (Gen 14:13). ii. Joseph was referred to as a Hebrew (Gen 39:14). iii. Egyptians might not eat bread with the Hebrews (Gen 43:32).

2. In the NT and OT the people of Hebrews refer themselves as Hebrews, strongly and confidently. Examples: i. "If a Hebrew man or a Hebrew woman be sold . . ." (Deut 15:12). ii. "He said unto them

1. Harvey, *True Israel*.
2. Young, *Analytical Concordance*, 473.

Appendix 1

"I am a Hebrew" (Jonah 1:9). iii. Apostle Paul referred to himself as a Hebrew of Hebrews (Phil 3:5).

3. Outsiders referred to them as Hebrews (1 Sam 4:6).
4. Some times this term might have been used derogatively by the outsiders. E.g., "The Hebrew servant, whom you have brought among us, came in to me to insult me" (Gen 39:17).

B. The language spoken or written among the Hebrews is known as Hebrew. Example: "He spoke unto them in the Hebrew tongue" (Acts 21:40). "It was written in Hebrew . . ." (John 19:20).

The above brief exploration shows that although the phrase "Hebrew"was used in the Bible in different circumstances the co-text of the passages indicate that noticeably it was used in the historical, social, cultural, and religious context of the people of Israel.

Etymology of the Concept "Hebrew"

According to the Even-Shoshan concordance the term עבר "Hebrew" occurs in the Bible about thirty-four times; and mainly it is used to refer the people of Israel and its members with an ethnic significance. The same term is also used to denote the language and grammar of the same ethnic group. Botterweck explains the term "Hebrew," translated as Εβραιος *Ebraios* into the Septuagint, as follows:

> (1) racially, one descended from Abraham (PH 3.5); (2) nationally, a Jew in contrast to a Gentile (2 Cor 11.22); (3) linguistically, a native Palestinian Jew who spoke Hebrew (possibly Aramaic) as a mother tongue in contrast to a Greek-speaking Jew who was probably an immigrant to Palestine.[3]

On the other hand, it is worth noting that this term is used mainly in the narrative texts both in singular and plural form. The word עברי "Hebrew" appeared for the first time in the Bible in Genesis 14:13 as "Abraham the Hebrew" (לאברם העברי).

The referent(s) of this expression is highly debated. Some biblical scholars argue that the Hebrews were one offshoot of Ha-Bi-Ru, a social class or an ethnic group in ancient Near East.[4] All arguments around this

3. Botterweck, "Hebrew."
4. Klein, "Ha-Bi-Ru," 46–47.

term can be summarized into four major etymological and philological explanations:

1. Some scholars such as Botterweck, among many others, argue that etymologically the expression Hebrew is related to עבר *(abar)*, implying to a territory beyond or on the other side of a river, which is the river Euphrates where Abraham came from.[5] It is also described based on the term עברי *ebri*, which could be understood as derived from the Hebrew root עבר—"to pass, to cross, to go beyond." Consequently, the translators of the Septuagint interpreted the term עבר as "one from the other side," i.e., beyond the Jordan. Therefore, in Genesis 14:13 they translated as "Αβραμ τω περατη" "Abram who crossed over," i.e., who became an immigrant.[6]

2. Some scholars, such as Wright, among others, also argue that it is related to *apiru/hapiru* which "refers to a certain social stratum common throughout the ancient Near East: landless people, political refugee, displaced people, outlaws."[7] Wenham suggests that, "Apiru/hapiru is usually on the periphery of society—foreign slaves, mercenaries, or even marauders,"[8] which is used to refer to Abraham, describing him as a fighter; as it is demonstrated by Abraham's fighting to rescue his nephew Lot.

3. However, this suggestion is rejected by Hamilton because of historical and philological discrepancy.[9] Botterweck, disagreeing with the suggestion of Apiru, argues:

   > But this proposal [Apiru/hapiru] strains the etymological and philological evidence and ignores the extant witness. We conclude from this that the two terms [hapiru/apiru and ibri] are not related. The term ibri is an ethnic term for proto-Israelites, descendants of Eber, and a gentilic term deriving from eber, "territory beyond," i.e., Mesopotamia, Abraham's original land.[10]

The referring expression "Hebrew" is related to Eber—the grandson of Shem, as a progenitor of the Hebrews. In this regard, the discourse structure of Genesis 10:21 struck my understanding. In this story Eber was

5. Botterweck, "Hebrew," 432.
6. Haldar, "Hebrew."
7. Wright, *Old Testament Ethics*, 158.
8. Wenham, *Genesis 1–15*, 313.
9. Hamilton, *Genesis 18–50*, 404–5.
10. Botterweck, "Hebrew."

Appendix 1

introduced in a focused way as if the whole genealogy was organized around him. In Genesis 11:16 he was referred again until his lineage came down to Terah, and then to Abraham. Thus the narrator puts Eber as a significant ancestor of Abraham.

1. Others argue that probably the "Hebrews" are a separate ethnic group in Canaan, though closely related to the Israelites.[11]

After evaluating the above alternative interpretations, I suggest that option 3 is more plausible and convincing because it fits the ancient Near East cultural and social context where many ethnic groups were called after one of their significant ancestors like Moabites, Ammonites, Edomites, etc. Thus, we can argue that probably, the term "Hebrews" was an ethnic name of the current Jews, related to their ancestor Eber. Yoshitaka Kobayashi observes this when he says "Terah and his family genealogically belonged to the Hebrews (or perhaps Apiru), who are the descendants of Eber in Gen 10:21, 25."[12]

The Term Hebrew and Its Derogative Use

Based on Potiphar's wife's referring to Joseph as "this Hebrew" (Gen 39:14) some scholars tend to conclude that originally this term was used by the outsiders to refer to the Hebrews derogatively, although, later on, the Hebrews themselves adapted it as their ethnic name. For example, von Rad interprets that originally it was used as "descriptive of a juridic-social position . . . Habiru originally described the legal position of servitude, or slavery, as opposed to the free person. Gradually, first by outsiders and then by Israelites themselves the word was used as a gentilicium."[13] However, the "Egyptians use of the name [Hebrew] does not prove that it is a derogatory appellative" because it could also mean normal ethnic referring expression.[14]

On the otherhand, it is clear that the Israelites referred themselves as Hebrews right from the beginning (Gen 40:15; 43:32; Exod 1:15; 2:11, 13; 1 Sam 13:3) "to distinguish [themselves] from a foreigner" which shows that this term is not used only by the outsiders derogatively.[15] For

11. Haldar, "Hebrew," 552.
12. Kobayashi, "Haran," 58.
13. Haldar, "Hebrew."
14. Harvey, *True Israel*, 118.
15. Hamilton, *Genesis 18–50*, 405.

example Jonah introduced himself to the captain as a Hebrew confidently (Jonah 1:9).

The Use of Hebrews, Jews, and Israelites as Synonym Terms

In the later generation, the Israelites apparently referred to themselves as Hebrews, Jews, or Israelites. As the historical records of the Bible show the referring expressions "Israel" and "Jews" were used after Jacob, who was the significant progenitor of this ethnic group.

The term "Israel" was introduced after Jacob while the term "Jews" was introduced after Judah who was one of the sons of Jacob. "Israel" is "the name of honor given to Jacob after his mysterious struggle with the angel.... When the immediate descendants of Jacob ... grew into a people they were called 'Israel' for what is now known as the Jewish people."[16] After the division of the kingdom, the southern kingdom consisting the tribes of Judah and Benjamin, took the name Judah while the remaining ten tribes of the north were called Israel.[17]

Thus, the terms Jews and Israelites, when they refer to the nation of Israel, denote political and religious significance of the Hebrews. Thus, Jews and Israelites are the later religio-political ethnic names of the Hebrews. Consequently, in the later context of the Israelites the terms Hebrews, Jews, and Israelites would be used interchangeably.[18] But one should be careful to apply these names to the appropriate context of this ethnic group's development in order to avoid anachronism.[19] Although we could describe these later referring expressions as synonyms to "Hebrew," the most ancient one is "Hebrew" because it is "applied to some of the most important people and to some of the earliest generations in the story of Israel: the name associated with antiquity, origins and people of central importance."[20]

---

16. Rabinowitz, "Israel."
17. Ibid.
18. Haldar, "Hebrew," 552.
19. Harvey, *True Israel*, 109.
20. Ibid., 110.

Appendix 1

Hebrew and Patriarchs

Abraham is one of the best-known figures in the Bible. He is a key figure in the history of both the Jewish and Arab people. He was a descendant of Eber and the grandfather of Jacob whose descendants became known as Israel, and great-grandfather of Judah, whose descendants became known as the Jews. He was also the father of Ishmael, from whom many of the Arab people are descended (Gen 21:9–13). Abraham was a *Hebrew*. But although he was the ancestor of *both* Jews and Arabs, Abraham himself was neither Jew nor Arab because they did not exist in the time of Abraham. Logically all the descendants of Abraham, both Arabs and Jews could keep the ethnic name "Hebrew," but they did not have too, because they could prefer to maintain new ethnic name beginning from their immediate ancestor, a descendant of Abraham, rather than preserving Hebrew.

According to the genealogical record, as presented in the book of Genesis, some of the most well-known terms relating to Israelite people, the *Semitic* genealogy, originated from Noah's son *Shem* while *Hebrew* is derived from *Eber*, the descendant of Shem and the ancestor of Abraham.

Abraham was a grandfather of Jacob and great-grandfather of Judah. From these two patriarchal figures, Jacob and Judah came as two other very well-known identity marking names: *Israelites* and *Jews*. Israelites are the descendants of Isaac's son Jacob, whom God renamed *Israel*, and from Jacob's son *Judah*, the terms *Jew* and *Jewish* were introduced as a new coinage of the ethnic group Israel.

The Terms Hebrew, Jew, and Israel, and the people Involved as Referents

The next question one could ask is that how do all of the three designations relate to the people involved? According to the narrative story of Genesis 10:21–31, the ethnic name Shemite is derived from Noah's son Shem and conversely the ethnic term "Hebrew" is derived from Shem's descendant Eber. Eber could be described as a Shemite, and the first Hebrew, but not an Israelite or a Jew because neither existed yet. Abraham was Eber's descendant and consequently he was a Shemite and a Hebrew, but not an Israelite or a Jew because neither existed yet. Isaac was Abraham's son and he was a Shemite and a Hebrew, but not an Israelite or a Jew because neither existed yet. Jacob, whom God renamed Israel, was Isaac's son and he was a Shemite and a Hebrew, but not a Jew because Jews were originated with his son Judah. The first Israelites were the children of Jacob. Judah was one of Jacob's twelve sons and he was a Shemite, a Hebrew, and an Israelite. Thus, the first Jews were the children of Judah. The descendants of the other eleven of Jacob's sons were not Jews, but were themselves named accordingly e.g. from Levi came the Levites, from Benjamin came the Benjamites and so on. Yet the current ethnic term Jew(s) may refer to any Israelite without any discrimination. Probably this is because of the significant political and social changes which affected the social structure of the community and the life of every member of the group descended from Jacob.

Conclusion

In conclusion, the term "Hebrew" is an ethnic name while "Israel" and "Jews" are originally politico-religious names, particularly when it is used to refer the people of Israel. The ethnic concept "Jew" was developed later from the tribe of Judah in the southern kingdom and Davidic dynasty. The southern kingdom comprises both Judah and Benjamites who feel as creams of the Israelites in terms of religious, political, and ethnic value or quality of the nation.

Appendix 2

Translation of Genesis 28:10–22

10 וַיֵּצֵא יַעֲקֹב מִבְּאֵר שָׁבַע וַיֵּלֶךְ חָרָנָה:
11 וַיִּפְגַּע בַּמָּקוֹם וַיָּלֶן שָׁם כִּי־בָא הַשֶּׁמֶשׁ וַיִּקַּח מֵאַבְנֵי הַמָּקוֹם וַיָּשֶׂם מְרַאֲשֹׁתָיו וַיִּשְׁכַּב בַּמָּקוֹם הַהוּא:
12 וַיַּחֲלֹם וְהִנֵּה סֻלָּם מֻצָּב אַרְצָה וְרֹאשׁוֹ מַגִּיעַ הַשָּׁמָיְמָה וְהִנֵּה מַלְאֲכֵי אֱלֹהִים עֹלִים וְיֹרְדִים בּוֹ:
13 וְהִנֵּה יְהוָה נִצָּב עָלָיו וַיֹּאמַר אֲנִי יְהוָה אֱלֹהֵי אַבְרָהָם אָבִיךָ וֵאלֹהֵי יִצְחָק הָאָרֶץ אֲשֶׁר אַתָּה שֹׁכֵב עָלֶיהָ לְךָ אֶתְּנֶנָּה וּלְזַרְעֶךָ:
14 וְהָיָה זַרְעֲךָ כַּעֲפַר הָאָרֶץ וּפָרַצְתָּ יָמָּה וָקֵדְמָה וְצָפֹנָה וָנֶגְבָּה וְנִבְרְכוּ בְךָ כָּל־מִשְׁפְּחֹת הָאֲדָמָה וּבְזַרְעֶךָ:
15 וְהִנֵּה אָנֹכִי עִמָּךְ וּשְׁמַרְתִּיךָ בְּכֹל אֲשֶׁר־תֵּלֵךְ וַהֲשִׁבֹתִיךָ אֶל־הָאֲדָמָה הַזֹּאת כִּי לֹא אֶעֱזָבְךָ עַד אֲשֶׁר אִם־עָשִׂיתִי אֵת אֲשֶׁר־דִּבַּרְתִּי לָךְ:
16 וַיִּיקַץ יַעֲקֹב מִשְּׁנָתוֹ וַיֹּאמֶר* אָכֵן יֵשׁ יְהוָה בַּמָּקוֹם הַזֶּה וְאָנֹכִי לֹא יָדָעְתִּי:
17 וַיִּירָא וַיֹּאמַר מַה־נּוֹרָא הַמָּקוֹם הַזֶּה אֵין זֶה כִּי אִם־בֵּית אֱלֹהִים וְזֶה שַׁעַר הַשָּׁמָיִם:
18 וַיַּשְׁכֵּם יַעֲקֹב בַּבֹּקֶר וַיִּקַּח אֶת־הָאֶבֶן אֲשֶׁר־שָׂם מְרַאֲשֹׁתָיו וַיָּשֶׂם אֹתָהּ מַצֵּבָה וַיִּצֹק שֶׁמֶן עַל־רֹאשָׁהּ:
19 וַיִּקְרָא אֶת־שֵׁם־הַמָּקוֹם הַהוּא בֵּית־אֵל וְאוּלָם לוּז שֵׁם־הָעִיר לָרִאשֹׁנָה:
20 וַיִּדַּר יַעֲקֹב נֶדֶר לֵאמֹר אִם־יִהְיֶה אֱלֹהִים עִמָּדִי וּשְׁמָרַנִי בַּדֶּרֶךְ הַזֶּה אֲשֶׁר אָנֹכִי הוֹלֵךְ וְנָתַן־לִי לֶחֶם לֶאֱכֹל וּבֶגֶד לִלְבֹּשׁ:
21 וְשַׁבְתִּי בְשָׁלוֹם אֶל־בֵּית אָבִי וְהָיָה יְהוָה לִי לֵאלֹהִים:
22 וְהָאֶבֶן הַזֹּאת אֲשֶׁר־שַׂמְתִּי מַצֵּבָה יִהְיֶה בֵּית אֱלֹהִים וְכֹל אֲשֶׁר תִּתֶּן־לִי עַשֵּׂר אֲעַשְּׂרֶנּוּ לָךְ:

10. Jacob set out from Beer Shebah and went to Haran. 11. He reached a certain place and he spent the night there because the sun was set and he took from the stones of that place put under his head and he slept at that place. 12. He had a dream and in his dream he saw a ladder set on the earth

and its top reached to the heaven and he saw the angels of God were going up and down on it/ascending and descending on it. 13. And he saw the LORD standing by him and he said: "I am the LORD God of your fathers Abraham and God of Isaac. The land on which you are lying I shall give it to you and to your descendant. 14. Your descendant shall be like the dust of the earth and you shall spread to the west and to the east, and to the north and to the south. And all the clans/families of the earth shall be blessed/shall bless themselves by you and your descendants. 15. Behold I am with you and protect you wherever you go and I will bring you back to this land because I shall not forsake/leave you until I have done what I said to you."

16. Jacob awoke from his sleep and said "Surely/I realized that the Lord is present in this place but I did not know." 17. And he was afraid that he said: "How awesome is this place! This is none other than the house of God. And this is the gate of the heaven." 18. Jacob woke up in the morning and he took the stone, which was under his head, and he set it as a pillar and he poured oil on its top. 19. And Jacob called the name of that place Bethel. But previously the name of that city was Luz.

20 And then Jacob made a *vow* saying "If God will be with me; and keep/protect me in this journey I am engaged on or undertaking; and give me food to eat and clothes to wear; 21 and I return back to my father's house in peace; then the LORD shall be my God, 22 and this stone which I set as a pillar shall be the house of God and I shall give tenth out of all you will give me."

Appendix 3

Institution of Tithing

Evidences about the practice of tithing in ancient Near East shows that it is a popular custom. Tithe was not practiced only by the Israelites, as it is attested in the most cultural world of the Mesopotamia, Egypt, South Arabia, and Ugarit. It has been observed that the practice of tithing in these cultures comprises both tax given to the government and an offering given to the deity.[21]

The concept of the מעשר 'tithe' in its derivative form as a verb is narrowed down specifically to the cultic practice of offering tithe to God or broadened to include even the sense of giving tax to kings. Examples:

- Gen 28:22: עַשֵּׂר אעשרנו עשר "giving the tenth" (Piel infinitive) אעשרנו "I will give the tenth" (Piel-imperfect/future)èI will surely give you the tenth.

- Deut 14:22: עשר תעשר עשר 'tithing you' (Piel infinitive); תעשר 'I shall tithe' (Peil imperfect/future)èyou shall truly tithe.

- 1 Sam 8:15, 17: יעשר Kal-imperfect (future) 'the king will take tithe.'[22]

In the Hebrew scripture the practice of tithe-offering is mentioned only twice in the narrative of the patriarchal religion (Gen 14:18–20; 28:22). But most of the evidences of the Hebrew Scripture about the concept of tithe imply that it is part of the thanksgiving to God for the blessing of abundance that the people of God receive from God. Tithing is not a one-time act, rather it is a continual act of his people as long as God's

21. Pagolu, *Religion of the Patriarchs*, 171–91.

22. One can observe from the above construction that according to the religious legislation of the cultic use of the tithe in the ancient Israelites, the intensive verbal form of the Hebrew verb is employed for tithing (Piel or Hiphil) while Kal (Qal?) imperfect is used for giving tax to the kings

Institution of Tithing

blessing continues. The following are the summary of some of the main features of the tithe in the ancient Israelite cultural context, which also indicate the aspect of the offering of the tithe:

1. It was perceived as given to God, to show the reverence and fear of him (Deut 14:23). In addition, in terms of Leviticus 27:30–34 and Numbers 18:21–31 it is presented as part of the religious worship.

2. Tithe was taken as an expression of thanksgiving to God for his provision and care. Thus it was expected to be accompanied with rejoicing (Deut 14:24–26). For example, Jacob made it as part of his vow to offer to God a tenth of all what God will bless him with, as a thanksgiving, if God answers his plea (Gen 28:22). The connection of giving tithe as a thanksgiving for receiving a blessing from God was well reflected in the book of the prophet Malachi:

> Bring the full tithe into the storehouse, so that there may be food in my house, and thus put me to the test, says the LORD of hosts; see if I will not open the windows of heaven for you and pour down for you an overflowing blessing. I will rebuke the locust for you, so that it will not destroy the produce of your soil; and your vine in the field shall not be barren, says the LORD of hosts. Then all nations will count you happy, for you will be a land of delight, says the LORD of hosts. (Mal 3:10–12)

Consequently, the giving of tithe was accompanied with a sacred meal which was eaten with praises and rejoicing, remembering the wonderful blessings of God (Lev 12:7; 14:23).

3. God allocated tithe offering to be given to his servants—priests and Levites. Consequently the tithe was legislated in the Israelite's law and it was dedicated to support the Levites and the priests (Deut 14:27; Num 18:20–22; Deut 26:12; Neh 10:37/38). Likewise, the tithe of every third year was allocated for the care of Levites, orphans, widows, and foreigners (Deut 14:28–29).

4. The tithe of the agricultural produce was allowed for the family celebration in order to rejoice for the agricultural provision of God (Deut 14:22–27).

5. The tithe should be given at the place which God chooses in one of the twelve tribes (Lev 12:6, 14).

6. Tithing is not a one-time action rather it is a continuous practice as long as the blessing of God continuous.

Appendix 3

The legislation given in Deuteronomy 14:22–29[23] shows that the main religious concept of the tithe in the ancient Israelite cultural context was rejoicing for the blessings they have received from God.

This scriptural evidences strengthens my conclusion that presumably the connection of Jacob's votive plea for "food to eat and clothes to wear" with his votive utterance to give tenth out of everything God will give him implies that he requested God for the blessing of prosperity, thus metarpresenting God's thought to bless him.

---

23. Set apart a tithe of all the yield of your seed that is brought in yearly from the field. In the presence of the LORD your God, in the place that he will choose as a dwelling for his name, you shall eat the tithe of your grain, your wine, and your oil, as well as the firstlings of your herd and flock, so that you may learn to fear the LORD your God always. But if, when the LORD your God has blessed you, the distance is so great that you are unable to transport it, because the place where the LORD your God will choose to set his name is too far away from you, then you may turn it into money. With the money secure in hand, go to the place that the LORD your God will choose; spend the money for whatever you wish—oxen, sheep, wine, strong drink, or whatever you desire. And you shall eat there in the presence of the LORD your God, you and your household rejoicing together. As for the Levites resident in your towns, do not neglect them, because they have no allotment or inheritance with you. Every third year you shall bring out the full tithe of your produce for that year, and store it within your towns; the Levites, because they have no allotment or inheritance with you, as well as the resident aliens, the orphans, and the widows in your towns, may come and eat their fill so that the LORD your God may bless you in all the work that you undertake.

Appendix 4

Interviews about the Vow and "Rape" of Dinah

These interviews aimed to discover two things:
1. To discover the Hadiyya and other related community's encyclopedic information about the concept of vow.
2. To discover whether the Hadiyya people perceive what Shechem did to Dinah as rape or as another way of marriage.

The major interview task was conducted on July 14–August 12, 2008, in Ethiopia and it involved sixty interviewees who comprised young, old, men, and women. Ten of them are unmarried young people: four girls and six men. The rest of the participants are all married: thirty men and twenty women. The interviewees are from different geographical locations of Ethiopia which include: Hadiyya, Addis Ababa, Central Shoa, Gondor, Gojam, Sidamo, Kambatta, Wollo, and Harar. I have also interviewed two Eritreans—one man and one woman. The majority of the participants are from the Hadiyya people—forty interviewees, and the rest are from the above mentioned places. The interview sessions were conducted in group context in different occasions and places; and I represent the summary of their responses here.

I thought it is appropriate to involve the majority of the participants from Hadiyya because the Hadiyya people are my focus group for the purpose of this research. Therefore, although I consider the contribution of the responses of the other interviewees, my conclusion of the empirical data is mainly based on the responses of the Hadiyya participants.

Appendix 4

Interview about the Concept of Vow in Hadiyya

Note: A vow could be made to deities like God, angel Gebreʼel, angel Michael, family spirits, Spirits which work through witchdoctors, etc.

1. *Why do you make a vow?* Except two interviewees, all the interviewees unanimously said that it is not intended to influence God rather it is caused by the distress of the person. It is a reflection of the emotion of the petitioner.

Note: In only one interview occasion only two scholars, one from Ethiopia and the other from Eritrea, responded that it was intended to influence God.

2. *Is it not possible to pray to God without making a vow?* Yes it is possible. Vow is a kind of commitment to express one's thanks and appreciation for what the deity has done. They indicated that it is intrinsic to bring such gifts to God as a thanks giving because he helped you to get out of your distress.

3. *To whom does one make a vow?* It is always made by the humans to the deity.

4. *When or in what circumstances do you make a vow?* When we are distressed.

5. *Where do you make a vow?* We can make a vow anywhere.

6. *When do you fulfill a vow?* If only when God answers our plea or petition.

7. *Does God make a vow to humans?* Never; we humans make a vow to God.

8. *Does one make a vow to another fellow man?* Never; we make vow only to God. We do not make vow to humans.

9. *How do you make a vow?* Several of them gave illustration from their own experience. I have incorporated one example here. An elderly man told his own experience as follows:

> Once I bought a goat and the goat fall sick. So I made a vow to God saying: "God if you heal this goat and if it produces many youngs then I will give you one out of them as a thanks giving." God healed the goat and eventually it produced so many of them. But I failed to fulfill my vow. Consequently, all the goats were hit by plague and all of them died. Thus I learned a lesson.

It is not an obligation to make a vow but once it is made it is seriously abiding."

10. *Can anybody make a vow?* Yes; even a thief can make a vow saying "God, if you give me success in this steeling I will do . . ."
11. *What will happen if one fails to fulfill his vow?* It is not good to fail to fulfill one's vow. Terrible thing will happen.
12. *Can you change a vow?* Never; you cannot change your vow.
13. *Are there some things which are not supposed to be offered as a vow offering?* No, you can offer anything. I was told that some people even offer lice, rat, walking to the sanctuary barefoot, standing naked etc.
14. *Can one annul a vow?* Never; once it is made it is abiding. But we are obliged to fulfill if and only if the deity answers one's plea.

Interview about whether Dinah was Raped

Research method: Read the narrative summary of the Dinah story to the audience and ask them what has happened to Dinah.

Summary of the story:
There is a story in Genesis 34 which tells us that a man called Jacob had a girl called Dinah. One day Dinah went out to visit with the girls of the land. While she was visiting with them a man called Shechem saw her, and he took her and he slept with her. Shechem loved the girl very much that he spoke to her in nice words and he told her that he loves her. Shechem was a son of Hamor who was the ruler of a city.

Shechem told his father Hamor that he loves Dinah very much. So he asked his father to go and negotiate with Dinah's family so that they can allow him to marry her. Therefore, his father went to Dinah's family and pleaded with them so that they should give their daughter to his son so that he can marry her. He told them that he can give them whatever they ask as a dowry. Both Shechem and his father pleaded with Jacob and with her brothers. Hamor spoke with them, saying "The soul of my son Shechem longs for your daughter; I pray you, give her to him in marriage. Make marriages with us; give your daughters to us, and take our daughters for yourselves. You shall dwell with us; and the land shall be open to you; dwell and trade in it, and get property in it." Shechem also said to her father and to her brothers. Let me find favor in your eyes, and whatever you say to me I will give. Ask of me so much as marriage present and gift,

Appendix 4

and I will give you accordingly as you say to me; only give me the maiden to be my wife" (Gen 34:8–12). Then I asked the interviewees:

According to this story, what happened to Dinah? Response: All participants said "*ooki gosimma*," which means "that was an abduction marriage." *Why?* Because it is evident that he kept the girl with him and he is negotiating with the girl's family for marriage. Probably the man abducted the girl because he new that they will not let him marry her. So first he had to take the girl and then negotiate.

Is it not rape? It is not, because if he intended to rape her he wouldn't keep the girl with him and he wouldn't go to negotiate for marriage.

Appendix 5

Conditionals and Metarepresentation

THE TRUTH FUNCTIONAL APPROACH to the propositional calculus and the semantic analysis of the conditional clauses linked by the connective "if" describes the conditionals as material implication or material conditionals. John I. Saeed calls the protasis of such expression "antecedent" and the apodosis "consequent." I wish to summarize Saeed's explanation of such connections of the two clauses in the truth table as follows:[24]

p	q	p→q
T	T	T
T	F	F
F	T	T
F	F	T

Saeed further explains the table by providing the following example: "If it rains then I'll go to the movies."

According to the table this conditional sentence can be false only if it rains and the person who commits himself to go does not go to the movies: p= T, q=F. If it doesn't rain (p=F), then the conditional claim whether he goes to the movie (q=T) or not (q=F), cannot be invalidated. Saeed explains such kind of relation of p is a sufficient condition for q (rain causes him to go to the movies) but not a necessary condition, because other things might cause him go.

However, Saeed admits that the conditional clauses in the actual language often have other features than the truth-conditional relation claims, because the truth-conditional description does not account for the human intuition about the other features of the conditional clauses. For example,

24. Saeed, *Semantics*, 91.

Appendix 5

the truth-functional description implies that there is always causal and consequent connection between protasis (antecedent or the *if*-clause) and apodosis (consequent or *then*-clause). This relation implies that if p=F then q=F; i.e., according to the above illustration, if it does not rain (p=F) then he will not go to the movies (q=F). However, the above truth-table claims p=F q=T, which will imply that even if it does not rain (p=F), still he will go (q=T) which will naturally invalidate the truth-functional claim. Saeed also further admits that the truth-functional approach does not account for the counterfactual conditionals like:

If I were an ostrich, then I would be a bird.
There is one other conditional which the truth-functional approach describes as "biconditionals." The biconditional clauses in English are connected by "if and only if." The relation between such clauses is symbolized by $\equiv$ or by $\leftrightarrow$. According to the truth functional approach the statement p $\equiv$ q is true only when p and q are true. In such construction p is a necessary condition for q.[25]

However, Noh argues that the truth-functional approach is not adequate to account for different features of the conditional expressions unless it is complemented with a pragmatic analysis.[26] This is because the traditional approach does not account for the non-basic conditionals (conditionals which do not denote cause and consequence like a votive atterance of Jacob). If God does not grant his plea, which could be described as F, and Jacob fulfils his vow any way it is not a vow at all, because it does not fulfil the contextual assumption ot the vow institution: vow making, vow granting and vow fulfilling (see my discussion in chapters 4, 5, and 6).

Besides, it is worth noting that Noh categorizes the conditional utterances as a metarepresentational utterances because the antecedents (protasis) are used to represent another representation. The metarepresentational utterances resemble the attributed utterance or thought in a particular context.[27] She further observes that in some cases both antecedents (protasis) and consequents (apodosis) may be used metarepresentationaly (used to represent another representation) in which case consequent (apodosis) may express the speaker's attitude to what is echoed in the antecedent.[28] Thus I consider that both the traditional and pragmatic approaches to the explaination of conditionals complement each other

---

25. Saeed, *Semantics*, 91–94.
26. Noh, *Metarepresentation*, 174–79.
27. Ibid., 186.
28. Ibid., 205–8.

because pragmatics complement the semantic (truth functional) approach by explaining the attitude and intention of the speaker for using the conditionals, in a particular context, by accessing the relevant contextual assumption by inferencing, being trigerred by the logical expresion. Besides, only the inferential processing aspect of the communication allows one to access the assumed relevant information, including the relevant encyclopedic information, of the relevant concept in a given context. For example, the binding feature of the vow institution and the adverse consequence of Jacob's laxity to fulfill his vow (which we discussed in this dissertation), which is some of the encyclopedic entries of the concept of vow and votive narrative in the cognitive environment of the hearers, cannot be explained by the truth conditional approach, because it is not explicitly stated by the conditional utterance. Rather, it was assumed that the hearers will imagine for themselves.[29] For example, the adverse consequence of the unfulfilled vow of Jacob, which was discussed in the dissertation, is beyond the propositional calculus and the semantic analysis of the conditional clauses of Jacob's votive utterances.

---

29. Carston, *Thoughts and Utterances*, 349–59.

Appendix 6

Some Real-Life Stories of Abductive Marriage among the Hadiyya People

The following examples of the abductive marriage are only a few of the many true stories of this practice. Each incident of these examples represents different features of the abductive marriage which would happen during the attempt. The main nature of the abductive marriage is that it is sexually violent and confrontational because it provokes the conscience of honor and shame of the involved social groups of the community.

Note: The names of the women involved are withheld in order to protect their identity.

Story of Woman A

A young girl came to visit her sister who was married in another village about two hours walk from their parent's home. A young man saw the girl and fell in love with her, so he consulted with his friends how to get her for marriage. Meanwhile the girl went back to her parents' home. However, one of his friends decided to go and persuade her sister so that she would arrange for the abductive marriage. Eventually the woman was persuaded and she agreed to work a conspiracy with the men. After all it is good for her because her sister will be closer to her.

The woman plotted the way as follows. She agreed to request her parents so that they send some wheat by her sister to the market and she will get it from there because she needed it badly. When her sister brings the wheat for her the young men will abduct her for the marriage. Thus she worked with the young man and his friends how to make the abductive

Some Real-Life Stories of Abductive Marriage among the Hadiyya People

marriage aattempt successful. The prospective husband bought dresses for the girl as a gift without the girl's knowledge. Then the men ambushed to abduct the girl. Eventually the innocent girl brought the wheat to the market for her sister only to find that she was betrayed by her sister. The men took the girl by force while she was screaming, and hid her in a place they felt was secure. The man had sexual intercourse with her.

Then the father of the boy was informed that his son has abducted the girl for the marriage. So he went to the parents of the girl with special gifts in order to negotiate for the marriage. Eventually both the girl and her parents consented for the marriage that they legalized it. The couple organized a post marriage wedding celebration. The couples are enjoying a happy marriage until today and they have several children.

Story of Woman B

According to the Hadiyya tradition young men used to go to a girl in order to explore and see whether the girl is desirable for marriage. Accordingly, two different young men who were interested to marry the girl came at the same time to see her for marriage. Both boys became highly interested in the girl so that the girl's parents did not know which one to choose. So the parents went to a witchdoctor to consult about the matter. The witchdoctor told them which one to choose, and they did as he said. Eventually the girl was legally betrothed to the young man. However, the other young man was jealous and he decided to marry the girl by abduction which he did. He took the girl and hid her in a secret place. This behavior made the clan of the fiancé of the girl furious because they felt that the clan of the abductor brought shame on the family and the whole clan of the fiancé. Therefore, they decided to hunt for the abducted girl and bring her for a wife for the fiancé in order to restore their honor, and revenge and humiliate the abductor, his family, and his clan. They found the girl after one week of searching and brought her with a great confrontation, enchantment, and dance to show that they are more powerful than the clan of the abductor; have restored their honor, and have reversed the shame on their opponent, his family, and his clan. Thus the abductive marriage was aborted after one week and she married her first fiancé. The couple have several children and they still live united in a good marriage relationship.

Appendix 6

Story of Woman C

Woman C was approached by a young man for a marriage when she was a girl and they were in love. The man gave the girl some gifts and he was planning to give dowry to legalize the agreement. However, the girl changed her mind and told him that she does not want to marry him. This behavior of the girl offended the man, so he decided to marry the girl by abduction. Supported by his friends, he ambushed and abducted the girl when she was coming from school and hid her in a particular place. When the parents of the girl heard that, they raised an alarm to their clan because they felt that this behavior of the boy was an offence to them and the whole clan. Thus, they were very angry because they felt that he threatened their honor. Therefore, they searched for the girl immediately in order to abort the abductive marriage and found her on the second day. They brought the girl home with a great enchantment and dance to show that they have restored their honor and reversed the shame on the abductor, his family, and his clan. They physically humiliated them. The clan of the abductor apologized for the attempted abductive marriage and pleaded with the clan and family of the girl so that they should give the girl in marriage. After a serious negotiation the family of the girl agreed to give the girl for marriage to the same man and asked the girl whether she was willing to marry him. The girl was also consented to marry him and she married him by a wedding ceremony. The couples are enjoying a happy marriage until today.

Story of Woman D

Woman D's sister was married in a village, very far from her parent's home. It was about two days walking distance. One day women D, when she was a girl, went to visit her sister. While she was with her sister a young man saw her and loved her, so he abducted her for marriage. This behavior of the boy offended the girl's family, so they decided to abort the marriage by confrontation. They searched for the girl for several days and eventually found her where the boy hid her. They attempted to take the girl home by force but the boy's side overpowered the girl's family and they retained the girl. Thus the girl's family went home humiliated once more. However, the girl tricked the boy. She disguised that she loved him. One day, after three weeks, in the early evening, the girl told her sister-in-law that she wanted to relieve herself outside and then come back home. So nobody followed

Some Real-Life Stories of Abductive Marriage among the Hadiyya People

her because they did not suspect her. The girl escaped. Immediately, the family of the abductor raised an alarm that they started hunting for the girl. When the girl realized that people are following after her, she begged one man to hide her in his house. The man hid her in his house and when they asked him whether he has seen a girl he told them that a girl has just passed running. They did not suspect him so they continued running to catch her. Early in the morning, the man accompanied the girl until she reached a safe place. Thus the girl escaped and reached her parents' home on the third day. Her parents took her to the hospital for treatment. Then she resumed her high school study and eventually she did her college study after finishing her high school.

Appendix 7

Excursus on Translating Gen 28:10—35:15

What is translation?

THE CURRENT COMMON TERM used as a title for the discipline of interpreting and translating a message from one language to another language is known as "Translation Studies."[30] During the early 1970 some scholars used the term "Translatology" to refer to the same discipline. The *Dictionary of Linguistics and Phonetics* explains that in applied linguistics the term "Translatology" subsumes both the process of interpretation and translation of oral and written texts. It also describes the oral translation of a written text or a written translation of an oral message into another language as "sight translation."[31] However, the term "Translatology" has not been accepted by the English speaking scholars because they consider it as an unsuccessful neologism.[32]

Shuttleworth summarizes how different scholars attempted to describe what translation is and he lists them as follows:

- Overt vs. covert translation or domesticating vs. foreignizing Translation;
- Diagrammatic translation;
- Inter-semiotic translation;
- Paraphrase and pseudo-translation;

30. Shuttleworth and Cowie, *Translation Studies*, 188.//
31. Crystal, *Encyclopedia*, 472.//
32. Neologism denotes a newly coined term supposed to be accepted in the main stream language, which eventually enters into common use.

- Replacement of textual material in one language (Source Language) by equivalent Textual material in another language (Target Language);
- An interpretation of verbal signs by means of some other language or inter-lingual translation;
- Conveying of meaning from one set of language signs to another set of language signs;
- A translation aimed in maintaining the effect of the original message in the translation which is secondary communication both in terms of meaning and style.[33]

Gentzler suggests that translation could be categorized into three areas:[34]

Intralingual translation which denotes paraphrasing of signs of one language with other signs of the same language;

Interlingual translation which denotes interpretation and translation of signs from one language with signs of another language;

Intersemiotic translation which denotes the process of conveying verbal signs from one language into non-verbal sign of another language like from language signs into music and art signs.

Gentzler also categorizes the translation theories which were introduced since mid-sixteenth century into five: (1) "[T]he North American translation workshop; (2) the 'science' of translation; (3) early translation studies; (4) polysystem theory; and (5) deconstruction."[35]

Most of these descriptions are normative in a sense that they tend to give guidance about what translation is supposed to be rather than simply describing what translation is. They are prescriptive not descriptive.[36] This distinction between prescriptive and descriptive definition of the translation is based on what one intends to define: "Translation" as the process or as the final product of the process. For example, on the one hand some scholars base their definition on the final product of the translation process and they avoid the prescriptive feature in their description.[37] On the other hand, some scholars propose a more comprehensive prescriptive definition of the current translation process based on the final product

---

33. See Shuttleworth and Cowie, *Translation Studies*, 181, for further insight about this categorization.
34. Gentzler, *Translation Theories*.
35. Ibid., 2.
36. Shuttleworth and Cowie, *Translation Studies*, 182.
37. Ibid.

Appendix 7

which varies according to the particular response to the needs it intends to address by the translation.[38]

However, all the above mentioned categorizations are based on the analogy of capturing a particular feature of the translation task. Hence, they are not comprehensive in terms of conceptualizing multifaceted task of translation process.[39] Consequently it has been proved that it is a challenge to establish a translation theory which comprises the sub-types of translation: translation as a process, translation as a product, translation as a function oriented target text (skopos theory), and translation didactics or instructions about how and what to do in translation.[40] In terms of applied translation it is impossible to exclude the above translation features one from the other.[41]

Multidisciplinary approach describes translation as an interdisciplinary task which involves cultural anthropology, different types of linguistic studies including socio and psycho linguistics, literature studies, different types of translations including machine translation, history, etc.[42] Gutt approaches translation studies from the relevance theoretic[43] perspective and describes it as an inferential communication, hence there is no need for a comprehensive translation theory.[44] The debate continues between those who argue that translation is simply a practical application which cannot be described as a theory and those who contend that a descriptive theory of the translation can be established.[45] In addition, there is a debate between accurate translatability and untranslatability of texts.[46]

---

38. Ibid., 182; Hickey, *Pragmatics of Translation*, 2.

39. Shuttleworth and Cowie, *Translation Studies*, 181.

40. Ibid., 187.

41. Gentzler, *Translation Theories*, 1.

42. Shuttleworth and Cowie, *Translation Studies* 184; Gentzler, *Translation Theories*, 1, 108, 203.

43. Relevance theory is a communication theory which recognizes that mental fuculty of the human being, which has capacity to draw relevant inferential conclusion from the behavior of people, enables people to communicate with each other. Communicators exploit this cognitive capacity so that they do not need to say everthing to the audience.

44. Gutt, *Translation*.

45. Hickey, *Pragmatics of Translation*, 2; Gentzler, *Translation Theories*, 76–79, 82.

46. Hickey, *Pragmatics of Translation*, 2.

Is Translation Possible?

It is an indisputable fact that languages are different in grammatical configuration which might have been caused by the conceptual incompatibility. Nevertheless, it is evident that ostensive translation between languages takes place effectively.[47] Conceptual incompatibility across languages which might have been caused by cultural difference or non existence of things in both language communities can not be a hindrance for translating the intended message of a text. Such incompatibility can be compensated by different translation techniques once a translator understood the intended message of the source text and any particular translation problem(s) he encounters in the translation process.[48]

A translator must be conversant with the source text side, the target text side, and social, cultural, and political differences between the two. All of these factors influence the mental and public representation of the texts.[49] Translation is a negotiation between the source text—its connection to other source literature, its language use, and its culture as implicated in the text and target text—its cultural, social, and political situation, concepts of translation, previous translation of the same source text, other texts, and etc of the receptor language.[50] In the process of all the translation tasks the translator's mental representation of the source text is supreme dominant because translators always aim to translate a text from the author's point of view of the source text.[51] Of course getting at the meaning of the source text is decisively inferential. In other words, one important feature regarding interpreting the source text is that it is inferential because naturally we do not limit our analysis on what is explicitly said, but also on "what it does not say or says only by implication."[52] However, the process of inferencing is decisively constrained by the public representation of the author of the source text and his/her point of view about the texts. Therefore, it is crucial for the translators to continue searching to access the cultural, social, political, institutional, experiential, etc.,

---

47. Hickey, *Pragmatics of Translation*, 1–2; Shuttleworth and Cowie, *Translation Studies*, 180.

48. See Shuttleworth and Cowie, *Translation Studies*, 180–181; Nida and Taber, *Translation*, 2, 98.

49. Wendland, *Cultural Factor*; Wendland, *Contextual Frames*; Wilt and Wendland, *Scripture Frames*.

50. Gentzler, *Translation Theories*, 4.

51. Ibid., 9, 13–14; Shuttleworth and Cowie, *Translation Studies*, 178.

52. Gentzler, *Translation Theories*.

Appendix 7

phenomenon that influenced the public representation of the source text. Richards observes this feature of the translation task when he claims that "translators, with proper education and practice, can come to know the proper methodology to achieve the correct understanding of the primary text."[53] Some of the relevant questions a translator should ask regarding the source text are what is that the source texts and its translation intend to achieve "and how they attempt to achieve it" and how both the writers of the source text and translated texts organize their public representation in terms of "cooperating with their readers, being polite and relevant, or how inter-cultural difference may be treated."[54] Thus, the final product of the translation reflects the translator's conclusion achieved by his choice and decision after exhausting all the possible resources in order to understand the source text correctly.[55] Thus, it is possible that a well equipped translator can make correct mental representation and public representation of the source text; hence creating an interpretive resemblance between both source text and receptor text.[56]

When we translate a culturally, temporally, geographically, and historically remote source text to a target community it is very important and necessary to help the target community access to relevant information of the contemporary cultural institutions, political and social situation, geographical and environmental phenomenon, and etc. of the source text(s) in order to guide the translators to reconstruct the original message and then represent a transparent target text. Thus we can help the recipients of the target text interact with the cultural constraints of the source language in order to understand the intended message.

In addition, experience shows that the translation process which will lead to a final product of a target text, acceptable by all concerned parties, requires a collaborative or joint action of all concerned parties in the process of translation. In such situation a translator should be ready and open to cooperate with all the concerned parties and other translation experts.

Sample Review of the Translated Versions of the Bible

As a background for my suggestion about how to translate the Hebrew concept of נדר and the votive narrative of Jacob I would like to do a brief

53. Hickey, *Pragmatics of Translation*, 6; Gentzler, *Translation Theories*, 14.
54. Hickey, *Pragmatics of Translation*, 5.
55. Shuttleworth, *Translation Studies*, 178.
56. Gutt, *Translation*, 105; Hickey, *Pragmatics of Translation*, 6.

Excursus on Translating Gen 28:10—35:15

review on other up-to-date Bible translations of the votive narrative of Jacob in order to see if there is any translation which translated the story from the votive narrative perspective. In this brief review I wish to consider only the translated versions which employ section-headings which is usually aimed to guide the readers.

New Revised Standard Version (1989)

This version divided Genesis 28:10—35:15 into 14 different sections:

1. 28:10-22: Jacob's dream at Bethel
2. 29:1-14: Jacob Meets Rachel
3. 29:15—30:24: Jacob Marries Laban's Daughters
4. 30:25-43: Jacob Prospers at Laban's Expense
5. 31:1-21 Jacob Flees with Family and Flocks
6. 31:22-42: Laban Overtakes Jacob
7. 31:43—32:2: Laban and Jacob Make a Covenant
8. 32:3-21: Jacob Sends Presents to Appease Esau
9. 32:22-32: Jacob Wrestles at Peniel
10. 33:1-17: Jacob and Esau Meat
11. 33:18-20: Jacob Reaches Shechem
12. 34:1-24: The Rape of Dinah
13. 34:25-31: Dinah's Brothers Avenge their Sister
14. 35:1-15: Jacob Returns to Bethel

New Revised Standard Version in Amharic (1992)

1. 28:10-22: The Dream Jacob Sow in Bethel
2. 29:1-14: Jacob Arrived to the House of Laban
3. 29:15-30: Jacob Service to Laban for Rachel and Leaha
4. 29:31—30:24: Children Born to Jacob
5. 30:25-43: Jacob complained with Labab about his Wage
6. 31:1-21: Jacob Flees from Laban secretly

Appendix 7

7. 31:22–42: Laban pursues Jacob
8. 31:43–55: An Agreement Made between Laban and Jacob
9. 32:1–21: Jacob's Preparation to meet Esau
10. 32:22–32: Jacob Wrestles with God
11. 33:1–20: Jacob Meets Esau
12. 34:1–31: The Rape of Jacob's Daughter Dinah
13. 35:1–15: God Blessed Jacob in Bethel

The New American Bible (1979)

1. 28:10–22: Jacob's Dream at Bethel
2. 29:1–14a: Arrival in Haran
3. 29:14b–30: Marriage to Leah and Rachel
4. 29:31—30:24: Jacob's Children
5. 30:25–43 Jacob outwits Laban
6. 31:1–24: Flight from Laban
7. 31:25–32:3: Jacob and Laban in Gilead
8. 32:4–22: Embassy to Esau
9. 32:23–33: Struggle with the Angel
10. 33:1–20: Jacob and Esau Meet
11. 34:1–12: The Rape of Dinah
12. 34:13–31: Revenge of Jacob's Sons
13. 35:1–16: Bethel Revisited

New International Version 2005

1. 28:10–22: Jacob's Dream at Bethel
2. 29:1–30: Jacob Arrives in Padan Aram
3. 29:31—30:24: Jacob's Children
4. 30:25–43: Jacob's Flocks Increase
5. 31:1–21: Jacob Flees from Laban

6. 31:22–55: Laban Pursues Jacob
7. 32:1–21: Jacob Prepares to meet Esau
8. 32:22–32: Jacob Wrestles with God
9. 33:1–20: Jacob Meets Esau
10. 34:1–31: Dinah and the Shechemites
11. 35:1–15: Jacob Returns to Bethel

NIV Amharic Version 2001

1. 27:41—28:9: Jacob runs to Laban
2. 28:10–22: Jacob's dream at Bethel
3. 29:1—30:24: Jacob arrives in Mesopotamia
4. 30:25–43: Jacob's flocks increase
5. 31:1–21: Jacob flees from Laban
6. 31:22–55: Laban pursues Jacob
7. 32:1–31: Jacob prepares to meet Esau his brother
8. 33:1–20: Jacob meets Esau
9. 34:1–31: Jacob's daughter raped
10. 35:1–15: Jacob returns to Bethel

We can observe from the section-heading organizations of the above sample versions that *none* of them treated the story as a votive narrative. Rather they treated the coherent episodes of the votive narrative as isolated episodes. To my surprise, even the Amharic translation of the story shows that, though the target audience is a vow conscious society, the translation was treated just like the English versions. Thus, the translators failed to reconstruct this votive narrative, interpret it, and translate it within the context of the institution of vow and within the framework of the votive narrative of Jacob in Bethel.

One may wonder "what was the reason?" The answer to this question, in terms of non-vow-conscious target readers, is that they cannot access to the primary audience's contextual assumption which the narrator assumed that they will naturally infer. Unless those assumptions are made accessible there is not way that they can process this narrative in the same way as the assumed primary audience did. Therefore, they need to be

Appendix 7

helped in this regard. Secondly, to answer in terms of the target audience who has similar practice of the institution of vow such as Amharic, probably they failed to reconstruct the story according to the votive narrative due to different reasons:

1. Probably they were influenced by other translations or translation aids and commentaries.
2. They failed to employ their assumptions of the institution of vow to reconstruct Jacob's votive narrative because of other different reasons which needs further investigation.

This calls for a suggestion of a better way of representation of this story into the target audiences in translation task. First of all, it is worth noting that, though translation is different from the primary communication, it is also a communication by the virtue of its communicative nature because understanding the translated message also involves inferential processing as the primary communication does, not decoding what has been encoded in the linguistic expression of the translation.[57] Translation scholars have noted that getting at the intended message "crucially involves the use of context."[58] According to the relevance theory, "[a] context is a psychological construct, a subset of the hearers' assumptions about the world" and will affect the interpretation of an utterance as well as any other communication stimulus, including translation.[59] For example the encyclopedic information about the institutional nature of the Hebrew concept "vow" comprises vow making, vow granting, and vow fulfilling. This nature is pertinent both in the actual practice of vow and in the mental representation of the concept vow and votive narratives. This nature is a mutually shared contextual assumption which was manifest to the primary audience which relevance theory describes as a "cognitive environment."[60] The question is then how can we help the target readers of the secondary communication (translation) to reconstruct these contextual assumptions about the vow so that they can create mutually shared cognitive environment like the primary audience about the same so that the contextual assumption of vow can manifest in their cognitive environment when they read this narrative unit? In other words, how can we make the cognitive environment of the secondary audience resemble with

---

57. Gutt, *Translation*, 22, 24ff., 76; Sim, *Handbook for Translators*, 34ff; 82, 148.

58. Gutt, *Translation*, 26; Nida and Taber, *Translation*, 107; Sim, *Handbook for Translators*, 48, 57ff.; Wendland, *Contextual Frames*.

59. Sperber and Wilson, *Relevance*, 15.

60. Ibid.

the cognitive environment of the primary audience regarding the institution of vow? This task is crucial for drawing relevant cognitive effect from the translation of the votive narrative of Jacob. Unless the reading of the translation of Jacob narrative is inferentially combined with the presumed contextual assumption of the ancient Israelites' institution of vow the intended communication of this votive narrative will not be effective.[61] In fact, as the above sample translation versions show, they will employ other unintended contextual assumption instead (searching for the relevance) if they are not able to access the intended contextual assumption of the primary audience.[62]

I believe it is possible to help our secondary audience in this matter because we assume that every normally thinking human being is capable of reconstructing such institutional contextual assumptions of other cultures in their cognitive environment, as long as they are helped sufficiently to access to it.[63] In this regard, several translation scholars have described the nature of contextual assumptions and suggested different ways of making such contextual assumption accessible to the target audience from different perspectives.[64] Particularly Hill describes and categorizes the contextual assumption which needs adjustment in the translation task into four types:[65]

1. Shared and believed to be shared with the communicator which does not need contextual adjustment.

2. Shared, but not believed to be shared which should be encouraged to be used

3. Not shared, but thought to be shared which should be corrected and

4. Not shared and not believed to be shared that they are not engaged and are unable to draw meaning. In this case the secondary audience must be taught about the need of reconstructing the contextual assumption they needed because, both they do not know it and do not know its relevance them.

Hill also suggests some strategies for supplying the necessary contextual adjustment—for example, in the text, in footnotes, in Bible

---

61. Gutt, *Translation*, 76; Sim, *Handbook for Translators*, 35, 111.

62. Sim, *Handbook for Translators*, 146.

63. Hill, *Communicating Context*, 100.

64. Gutt, *Translation*; Hill, *Cultural Crossroads*; Sim, *Handbook for Translators*, 38ff.

65. Hill, *Communicating Context*, 450-54.

Appendix 7

background booklets, films, teaching, etc.—and she remarks that such contextual adjustment has proven helpful. Therefore, I propose that such contextual adjustment should be made in the task of translating the Hebrew concept נדר and Jacob's votive narrative of Genesis 28:10—35:15.

Bibliography

Alders, G. C. *Bible Students Commentary: Genesis Volume II.* Grand Rapids: Zondervan, 1981.
Allwood, Jens. "Meaning Potentials and Context: Some Consequences for the Analysis of Variation in Meaning." In *Cognitive Approaches to Lexical Semantics,* 29–62. Berlin: de Gruyter, 2003.
Alter, Robert. *The Art of Biblical Narrative.* New York: Basic, 1981.
Archer, G. L. "Hebrew." In *The Zondervan Pictorial Encyclopedia of the Bible (vol. 3),* edited by Mirill Tenny and Steven Barab, 65–76. Grand Rapids: Zondervan, 1975.
Arnold, Bill T., and H. G. M. Williamson, editors. *Dictionary of the Old Testament Historical Books.* Downers Grove, IL" InterVarsity, 2005.
Austin, J. L. *How to Do Things with Words.* Oxford: Oxford University Press, 1962.
Baarda, Tjitze. "The Shechem Episode in the Testament of Levi: A Comparison with Other Traditions." In *Sacred History and Sacred Texts in Early Judaism: A Symposium in Honor of A. S. Van Der Woude,* edited by F. N. Bremmer and F. Garcia Martinez, 11–71. Kampen: Kok Pharos, 1992.
Bader, Mary Anna. *Sexual Violation in the Hebrew Bible: A Multi-Methodological Study of Genesis 34 and 2 Samuel 13.* New York: Lang, 2006.
Bar-Efrat. *Narrative Art in the Bible.* London: T. & T. Clark, 1992.
Bechtel, Lyn M. "Shame as a Sanction of Social Control in Biblical Israel: Judicial, and Social Shaming." *Journal for the Study of the Old Testament* 49 (1991) 47–76.
———. "What if Dinah Is Not Raped? (Genesis 34)." *Journal for the Study of the Old Testament* 62 (1994) 19–36.
Berlinerblau, Jacques. *The Vow and the Popular Religious Groups of Ancient Israel: A Philological and Sociological Inquiry.* Sheffield, UK: Sheffield Academic Press, 1996.
Blakemore, D. "The Organization of Discourse." In *Linguistics: The Cambridge Survey,* edited by F. Newmeyer, 229–50. Cambridge: Cambridge University Press, 1988.
Blass, Regina. *Relevance Relations in Discourse: A Study with Special Reference to Sissala.* Cambridge: Cambridge University Press, 1990.
Blyth, Caroline. "Terrible Silence, Eternal Silence: A Consideration of Dinah's Voicelessness in the Text and Interpretive Traditions of Genesis." PhD diss., University of Edinburgh, 2008.
Botterweck, G. Johannes. "Hebrew." In *Theological Dictionary of the Old Testament,* vol. 1, 428–32. Grand Rapids: Eerdmans, 1999.
Brand, Chad, et al., editors. *Holman Illustrated Bible Dictionary.* Nashville: Broadman & Holman, 2003.

Bibliography

Braukampex, Ulrich. "The Correlation of Oral Tradition and Historical Records in Southern Ethiopia: A Case Study of the Hadiyya/Sidaama Past." *Journal of Ethiopian Studies* 11.2 (1973) 29–50.
Brisman, Leslie. *The Voice of Jacob: On the Composition of Genesis*. Bloomington, IN: Indiana University Press, 1990.
Brown, Francis, S. R. Driver, Charles A. Briggs. *The New Brown-Driver-Briggs-Gesenius Hebrew and English Lexicon*. Peabody, MA: Hendrickson, 1979.
Brown, Gillian, and George Yule. *Discourse Analysis*. Cambridge: Cambridge University Press, 1983.
Brueggemann, Walter. *Genesis: Interpretation: A Bible Commentary for Teaching and Preaching*. Atlanta, John Knox, 1982.
Bryce, Trevor. *Life and Society in the Hittite World*. Oxford: Oxford University Press, 2002.
Calvin, John. *The First Book of Moses Called Genesis*. Grand Rapids: Eerdmans, 1843–45.
Candlish, Robert S. *Studies in Genesis: Expository Message*. Grand Rapids: Kregel, 1979.
Carston, Robyn. *Thoughts and Utterances: The Pragmatics of Explicit Communication*. Oxford: Blackwell, 2002.
Carston, R., and G. Powell. "Relevance Theory—New Directions and Developments." In *The Oxford Handbook of Philosophy of Language*, edited by E. Lepore and B. Smith, 341–60. Oxford: Oxford University Press, 2005.
Cartledge, Tony W. *Vows in the Hebrew Bible and the Ancient Near East*. Sheffield, UK: Sheffield Academic Press, 1992.
Ceruli, Ernesta. *People of South-West Ethiopia and Its Border Land*. London: London International African Institute, 1956.
Charles, R. H. *The Book of Jubilees: Translated from the Ethiopic Texts*. Eugene, OR: Wipf & Stock, 2001.
Chepey, Stuart. *Nazirites in Late Second Temple Judaism: A Survey of Ancient Jewish Writing, the New Testament, Archaeological Evidence, and Other Writings from Late Antiquity*. Leiden: Brill, 2005.
Coppes, Leonard J. "Make a Vow." In *Theological Wordbook of the Old Testament*, edited by R. Laird Harris, 557–58. Chicago: Moody, 1980.
Coats, George W. *Genesis with an Introduction to Narrative Literature*. Grand Rapids: Eerdmans, 1983.
Cotter, David W. *Studies in Hebrew Narrative & Poetry*. Collegeville, MN: Liturgical, 2003.
Crystal, David. *The Cambridge Encyclopedia of Language*. Cambridge: Cambridge University Press, 1990.
———. *A Dictionary of Linguistics and Phonetics*. Oxford: Blackwell, 2003.
Dilley, Roy. "Introduction: The Problem of Context." In *The Problem of Context*, edited by Roy Dilley, 1–46. New York: Berghahn, 1999.
Driver, S. R. *The Book of Genesis*. Westminster Commentary. 3rd ed. New York: Gorham, 1904.
Dumbrell, W. J. "The Role of Bethel in the Biblical Narrative from Jacob to Jeroboam I." *Australian Journal of Biblical Archaeology* 2.3 (1974–75) 65–76.
Edelman, Diana V. "Mahanaim." In *The Anchor Bible Dictionary*, vol. 4, edited by David Noel Freedman, 472. New York: Doubleday, 1992.

Edzard, Dietz O. "The History of Ancient Mesopotamia." In *The New Encyclopedia Britannica, vol. 23*, 15th ed., 860-76. Chicago: Encyclopedia Britannica, 2003.

Eisenstadt, Samuel N. "Social Institutions." In *International Encyclopedia of the Social Sciences, vol. 13*, edited by David L. Sills, 409-20. New York: Macmillan, 1968.

Epstein, Rabbi Isidore. *The Babylonian Talmud: Seder Nezikin*. London: Soncino, 1935.

———. *The Babylonian Talmud: Seder Nashim*. London: Soncino, 1936.

———. *The Babylonian Talmud: Seder Moed*. London: Soncino, 1938.

———. *The Babylonian Talmud: Seder Kodashim*. London: Soncino, 1948.

Ferris, Paul Wayne. "Hebron." In *The Anchor Bible Dictionary, vol. 3*, edited by David Noel Freedman, 107-8. New York: Doubleday, 1992.

Fewell, Danna Nolan, and David Gunn. "Tipping the Balance: Sternberg's Reader and the Rape of Dinah." *Journal of Biblical Literature* 110 (1991) 193-12.

Fields, Weston W. *Sodom and Gomorrah: History and Motif in Biblical Narrative*. Sheffield, UK: Sheffield Academic Press, 1997.

Fishbane, Michael. *Text and Texture: Close Reading of Selected Biblical Texts*. New York: Schocken, 1979.

Fitzmyer, Joseph A. *Responses to 101 Questions on the Dead Sea Scrolls*. New York: Paulist, 1992.

Fleshman, Joseph. "Why Did Simeon and Levi Rebuke Their Father in Genesis 34:31." *Journal of Northwest Semitic Languages* 26.1 (2000) 101-12.

Fokkelman, J. P. *Narrative Art in Genesis*. Eugene, OR: Wipf & Stock, 1991.

Follingstad, Carl M. *Deictic Viewpoint in Biblical Hebrew Text: A Syntagmatic and Pragmatic Analysis of the Particle Ki*. Dallas: SIL International, 2001.

Francisco, Clyde T. "Genesis." *General Articles: Genesis—Exodus*, 101-288. Vol. 1 of *The Broadman Bible Commentary*, edited by Clifton J. Allen. Nashville: Broadman, 1969.

Gentzler, Edwin. *Contemporary Translation Theories*. Clevedon, UK: Multilingual Matters, 2001.

Goldingay, John. "The Patriarchs in Scripture and History." In *Essays on the Patriarchal Narratives*, edited by A. R. Millard and D. J. Wiseman, 11-42. Leicester, UK: InterVarsity, 1980.

Grimes, Barbara F. *Ethnologue: Language of the World, Fifteenth Edition*. Dallas: SIL International, 2005.

Gunkel, Hermann. *Genesis*. Mercer Library of Biblical Studies. Macon, GA: Mercer University Press, 1997.

Gutt, Ernst-August. *Translation and Relevance: Cognition and Context*. Manchester: St. Jerome, 2000.

Haldar, A. "Hebrew." In *The Interpreters Dictionary of the Bible: An Illustrated Encyclopedia, vol. E—J*, edited by George Buttrick, 552-53. New York: Abingdon, 1962.

Hamilton, Victor P. *The Book of Genesis: Chapters 1-17*. The New International Commentary on the Old Testament. Grand Rapids: Eerdmans, 1990.

———. *The Book of Genesis: Chapters 18-50*. The New International Commentary on the Old Testament. Grand Rapids: Eerdmans, 1995.

———. "Shebuha." In *Theological Wordbook of the Old Testament, Vol. 2*, edited by Laird Harris, 899-901. Chicago: Moody, 1980.

Hankore, Daniel. "Nominalization in Hadiyya." M.A. thesis, Nairobi Evangelical Graduate School of Theology, 1998.

Bibliography

Hartley, John E. *New International Biblical Commentary: Genesis.* Peabody, MA: Hendrickson, 2000.

Harvey, Graham. *The True Israel: In Ancient Jewish and Early Christian Literature.* Boston: Brill, 1996.

Hayas, John H., and Carl R. Holladay. *Biblical Exegesis: A Beginner's Handbook.* London: SCM, 1982.

Heller, Roy L. *Narrative Structure and Discourse Constructions: An Analysis of Clause Function in Biblical Hebrew Prose.* Winona Lake, IN: Eisenbrauns, 2004.

Hickey, Leo. *The Pragmatics of Translation.* Clevedon, UK: Multilingual Matter, 1998.

Hill, Harriet Swannie. *The Bible at Cultural Crossroads: From Translation to Communication.* Manchester, UK: St. Jerome, 2006.

———. "Communicating Context in Bible Translation among the Adioukrou of Cote D'Ivoire." Ph.D. diss., Fuller Theological Seminary, 2003.

Hoffmeier, James K. "Egyptians." In *Peoples of the Old Testament World*, edited by Edwin M. Yamauchi, 251–89. Grand Rapids: Baker, 1994.

Holladay, Carl R. *The Epic Poets Theodotus and Philo and Ezekiel the Tragedian. Fragments from Hellenistic Jewish Authors.* Atlanta: Scholars, 1989.

Hutchinson, John, and Anthony D. Smith. *Ethnicity.* Oxford: Oxford University, 1996.

Jaworski, Adam, and Nikolas Coupland, editors. *The Discourse Reader.* London: Routledge, 1999.

Kass, Leon R. *The Beginning of Wisdom: Reading Genesis.* New York: Free, 2003.

Kelley, Page H. *Biblical Hebrew: An Introductory Grammar.* Grand Rapids: Eerdmans, 1992.

Kilpatrick, G. D. "Aaron, Bethel, and the Priestly Menorah." *Journal of Jewish Studies* XXVI.1–2 (1975) 39–49.

Kissling, Paul. *The College Press NIV Commentary: Genesis Volume 2.* Jopline, MO: College, 2009.

Klein, Ernest. *A Comprehensive Etymological Dictionary of the Hebrew Language for Readers of English.* Jerusalem: The University of Haifa, 1987.

Klein, Meredith G. "The Ha-Bi-Ru—Kin or Foe of Israel?" *Westminster Theological Journal* 10 (1958) 46–70.

Klinger, Elmar. "Vows and Oaths." In *The Encyclopedia of Religion*, edited by Mircea Eliade, 301–5. New York: MacMillan, 1987.

Kobayashi, Yoshitaka. "Haran." In *The Anchor Bible Dictionary*, vol. 3, edited by David Noel Freedman, 58–59. New York: Doubleday, 1992.

Kohlenberger III, John R., and James A. Swanson. *The Hebrew—English Concordance to the Old Testament: With the New International Version.* Grand Rapids: Zondervan, 1998.

Kress, Gunther, and Theo van Leeuwen. "Representation and Interaction: Designing the Position of the Viewer." In *The Discourse Reader*, edited by Adam Jaworski and Nikolas Coupland, 377–403. London: Routledge, 1999.

Labove, William. "The Transformation of Experience in Narrative." In *The Discourse Reader*, edited by Adam Jaworski and Nikolas Coupland, 221–35. London: Routledge, 1999.

Lauterbach, Jacob Zallel. "Vows." In *The Jewish Encyclopedia*, edited by Isidore Singer et al., 451–52. New York: Ktav, 1906.

Bibliography

Leeb, Carolyn. "Translating the Hebrew body into English Metaphor." In *The Social Science and Bible Translation*, edited by Dietmar Nefeld. Atlanta: Society of Biblical Literature, 2008.

Lehrer, Keith. "Meaning, Exemplarization and Metarepresentation." In *Metarepresentations: a Multidiscipilinary Perspective*, edited by Dan Sperber, 299–310. Oxford: Oxford University Press, 2000.

Leick, Gwendolyn. *Sex and Eroticism in Mesopotamian Literature*. London: Routledge, 1994.

Levine, Michelle J. "The Inner World of Biblical Character Explored in Nahmanides' Commentary on Genesis." *Journal of Jewish Studies* LVI.2 (2005) 306–34.

Levinson, Stephen C. *Pragmatics*. Cambridge: Cambridge University Press, 1983.

Linde, Charlotte. "Narrative in Institutions." In *The Handbook of Discourse Analysis*, edited by Deborah Schiffrin, Deborah Tannen and Heidi E. Hamilton, 518–35. Oxford: Blackwell, 2001.

Marcus, David. *Jephthah and His Vow*. Lubbock, TX: Texas Tech, 1986.

Marguerat, Daniel, and Yvan Bourquin. *How to Read Bible Stories: An Introduction to Narrative Criticism*. London: SCM, 1999.

Mathews, Kenneth A. *The New American Commentary an Exegetical and Theological Exposition of Holy Scripture: Genesis 11:27—50:26*. Vol. 1B of *New International Version the New American Commentary*. Nashville: Broadman & Holman, 2005.

Mielziner, Moses. *Introduction to the Talmud*. New York: Bloch, 1968.

Miller, James E. "Sexual Offences in Genesis." *Journal for the Study of the Old Testament* 90 (2000) 41–53.

Morris, Henry M. *The Genesis Record: A Scientific and Devotional Commentary on the Book of Beginning*. Grand Rapids: Baker, 1976.

Nida, Eugene, and Taber, Robert. *The Theory and Practice of Translation*. Leiden: Brill, 1969.

Noh, Eun-Ju. *Metarepresentation*. Amsterdam: Benjamins, 2000.

Oblath, Michael. "'To Sleep, Perchance to Dream:' What Jacob Saw at Bethel (Genesis 28:10–22)." *Journal for the Study of the Old Testament* 95 (2001) 117–26.

Oppenbeim, A. Leo. *Ancient Mesopotamia: Portrait of a Dead Civilization*. Chicago: The University of Chicago Press, 1964.

Pagolu, Augustine. *The Religion of the Patriarchs*. Sheffield, UK: Sheffield Academic Press, 1998.

Parker, Simon B. *Ugaritic Narrative Poetry*. Atlanta: Scholars, 1997.

Parry, Robin A. *Old Testament Story and Christian Ethics: The Rape of Dinah as a Case Study*. Milton Keynes, UK: Paternoster, 2004.

———. "Source Criticism & Genesis 34." *Tyndale Bulletin* 51 (2000) 121–38.

Patterson, R. D. "Sulam, Ladder." In *Theological Wordbook of the Old Testament*, edited by R. Laird Harris, 626–27. Chicago: Moody, 1980.

Payne, J. Barton. "Israel." In *Theological Wordbook of the Old Testament*, edited by R. Laird Harris, 883. Chicago: Moody, 1980.

———. "Jacob." In *Theological Wordbook of the Old Testament*, edited by R. Laird Harris, 691–92. Chicago: Moody, 1980.

Pelikan, Jaroslav. *Luther's Works, Vol. 6: Lectures on Genesis Chapters 31–37*. Saint Louis: Concordia, 1970.

Pink, Arthur W. *Gleanings in Genesis*. Chicago: Moody, 1922.

Powell, Mark Allan. *What Is Narrative Criticism?* Minneapolis: Fortress, 1990.

Bibliography

Rabinowitz, Louis Isaac. "Israel." In *Encyclopedia Judaica*, vol. 9, 106. Jerusalem: Macmillan, 1971.

———. "Vows and Vowing." In *Encyclopedia Judaica*, vol. 9, 227–28. Jerusalem: Macmillan, 1971.

Rønne, Finn Aa. "Kontinuitet og Forandring: Opkomsten og Udviklingen af Protestantisk Kristendom i Kambaataa-Hadiyya, Ethiopien 1928 til 1974." PhD diss., Kobenhavns Universitet, 2002.

Ross, Allen P. "Genesis." In *The Bible Commentary on Old Testament: An Exposition of the Scriptures by Dallas Seminary Faculty*, 15–100. Wheaton, IL: Victor, 1985.

Ryken, Leland. *Complete Literary Guide to the Bible*. Grand Rapids: Zondervan, 1993.

Saeed, John I. *Semantics*. 2nd ed. Oxford: Blackwell, 2003.

Schiffman, Lawrence H. "Oaths and Vows." In *Encyclopedia of the Dead Sea Scrolls, Vol. 2*, edited by Lawrence H. Schiffman and James C. Vanderkam, 621–23. Oxford: Oxford University Press, 2000.

Schoville, Keith N. "Canaanites and Amorites." In *Peoples of the Old Testament World*, edited by Alfred J. Hoerth, Edwin M. Yamauchi, and Gerald L. Mattingly, 157–81. Grand Rapids: Baker, 1994.

Scott, Jack B. "Alah." In *Theological Wordbook of the Old Testament, vol. 1*, edited by R. Laird Harris, 45. Chicago: Moody, 1980.

Scott, William R. *A Simplified Guide to BHS*. Richland Hills, ON: Bible, 1995.

Shuttleworth, Mark, and Moira Cowie. *Dictionary of Translation Studies*. Manchester: St. Jerome, 1997.

Sim, Ronald J. "Intepretatively Used Language in Genesis." Paper Presented at SBL Annual Meeting, New Orleans, 21–24 Nov, 2009.

———. *Predicate Conjoining in Hadiya: a Head-driven PS Grammar*. Edinburgh: University of Edinburgh, 1989.

———. *Retelling Translation: A Handbook for Translators*. Unpublished manuscript, 2006.

Skinner, John. *Critical and Exegetical Commentary on Genesis*. 2nd ed. Edinburgh, T. & T. Clark, 1980.

Slayton, Joel C. "Penuel." In *Anchor Bible Dictionary, vol. 5*, edited by David Noel Freedman, 222–23. New York: Doubleday, 1992.

Smick, Elmer B. "Berit, 'Covenant.'" In *Theological Wordbook of the Old Testament, vol. 1*, edited by R. Laird Harris, 128–30. Chicago: Moody, 1980.

Speiser, E. A. *Genesis*. New York: Doubleday, 1982.

Sperber, Dan, and Deirdre Wilson. *Relevance: Communication and Cognition*. 2nd ed. Oxford: Blackwell, 1995.

Sperber, Dan. "Introduction." In *Metarepresentations: A Multidisciplinary Perspective*, edited by Dan Sperber, 3–13. Oxford: Oxford University Press, 2000.

Sternberg, Meir. "Biblical Poetics and Sexual Politics: From Reading to Counterreading." *Journal of Biblical Literature* 111.3 (1992) 463–88.

———. *The Poetics of Biblical Narrative: Ideological Literature and the Drama of Reading*. Bloomington, IN: Indiana University Press, 1985.

Steinberg, Naomi. *Kinship and Marriage in Genesis: A Household Economics Perspective*. Minneapolis: Fortress, 1993.

Strahan, James. *Hebrew Ideals in Genesis*. Grand Rapids: Kregel, 1982.

Taylor, Joan E. "The Asherah, the Menorah and the Sacred Tree." *Journal for the Study of the Old Testament* 66 (1995) 29–54.

Bibliography

Unger, Merill F. *The New Unger Bible Dictionary*. Chicago: Moody, 1988.
Vaux, Roland de. *Ancient Israel: Its Life and Institution*. London: Darton, Longman & Todd, 1973.
———. *Ancient Israel: Religious Institution*. New York: McGrew-Hill, 1965.
Venter, M. Pieter. "A Triadic Construct in Jubilee 30." Paper presented at SBL International Meeting, Rome, July 2009.
von Rad, Gerhard. *Genesis: A Commentary*. Philadelphia: Westminster, 1972.
Walters, Stanley D. "Jacob Narrative." In *The Anchor Bible Dictionary, vol. 1*, edited by David Noel Freedman, 599–608. New York: Doubleday, 1992.
Waltke, Bruce K., and Murphy O'Connor. *An Introduction to Biblical Hebrew Syntax*. Winona Lake, IN: Eisenbrauns, 1990.
Walton, Kevin. *Thou Traveller Unknown: The Presence and Absence of God in the Jacob Narrative*. Carlisle, UK: Paternoster, 2003.
Wenham, Gordon J. *Genesis 1–15*. Word Biblical Commentary. Nashville: Thomas Nelson, 1987.
———. *Genesis 16–50*. Word Biblical Commentary. Nashville: Thomas Nelson, 1994.
Wendland, Ernst. *Contextual Frames of Reference in Translation: A Coursebook for Bible Translators and Teachers*. Manchester, UK: St. Jerome, 2008.
———. *The Cultural Factor in Bible Translation*. London: United Bible Societies, 1973.
Westermann, Claus. *Genesis 12–36*. Translated by John J. Scullion. Minneapolis: Augsburg, 1985.
———. *The Promise to the Fathers: Studies on the Patriarchal Narratives*. Philadelphia: Fortress, 1976.
Whiston, William A. M. *Josephus: The Complete Works*. Nashville: Thomas Nelson, 1998.
Wilson, D., and T. Matsui. "Recent Approaches to Bridging, Truth, Coherence, Relevance." In *Lengua, Discurso, Texto*, edited by J. J. de Bustos Tovar, 103–31. Madrid: Visor, 2000.
Wilson, Deirdre. "Metarepresentation in Linguistic Communication." In *Metarepresentations: A Multidisciplinary Perspective*, edited by Dan Sperber, 411–41. Oxford: University Press, 2000.
Wilt, Timothy, and Ernst Wendland. *Scripture Frames and Framing: A Workbook for Bible Translators*. Stellenbosch: Sun, 2008.
Wiseman, P. J. *Ancient Records and the Structure of Genesis: A Case for Literary Unity*. Nashville: Thomas Nelson, 1985.
Wolde, Ellen van. "Does '*Inna*' Denote Rape? A Semantic Analysis of a Controversial Word." *Vetus Testamentum* 52.4 (2002) 528–44.
Wright, Christopher J. H. *Old Testament Ethics for the People of God*. Leicester, UK: InterVarsity, 2004.
Yamada, Frank M. "Configurations of Rape in the Hebrew Bible: A Literary Analysis of Three Rape Narratives." PhD diss., Perkins School of Theology, New York, 2004.
Young, Robert LL. D. *Young's Analytical Concordance to the Bible*. Grand Rapids: Eerdmans, 1936.
Zertal, Adam. "Shechem." In *The Anchor Bible Dictionary, vol. 5*, edited by David Noel Freedman, 1186–87. New York: Doubleday, 1992.
Zimmerli, Walther. *I Am Yahweh*. Atlanta: John Knox, 1982.

Scripture Index

Genesis

3:14	81
5:3	23
10:21—11:24	24, 215
10:21–31	218
11:16	216
12:1–3	107, 109
12:7	105
13:14–16	105, 107, 109
14:18–22	78, 222
15:18	79, 104
17:14	82
17:18	105
18:2	103
21:9–13	218
21:22–31	79
24:2, 3	78
24:7	105
24:28	79
40:15	216
43:32	216
45:1	103
39:14	216

Exodus

1:15	216
2:11, 13	216
18:13–14	103
34:20	62

Leviticus

5:1	78
7:16	66, 69, 72
12:6, 7, 14	223
14:23	223
19:12	82
22:21	69
26:15–16	82
27:2–10	60, 69, 72, 73
27:26, 28	66, 73
27:30–34	223

Numbers

6:1–21	63, 64
15:3, 8	69
18:20–31	223
21:1–3	59, 63, 66, 68, 72
30:3–15	60, 69, 82

Deuteronomy

12:6, 11	72
12:26	66, 69
14:22–29	222–24
16:16	62
17:8	72
23:18–23	59, 66, 67, 69, 71, 73, 82
26:12	223
27:15–26	81

Joshua

9:14	79
9:20	82

Scripture Index

Judges
11:30–37	3, 59, 67, 68
13:3–5	64
14:19	64
18:31	111

Ruth
1:17	78

1 Samuel
1:10—12:11	3
1:10–24	58, 59, 63, 66–68
8:15, 17	222
13:3	216
14:24–46	77, 82
18:3	79
20:13	78
28:15, 17	222

2 Samuel
15:7–8	59, 68
21:1–14	82

1 Kings
8:31	78
12:29–33	100

1 Chronicles
4:48	111
11:3	79

2 Chronicles
18:1–27	12

Ezra
1:4	111

Nehemiah
6:10	111
10:37–38	223

Job
22:27	66, 72

Psalms
22:21–25	66, 70, 72
42:4	111
56:2	64
61:5–8	66, 70, 72
66:13, 18	66, 73
116:14, 17–18	58, 66, 70, 72
132:2	59

Proverbs
7:14	58, 66, 73
29:24	78

Ecclesiastes
5:1	111
5:4, 6	58–60, 65, 67, 69, 73

Isaiah
19:21	58, 71
45:23	79

Jeremiah
44:12	78
44:25, 26	58, 59, 71, 79

Daniel
1:2	111
12:7	78

Amos
3:14	100

Jonah
1:16	58, 71
2:10	71

Nahum

1:15   58, 66, 71

Malachi

1:14   58–60, 71
3:10–12   223

Hebrews

6:13   79

Author Index

Bader, Mary Anna, 129, 132
Bechtel, Lyn M, 180–82, 189, 191
Blyth, Caroline, 191
Botterweck, G Johannes, 214, 215
Bourquin, Yvan, 131
Brisman, Leslie, 32, 98, 170
Brown, Gillian, 35, 126, 129–31
Brueggemann, Walter, 158, 170
Butler, C.E, 97

Candlish, Robert S, 174
Cartledge, Tony, 41, 49, 51, 57, 58, 63, 64, 117–19, 126, 134, 136
Charles, R.H, 189
Coats, George W, 20, 25
Cotter, David W, 20, 25
Coupland, Nikalas, 4, 130

Dilley, Roy, 45
Dumbrell, W.J, 198

Edzard, Dietz O, 49

Ferris, Paul Wayne, 97
Fewell, Danna Nolan, 177, 178
Fishbane, Michael, 19, 22, 27, 33, 34
Fokkelman, J.P, 100
Follinstad, Carl M, 104

Gentzler, Edwin, 237
Goldingay, John, 32
Gunkel, Hermann, 23, 24, 29, 112, 134, 139, 142, 189
Gunn, David, 177, 178
Gutt, Ernst August, 238

Hamilton, Victor P, 30, 33, 215
Harvey, Graham, 213
Heller, Roy L, 113
Henry, Matthew, 169
Hill, Harriett Swannie, 245

Jaworski, Adam, 4, 130

Kass, Leon R, 21, 22, 31, 36, 96
Kissling, Paul J, 25, 26
Kress, Gunther, 129

Labove, William, 128, 129
Leeb, Carolyn, 191
Leeuwen, Theo van, 129
Lehrer, Keith, 91, 92
Linde, Charlotte, 5

Marcus, David, 53
Marguerat, Daniel, 131
Morris, Henry M, 97

Noh, Eun-Ju, 93, 94, 123, 230

Pagulo, Augustine, 40, 62, 99, 112, 132, 134, 156
Parry, Robin, 158, 164, 166, 167, 172, 176, 182, 187, 188, 190
Pink, Arthur W, 174

Rad, Gerhard von, 22, 26, 216
Richards, 240
Ridling, Zaine, 98
Rønne, Finn, 6, 44

Saeed, John I, 229

Author Index

Schiffman, Lawrence H, 74
Shuttleworth, Mark, 236
Sim, Ronald J, 7, 104, 127
Skinner, John, 27
Sperber, Dan, 18, 90, 91, 120
Sternberg, Meir, 131, 171, 172, 177–79, 191
Strahan, James, 174

Venter, Pieter M, 181

Walters, Stanley D, 19
Walton, Kevin, 22, 23, 30, 34, 36

Wenham, Gordon J, 22, 24, 28, 33, 39, 40, 97, 107, 108, 111, 129, 134, 137, 138, 140, 156, 160, 170, 188, 215
Westermann, Claus, 22, 28, 32, 111, 113, 134
Wilson, Deirdre, 18, 88, 89, 90, 120
Wiseman, P.J, 28
Wolde, Ellen van, 189, 190
Wright, Christopher J.H, 215

Yule, George, 35, 126, 129–31

Zimmerli, Walther, 106

Subject Index

Abductive marriage, 38, 164, 182, 183, 185–95, 199, 231
Ad hoc concept, 14
Anthropology, 179, 180, 238

Boundaries, 19, 20, 21, 23, 138

Coherence, 2, 3, 16, 18, 19, 41, 43, 88, 133, 142, 199, 202
Commissive
    Speech act, 14, 44, 78–81, 85, 103, 105, 108, 109, 119, 125, 127, 148, 158, 203, 204, 209, 210
    Utterance, 117
Communicative intention, 2, 3, 4, 5, 13, 14, 15, 18, 45, 64, 95, 132, 202, 206, 207
Contextual
    Adjustment, 12, 208–10, 212, 245, 246
    Assumption, 5, 6, 10, 12, 13, 15, 21, 66, 85, 86, 101, 106, 109, 110, 113, 114, 137, 160, 165, 187, 188, 197, 202–4, 206–9, 211, 212, 230, 231, 243–45
    Framework, 19, 20, 30, 34–36, 202
Covenant, 25, 27, 30, 33, 35–39, 44, 45, 77, 79, 80, 82, 85, 99, 106, 107, 109, 122, 123, 133, 137, 171, 203
Curse, 45, 81, 82

Feminist, 176–79

Hadiyya people, 6–8, 45, 46, 84, 163, 183, 184, 185, 186, 187, 192, 203, 205, 206, 225, 232

Implicature, 8–10, 13, 38, 93, 107, 109, 121, 122, 148, 150, 157, 158, 188
Informative intention, 4, 13, 14, 90, 128, 156
Interpretive resemblance, 10, 11, 40, 45, 92, 107, 109, 117, 121, 122, 124, 125, 204, 207, 240

Literary
    Document, 3, 4
    Structure, 5, 18, 19, 25–37, 41, 70, 100, 136

Metarepresentation, 11, 12, 88–95, 101–5, 109, 110, 113, 115, 117, 119, 121–24, 134, 135, 139–40, 147–49, 152, 153, 204, 224, 230
Narrative unit, 1–3, 5, 15, 16, 19, 20, 23–26, 32, 34–37, 39, 41–43, 88, 115, 118, 126, 133, 137, 146, 152, 157, 160, 171, 176, 199, 201–3, 205, 208, 244

Oath, 37, 44, 45, 76, 78–82, 85, 203
Ostension, 2, 4, 5, 8–10, 12–14, 16, 62, 90, 100, 101, 124, 126–28, 132, 147, 151, 156, 161, 164, 182, 205, 206, 239

Subject Index

Relevance theory, 1, 3–5, 8, 9, 11, 13, 14, 18, 88, 110, 120, 127, 204, 206, 244

Source criticism, 3, 164, 175, 176
Swearing, 37, 44, 77, 78–82, 106

Tithing, 66, 120, 121, 124, 222–24
Truth-functional, 94, 116, 117, 229–31

Vav consecutive, 61, 68, 113, 118
Votive
  Commitment, 66, 73, 85, 127, 133, 135, 161, 203, 204
  Plea, 16, 41, 46, 47, 59, 67, 116, 119, 124–28, 132–41, 147–53, 155–57, 161, 163, 166, 197, 203, 204, 210, 211, 224
  Pledge, 65, 134–36, 157, 158, 161
  Promise, 47, 67, 121, 124, 127, 128, 135, 150, 157–63, 197, 204, 205, 212
  Utterance, 16, 40, 41, 42, 45, 64, 70, 100, 114–20, 122–27, 132, 133, 135, 139, 147, 161, 197, 204, 224, 231
Vows
  Always a conditional commitment, 60, 203
  Ancient Near East, 6, 49–56, 203
  Aramaic, 54
  As praise to God, 65
  As strictly binding utterance, 59, 203, 226, 227
  Assyrian, 50, 83
  Babylonian, 50, 85
  Between God and humans, 57, 86, 203
  Contrast with covenant, 79, 80, 203
  Contrast with oath, 78, 80, 203
  Contrast with swearing, 78, 80
  Echoic, 38, 40, 103, 117
  Egyptian, 51
  Fulfilling, 101, 160, 204–7, 230, 244

  Granting, 114, 119, 133, 160, 201, 204, 205, 207, 211, 230, 244
  Hadiyya, 6, 15, 44–49, 82, 84, 85, 163, 203, 209
  Hittite, 52
  In Book of Jubilees, 76
  In context of distress, 58, 203, 226
  In Dead Sea Scrolls, 73
  In Hebrew Scriptures, 56, 81, 82, 83, 85, 203, 207, 209
  In narrative books, 68
  In Psalms and Wisdom books, 69
  In Talmud, 74
  In the Prophets, 71
  In Torah, 68
  Institution, 3, 209, 230, 231, 245
  Location and time of fulfillment, 66
  Making, 43, 46, 49–59, 62, 64, 65, 68, 71, 72, 74, 76, 80, 84, 85, 86, 88, 95, 113, 114, 116, 117, 133, 160, 201, 203, 205, 207, 211, 230, 244
  Offering, 47, 60, 66, 72–74, 83, 84, 86, 227
  Phoenician, Punic, Neo-Punic, 54
  Sumerian, 50
  Ugaritic, 52
  Unfulfilled, 43, 45, 49, 51, 59, 74–76, 82, 163, 83, 187, 196, 197, 200, 201, 203–5, 210, 211, 231

Utterances
  Binding, 59, 78, 80, 81, 82, 212
  Commissive, 117
  Conditional, 94, 230, 231
  Echoic, 12, 41, 88, 92–95, 110, 117, 119, 122, 204
  Optimally relevant, 14
  Votive, 16, 40, 41, 42, 45, 64, 70, 100, 114–20, 122–27, 132, 133, 135, 139, 147, 161, 197, 204, 224, 231

www.ingramcontent.com/pod-product-compliance
Lightning Source LLC
Chambersburg PA
CBHW050345230426
43663CB00010B/1992